
philadelphia communists, 1936–1956

DISCARDED

paul lyons

philadelphia communists, 1936–1956

temple university press   philadelphia

Temple University Press, Philadelphia 19122
© *1982 by Temple University. All rights reserved*
Published 1982
Printed in the United States of America

Library of Congress Cataloging in Publication Data
Lyons, Paul.
  Philadelphia communists, 1936–1956.
  Bibliography: p.
  Includes index.
  1. Communist Party of the United States of
America—History.   2. Communism—Pennsylvania—
Philadelphia—History.   3. Communist—Pennsylvania
—History.   I. Title.
JK2391.C53P485   324.273'75'09   82-2019
ISBN 0-87722-259-2   AACR2

To Mary,
for healing wounds

History as a way of learning can offer examples of how other men faced up to the difficulties and opportunities of their eras. Even if the circumstances are noticeably different, it is illuminating, and productive of humility as well, to watch other men make their decisions, and to consider the consequences of their values and methods.

William Appleman Williams

Marxism is distinguished from the old utopian socialism by the fact that the latter wanted to build a new society not out of the masses of human material created by bloody, dirty, money-grubbing, rapacious capitalism, but out of especially virtuous people raised in special greenhouses and hothouses.

V. I. Lenin

contents

acknowledgments *xi*

one **introduction** *3*

two **radicalization** *19*

three **organization and subculture** *49*

four **ethnicity** *70*

five **marriage, family, and sex roles** *87*

six **the communist as organizer** *109*

seven **problems and crises, 1939–1956** *138*

eight **coping** *169*

notes *191*

bibliographic essay *231*

interviews *239*

index *241*

acknowledgments

In writing this book I have benefited from the support and criticism of many friends and colleagues. I am most indebted to all of them for providing sustenance, especially during those moments when it seemed that I would not finish.

I would like to thank the Bryn Mryn Graduate School of Social Work and Social Research for supporting generously a research project that could easily have been hampered or blocked by conventional definitions of appropriate subject matter. Dr. Dennis Brunn, my initial dissertation director, merits gratitude for his continuing encouragement and unflagging interest. I wish to thank Dr. Milton Speizman for his perceptive insights, supportive criticism, and admirably thorough supervision; I am most grateful for his willingness to direct a dissertation already in progress.

I am also indebted to Dr. Robert Zaslavsky of the Library staff at Bryn Mawr College for his helpfulness and to Dianne Wills for her very professional typing services.

xi

Appreciation must also be expressed to Dr. Lewis Leitner, Dean of the Social and Behavioral Sciences Division, Stockton State College, for facilitating typing services for me. Of course I must also thank Linda Arroyo, Gwen McClarren, Marcy Sciscoe, and Kathleen Wood for supplying those services.

I received valuable criticism from Joan Mandle, Ann Beuf, Mark Naison, Maurice Isserman, and Roger Keeran. Although I did not always follow their suggestions, my book has gained a sharper focus through their comments.

The conversion of a dissertation into a book requires considerable and often tedious effort. I am most grateful for the support that Temple University Press has provided. In particular, I would like to thank Ken Arnold, the editor-in-chief, for his ongoing support and his always thoughtful criticisms. Also I want to commend Jane Barry for a copyediting effort that tightened up my often clumsy prose.

I wish to thank members of my family for bearing with me; I hope that Jennifer and Nate have caught some sense of the extraordinary within the ordinary from my pursuits. My wife, Mary, has had to bear the brunt of my single-mindedness, and I want to express my love and gratitude to her. She best understands what has driven me.

Finally, it is imperative for me to express infinite appreciation to all of the veterans of the Communist Party in Philadelphia who have graciously allowed me to tell at least a part of their stories. They have literally opened their doors to me, provided me with inestimable advice and critical leads, and, with curiosity and intelligence, become partners in a search for meaning. In particular I wish to thank Isadore Reivich, Vincent Pieri, and Albert Silverman for their support, knowledge, and criticism. Without their efforts, their encouragement, this study would never have been either commenced or completed.

Paul Lyons

Philadelphia, Pa.
January 1982

philadelphia communists, 1936–1956

one

introduction

The first teach-ins in the spring of 1965 marked my transformation into a radical or, as I rather casually defined myself, a "New Leftist." The fact that I was a Marxist was significant, but of comparable import was the fact that in a whole variety of ways, not the least of which was my love for rock and roll, I felt part of a generational moment.

My generational sense was tempered by the academic training I received from Marxist intellectuals who eschewed both the old, turgid Marxist-Leninist rigidities and the activist imperatives of SDS. In this regard, my New Left identity was anomalous: very few of my movement friends had had enlightening or valuable academic experiences, least of all with Marxist professors.

What I shared with my generational cohorts was a knee-jerk contempt for what we called the "Old Left," most particularly the Communist Party, but the "Trots" as well. Some "red-diaper babies," children of Old Leftists, spoke impatiently of the old

3

battles they were forced to endure between Stalinist uncles and Shactmanite cousins. More important, the pioneers of the New Left, the SDS founders, had direct experience with the old ideological wars and, as a result, helped to frame an image of the Old Left as dogmatic, foolish, and irrelevant.[1]

My own rather limited experiences confirmed such a contemptuous stance. At a Party-sponsored forum, one encountered several dozen old people seemingly battling ideological ghosts of an idiosyncratic past, mouthing passionate abstractions, still holding to "the correct line." The Old Left seemed positively geriatric, and like most of my throw-away nation, Left, Center, or Right, I was insensitive to old folks. They were simply "old farts," relegated to the dust-bin of history by those contemptuous of the past.

Indeed, the seminal intellectual influences of the sixties heavily weighted criticism against the Old Left. C. Wright Mills called on the young intelligentsia to abandon the "labor metaphysic" and to seek allies among their Third World peers. William Appleman Williams focused the attention of a generation of young revisionist historians on the expansionist nature and co-opting genius of "corporate liberalism." Most New Leftists used such lessons to excoriate Communist Party strategy as "economistic" and "revisionist" (that is, passively awaiting the unfolding of History) and to view Old Left tactics (for example, refusing to struggle openly for socialism) as cowardly and enfuriating.[2]

The socialism we wished to proclaim was inspired by the visions of the young Marx of the *1844 Manuscripts*.[3] Alienation, rather than exploitation, was the central category of experience for sixties radicals. We faced what Herbert Marcuse called a "one-dimensional society,"[4] with both Western capitalist and Soviet models, which was organized to perpetuate humanity's alienation from such essential attributes as freedom, creativity, and harmony through bureaucratic, co-optive mechanisms topped by material benefits—that is, the system delivered the goods. The counterpoint to alienation was necessarily "liberation," or if that was only a distant hope, then at least a "great refusal" to participate in the "Happy Consciousness."[5] We were enamored with the utopian visions of Wilhelm Reich and Norman O. Brown[6] and found precious little succor in puritanical Soviet experience.

New Leftists seemed to believe that radicalization would result from a more open and strenuous advocacy of a participatory democracy, which would temper Marxism with a touch of Christian blessed community, a strain of irreverence inspired by Groucho rather than Karl, and a healthy dose of erotic exuberance. We tried to pinpoint the psychic barriers that blocked people off from radical insights. Our essentially romantic question centered on what prevented people from being radical. What were the qualities of alienation that blocked humanity from "the complete return of man to himself as a social (i.e., human) being"?[7]

The literature dealing with the Communist Party and with radicalism in general, on the other hand, typically asks a different question: why do people become radical?[8] Such studies place the radical experience within the context of deviance, searching out the paths that have led characteristically neurotic people to act out their pathologies through politics.[9] As a result, the study of radicalization and radicals is often limited to a branch of social psychology. A variation of such an approach is to consider radicalization as an understandable phase in the maturational process, a generational struggle finding articulation within particular historical circumstances. As such, it will soon pass.

While the question of how human beings become radicals is of obvious importance, of equal weight are the consequences of radicalization, and in particular the question how and why one remains a radical.[10] The longitudinal question is of particular relevance in dealing with American radicals.

The United States remains a land of what Louis Hartz called the Liberal Tradition,[11] that is, a bourgeoise hegemony of social-contract theory. It is a nation weened on popularizations of English seventeenth-century political thought, which is often reduced to life, liberty, and the pursuit of happiness through a commitment to private property.

Although injustice has been persistent among our "people of plenty," such incidents are perceived as exceptional, not endemic, anomalous blots on the democratic conscience. Advocates of social change have therefore characteristically been reform-minded, ameliorative, muckraking adherents of the evolutionary and piecemeal approach. In special hothouse circumstances, all in the past, of course, some have become radicals and revolutionaries. Fortunately, from the vantage point of the "vital center," youthful indignation soon yields to mature and sober pragmatism; radicals are compelled toward responsible liberalism not only by the aging process itself but also by the system's ability to absorb dissent and incorporate ameliorating programs.[12] Our historical legacy notes with self-satisfaction the evolution of Debsian Socialists into Wilsonian Progressives, and Depression-era Communists and Socialists into New Deal Democrats. Recently we have witnessed the continuation of celebration as sixties radicals metamorphose into over-thirty reformers "working within the system."

(Within this study, capitalized political designations [e.g., Communist, Socialist, or Fascist] indicate formal, institutional affiliations, such as membership in particular parties. Political designations not capitalized indicate ideological inclinations but not necessarily institutional affiliations. The broadest categories are based on the directional signals originated during the French Revolution: Left and Right. In this study "the Left," "left wing," and "radical" indicate alignment with anticapitalist political formations generally associated but not limited to Marxian socialism. A capitalized "Progressive" indicates affiliation with Henry Wallace's Progressive Party of 1948; uncapitalized "progressive" indicates ideological commitment to liberal, New Deal–style social reform. Within the Communist Party tradition, "progressive" also indicates a willingness to work cooperatively with radicals in Popular Front alliances and to eschew anti-Communism both domestically and in foreign policy.)

More depressing is the phenomenon of radicals becoming reactionaries, hucksters, religious faddists, and, finally, scoundrels or fools. The prevailing social psychology suggests that the radical-to-liberal transformation reflects the short-term deviance of healthy personality, whereas the turn toward the corrupt and the bizarre signals the persistence of pathology. In brief the radical-turned-liberal "grew up"; the radical-turned-conservative simply shifted focus within a paranoid style of stereotypical thought.[13] The liberal, centrist bias of such vulgar psychologizing should be apparent.

We are left with the radical who remains radical throughout a lifetime. Is such a person an "authoritarian personality" or merely quaint? We need to explore the resources that sustain such radicals against the deep and subtle hegemonic forces of the "American way of life." After all, in what other modern culture is the dominant value system so monolithically identified with the nation itself?

Peter Clecak delineates with remarkable insight the paradoxes that work against the construction of an indigenous American radical movement and generate frustration, excess, and demoralization.[14] To be a socialist in a land without a socialist movement and without a class-conscious proletariat is painful. It is particularly agonizing when the times seem ripe for fundamental change and one's ideological framework demands transformations that simply do not occur. Objective conditions are out of kilter with political realities.

The radicals of the thirties, like those of the sixties, experienced the times as historically propitious; both radical generations seemed to be riding a wave of the future—in the former case that of the industrial workers, in the latter, a complicated mix of students, youth, blacks, Third World peoples, women, and gays. At a certain point, such radicals felt that history was indeed on their side.

By the late forties, however, the older Communist Party generation of the Depression era knew that history had taken a different and disappointing turn. They had invested considerable faith in the Idea of Progress, Marxian-style, only to come up against mortality, ideological and personal. Communism was not turning out to be twentieth-century Americanism but instead a beleaguered and increasingly marginal rearguard with an increasingly suspect sponsor.

After moving to Philadelphia in 1967, I made some contacts with a few former Communists. They seemed to have a sense of the long haul that I had not noticed before. (Of course, I had never looked!) They seemed to have reservoirs of patience that did not reek of selling or burning out. I became friends with three Old Left men, all of whom had entered the Party in the thirties and had left it in the aftermath of the multiple trauma of Khrushchev's Twentieth Party Congress revelations about Stalin, the Soviet intervention in Hungary, and the exposure of Soviet anti-Semitism. Yet all three continued fighting for socialism—which included working for piecemeal reforms—after leaving the Party. They, along with other ex-communists I encountered, worked in civil rights and peace groups and neighborhood associations fighting for integration.

Over a ten-year period in Philadelphia, I met many other veterans of that Depression generation of Communists—at rallies, at educational conferences, within the university, and sometimes through their children, who were my peers. I discovered, almost by accident, that the Communist Party had spawned an impressive network of radicals in a variety of political and cultural settings.

This remarkable network of old comrades rested on the ongoing social contact of scores of friends, acquaintances, and even enemies over more than four decades. They kept in touch, socialized, and still sparred with each other, sometimes harshly, sometimes nostalgically. My own generation seemed to have great difficulty in this sphere over a mere decade. Many of my friends had moved away, radical variants of the American gypsy, without the excuse of corporate orders. We were not even good letter writers and often made excuses about the costs of coast-to-coast phone calls. It saddened me. Clearly there was some reason to envy these Old Leftists their more stable networks. Too many of my generation, born in sprawling suburbs, did not have the rootedness of the urban- and ethnically based old Communists.

The crystalizing event in my developing fascination with Philadelphia's Old Left community came at a memorial service for the mother of a friend of my stepdaughter. She had been an energetic and productive educational innovator in the area. I already knew that her parents were 1905ers, Russian Jewish radicals who had carried their political idealism to the New World at the start of the century. She had even been named for a great Bolshevik leader, although she was known publicly by a less controversial derivative.

Upon entering the auditorium, I half-consciously began to note the presence of several veterans of the Old Left network, though I could not identify them all by name. Indeed, delivering one of the memorial service addresses was one of my three Old Left friends; he had known the dead woman since she was a little girl. By the close of the services it became apparent that scores of participants in this remarkable network were present. It was a rather frail and insignificant network as civil society goes, and yet it sustained several of its own cultural and social organizations, filled important positions in many progressive political groups, and was on call for a host of programs that made local and national life a bit more humane.

My story begins at that point. Were these old radicals typical of their political generation? Why had they not burnt out or sold out? Was I romanticizing a small, unrepresentative sample? Was I merely reading the surface, unaware of uglier and less noble features beneath?

The literature about the Communist Party, U.S.A., offered few answers or even hints. Most of it focused on the national and international dynamics of the Party or on a social-psychologizing of Communists.[15] There seemed to be no considerations of what it was actually like to be a Communist. More intriguing, at least to me, was how local radical activists experienced national and international events and issues within their own immediate environments. For example, what did the Nazi-Soviet Pact mean to a steel plant organizer whose primary associations were with fellow activists within a Party industrial branch? What did the flip-flops of Soviet policy mean to a rank-and-file member of a neighborhood club who sold his quota of *Sunday Workers* and attended Party functions and rallies? How did members experience their participation in a worldwide movement in the context of local friendships, local efforts, and local victories and defeats?

My own experience within the New Left led me to anticipate that local peer-group pressure played a remarkably large role in the personal responses to political events. There was the bright and perceptive guy who had worked with those fanatical Labor Committee people, and the energetic and decent woman in Progressive Labor, and, of course, the sharp and hard-working people I knew who opted for the Communist Party in the aftermath of the collapse of the New Left. Several acquaintances had joined the Weather Underground despite their academic accomplishments and apparent street smarts. The key seemed to be in social networks, their radical comrades and friends, particularly their "significant others," admirable leaders, inspirational co-workers. Radical politics, like any other variety, seemed to be as much a matter of loyalties as of conscience and ideology. Certainly one encountered within the Left true believers, authoritarian personalities, power-trippers, and fools. The bulk, however, seemed to be people with fairly normal, if not superior, quotients of common sense and intelligence.

This study is the result of my probes. My goal was to construct a model of a local Party experience—not so much a history or an institutional analysis as an anthropological, ethnographic account. The focus is the experience of becoming, being, and remaining a radical in a particular local setting. My three Old Left friends were of invaluable assistance in helping me contact a large enough sample to construct such a model.[16]

■ *methodology*

Oral history has become a contemporary fad. As Tamara Hareven wryly notes, "Like the computer, the recorder has not only facilitated the gathering and preservation of data; it has also generated a mystique of authenticity which is conveyed through the magic of technology."[17] Hareven appropriately sees oral history as "a subjective process, . . . an expression of the personality of the interviewees, of their cultural values, and of the particular historical circumstances which shaped their point of view." As such it is "a record of perceptions, rather than a re-creation of historical events." Oral history, despite the tendency to confuse sophisticated technology with a guarantee of objectivity, requires corroboration.[18]

After much consideration and advice from cooperative Philadelphia Old Leftists, I decided to eschew the gadgetry and rely on traditional notetaking. The prospective sample included few well-known figures, being made up for the most part of local former members with good reasons for avoiding publicity. Many Communist veterans bear painful and deep scars inflicted by governmental persecution and harrassment that affected vocation, neighborhood and family. Although a few would consent to taping, I anticipated that the electronic machinery would subtly intimidate and put even them on guard.

To further secure cooperation, I devised a coded system of numbers and aliases to protect my research files and assure those interviewed that any published results would protect anonymity. Only two people preferred to be identified. Other Philadelphia Communists are presented either under cover names or, to ensure that biographical details cannot lead to identification, in composite form. The integrity of the process rests on the accuracy of the interview transcriptions. However, given the special circumstances of such interviewees, I have engaged in some camouflage.[19]

The sample is both geographically and generationally bound. All of those interviewed spent at least a substantial part of their political lives, that is, their Communist Party experiences, in greater Philadelphia. Living and healthy pre-Depression Party members are relatively few in number. The experiences of such Communists, who were either charter members or who joined in the twenties, remains a valuable research area; I decided, however, to focus on the Communists of the Depression generation, with a few exceptions included for purposes of comparative analysis.

Relying on the few close contacts mentioned above, I began to collect the names and addresses of Old Leftists in the area. As usually happens, the list grew as interviews yielded new possibilities. Clearly this study would not have been possible without the initial support of key contacts. In many instances, I would telephone a possible subject, describing the study and requesting an interview. Many Old Leftists were initially suspicious, for obvious reasons, and wanted to know how I came to know of their names. In a few instances, in fact, contacts were reprimanded for providing names. In most cases, fortunately, Communist veterans either found my connections comforting or simply delayed scheduling an interview until they had checked with contacts about my reliability.

Even after they had checked my references, many Old Leftists were initially suspicious and cautious in their responses. I therefore framed the interviews more extensively than I had planned to. I informed people of the kinds of questions that directed the study and how I had selected this particular topic. I expressed my empathy for Old Left experiences clearly but generally so as not to give clues to particular political preferences and, therefore, to desired or anticipated responses.

The interviews were essentially autobiographical, although in a few cases sources served as important guides to organizational and strategic issues. Most interviews began with the informant's family and proceeded through his or her life story. The emphasis, most of which emerged naturally in freely flowing discourse but which I at times directed, was on family background, the process of radicalization, organizing experiences, the significance of marriage and family, the role of ethnicity, the influence of the local Party subculture and social network, and, broadly, responses to the various crises in the Party's history from the late thirties through the mid-fifties. I concluded most interviews with questions about people's post-Party experiences and perspective. Interviews ranged from ninety minutes to almost four hours, most typically lasting for two to three hours. I interviewed a few people more than once.

I was able to accumulate the names of ninety-five Philadelphia Old Leftists from helpful sources, and thirty-six allowed me to interview them. Of the remainder, five were no longer in the area, one had died, sixteen could not be located, and seventeen were eliminated because they would tilt the sample away from any semblance of ethnic representation (see Chapter Four for the ethnic composition of the Communist Party in Philadelphia). Seven were judged inappropriate because of their age or lack of extensive experience in Philadelphia. Finally, thirteen people declined to be interviewed, most for personal reasons, a few on what they called Party instructions.

The thirty-six interviews, all Philadelphia-based, represent a unique sample. Gabriel Almond interviewed sixty-four former American Communists and also gained information supplied by psychotherapists who provided services to another thirty-five former Communists. Not only was Almond's sample geographically undefined, but more than half of his subjects had left the Party by 1940 and none were products of the fifties schisms.[20]

Vivian Gornick's more journalistic study involves a sample of more than forty Old Leftists but organizes them impressionistically.[21] Arthur Liebman, in his massive and invaluable study of Jewish radicalism, interviewed thirty-five old Party members, mostly in New York City, but used the interviews only to illustrate his narrative analysis.[22]

As Nathan Glazer asks, "How is one to find a random sample of former Communists?"[23] One hopes at best to find a reasonably representative sample. Judging from the consistency of responses from many Philadelphia sources, this sample approaches such a level of representation, racially, ethnically, sexually, and ideologically.

This is a study of the Depression generation of Philadelphia Communist activists. Given the incredibly high turnover within the Party, nationally and locally, those interviewed make up a sample that is skewed toward long-term, more intensively involved, and relatively affirming members and former members. They are part of the Depression generation identified not by "an interval of time," but by "an energy field that provides a framework for one of several experiences held to be crucial and worth remembering."[24] What sets them off from other thirties products is the intensity with which they responded to those experiences and the particular framework with which they identified. In addition, they are notable for their durability, for the way in which the framework and the vision generated in the thirties have remained constant, though with revisions, over at least four decades.[25]

In interviewing participants about events and feelings of the past, I sought to remain as sensitive as possible to the inevitable tendency to color and distort. Often the narratives and observations of several veterans aided in deciphering an experience or event. Of critical importance, as well, was a thorough familiarity with Party literature, particularly the *Daily Worker* and, in the late forties and fifties, the Pennsylvania Sunday supplement, often called the *Pennsylvania Worker*. The various memoirs, autobiographies, biographies, histories, and sociological studies dealing with the CPUSA have been invaluable. Although formal Party records are not available, I made maximum use of accumulated memorabilia and cross-checked the recollections of individuals.

The ability of most Old Leftists to describe and evaluate their lives with considerable self-criticism, if not detachment, is most impressive. These were and are passionate people for the most part, interested in understanding the significance of their political careers and institutional affiliations. My greatest difficulty in gathering a representative sample was finding informants who still held orthodox Communist views. Primary contacts tended to be of a particular type: people who left the Party in the mid-fifties and have since become anti-Stalinist but not anti-Communist democratic socialists. Fortunately, enough orthodox—that is, still essentially pro-Soviet and Stalinist—veterans agreed to be interviewed. With perhaps one exception, the bitter and the disillusioned do not appear in the sample.

■ *point of view*

This study will, I hope, help to flesh out a more dense and comprehensive history of the American Communist Party that takes local dynamics into full account. My first goal is to provide my own generation and later generations of radicals with some insight into the qualities that sustain or subvert the stability and vitality of a local radical community.

Every research effort operates on certain hunches, if not biases. Mine are significant to the particular approach I have chosen. The reader will have to determine whether my predispositions mar the evidence I present.

Despite a few moments of ecstatic and millenial expectations, I have been a fairly consistent advocate of democratic socialism and a Marxist approach to the study of society and culture. As such, I am critical of social democratic politics as prone to self-satisifed trusteeship of capitalist goals, of Soviet-style Communism as fundamentally corrupt and hostile to basic civil liberties, and of anarchism and various forms of Maoist Communism as utopian and therefore susceptible to excess. Modern history seems to indicate that an authoritarian model of economic development directed by a Marxist-Leninist party through the state makes some sense for poor and backward nations, although such disasters as the Pol Pot regime in Cambodia force one to a chilling recognition of the consequences of left-wing fanaticism. In Western and advanced nations, experience rather than theory informs one that working-class movements tend to opt for either social democratic formations (including American liberal and British laborite variants) or authoritarian Communist trade-union and party ones. Why this is so is a query that deserves the utmost study and yet so far has received virtually no serious attention, other than a blaming of false leadership. Suffice it to say that a commitment to democratic socialism often seems to be closer to a Kantian imperative than to a Hegelian historical synthesis. What is there in the make-up of a worker, or indeed of any nonexploiter, that tolerates impositions from capitalists, labor bureaucracies, and state officialdom? Answers do not come easily, and yet I persist in attempting to move beyond a Scylla and Charybdis of revision and repression, of social democratic sell-out and Stalinist cynicism.

My attempt focuses on the following problem: how can a sober, pragmatic movement in touch with the everyday realities of immediate reform maintain its revolutionary cutting edge? This is the political counterpart of the personal problem of how to be *in* but not *of* the world. The question has been addressed strategically through the concept of structural reforms.[26] The British writer Stanley Moore offers the most useful and modest approach to this dilemma arguing, in brief, that the commitment to a transition from the socialist to the communist stage—that is, from a postcapitalist order with reward based on one's contributions to a *gemeinschaft* with no division of labor and reward based on need—must be rejected as utopian. Basing his analysis upon the experiences of left-wing totalitarianism, Moore eschews the Marxian vision of communism as "romantic and utopian in theory, oppressive and reactionary in practice."[27] He distinguishes a "sociology of change" rooted in Marx's empirical analysis of capitalism from a "dialectic of liberation" resting on "a quantum leap out of history" into communitarian utopia.[28]

Such an assertion is not sufficient. Marxism must disengage itself from its utopian vision, from its anticipation of the end of alienation, from its dreams of utter harmony and community, from its belief that the state will wither away. But must it necessarily, inexorably, be reduced to the kind of reformism associated with social democracy or the Alice-in-Wonderland elitism of Communist Party hegemony?

A sober assessment of human capability does not necessarily lead to a rejection of social justice and equality. Lenin was capable of the following exultation:

> Revolutions are the locomotives of history, said Marx. Revolutions are festivals of the oppressed and the exploited. At no other time are the mass of the people in a position to come forward so actively as creators of a new social order, as at the time of revolution. At such times the people are capable of performing miracles, if judged by the limited, philistine yardstick of gradualist progress.[29]

Yet he was, at the same time, the consummate realist, eschewing ideological and romantic definitions belied by material realities. His euphoric lapses in *State and Revolution* are more than balanced by his single-minded attention to actual behavior.[30] One must make the revolution with human beings as they actually are, not as one wishes they were; and one sustains the revolution by continuing to pay attention to human behavior.

The Old Leftists I have interviewed straddled such dilemmas with little self-consciousness or reflection of their own behavior. They were for the most part not psychologically sophisticated. In many ways they were conservative—not Victorian or prudish, but solidly old-fashioned in their basic values. I am intrigued by the relationship between their personal and primary group-behavior and their political and institutional beliefs and activities. In particular, I want to understand the strengths and weaknesses of their particular mix of character, ideology, and organization. I do not wish to project these Old Leftists as models for newly chastened sixties radicals; rather, my intention is to use Communist Party experiences to raise questions about the relationship between radicals' way of life and their effectiveness in organizing constituents.

There is a need to approach such a task with great humility. The veterans of the Communist Party often behaved badly, brutalizing comrades, manipulating constituents, and treating loved ones hypocritically and insensitively. Yet we of the following political generation have also proved capable of atrocious behavior, tolerating injustice in the name of abstractions, sanctioning adventurism and terrorism, generating dogmatism, phrase-mongering, and all the posturings associated with the Old Left. And the cruelties, mostly unintended, of our personal relations have been at least as damaging as those of our political elders.

Those of us who have been humbled by our own loss of innocence and approach to maturity have found it necessary to take another look at the radicals and organizers of the previous political generation. Their failures now look less pathetic and cowardly; their moderation now seems less irresponsible and "revisionist." Like the child who finally discovers, somewhere in early adulthood, that his parents have grown wiser, we radicals of the sixties, coming to grips with the realities of defeats, setbacks, even mortality, must take a more realistic and respectful look at another political generation that struggled, in a different context, with similar problems.

My goal is not to deify previously condemned activists. The men and women who made up the CPUSA were neither saints nor knaves, though sometimes, in seeking forms of sainthood, they tragically and inexorably produced its opposite. Ultimately, they were people committed to a vision of social justice and a strategy of social change that make them my political forebears. And like my biological parents, they merit a love that includes—in fact, requires—recognition of their faults and errors. Needless to say, such a love also rests on an honoring.

two

radicalization

It may be only in the United States that one addresses the process of radicalization as a problem. To ask why someone became a radical presupposes that a particular deviancy must be explained. The literature on radicals and radicalization is replete with analyses with a psychological bent. Radicalization has been reduced to a phase of the identity crisis, an Oedipal conflict between generations, a manifestation of authoritarian personality structures, and a consequence of Dr. Benjamin Spock's allegedly permissive child-rearing techniques.[1]

The gestation of the particular type of radical who becomes a member of the American Communist Party inspires an even greater emphasis on deviance, theological as well as psychological in nature. The demonology of many studies of Communist Party members is best considered a sad reflection of what we must now call the First Cold War of the late forties and early fifties, when all but the most fair-minded liberal scholars succumbed to McCarthyism.

In recent years, scholars have shown a more respectful interest in both the general question of radicalization and the more specific issue of American Communism. The breakdown of Cold War stereotypes during the 1960s made it more difficult to trace all radicals to alien roots. Of equal significance, scholars influenced by that decade of movement and resistance began to ask more pertinent questions about the process of radicalization. They sought to understand what produces radicals, particularly in a culture without a densely textured radical tradition. What are the personal, familial, institutional, and cultural factors that bring individuals into radical groups and movements?

■ *historical context*

First and foremost one must address the historical context within which radicalization occurs. In particular, one must place the twenty-six men and ten women interviewed in this study within the context of both the Communist Party and the political landscape following the Great Crash of 1929. These Philadelphia-based activists, political children of the Depression and Roosevelt's New Deal, of the rise of fascism and the diverse popular movements among industrial workers, farmers, the unemployed, blacks, and tenants, are essentially a thirties generation. For example, the mean year of radicalization is 1936, the year of Roosevelt's second election victory, of the beginning of the Spanish Civil War, and of the rise of the Congress of Industrial Organizations (CIO). The mean age of radicalization is 19.6; the median is 20. These Philadelphia Communists began as a youth movement in a particular period of historical and cultural upheaval.

The French political sociologist Annie Kriegel suggests that a political generation experiences a "knot," that is, a "point of origin and of reference" that creates a group identity.[2] Although not all generational cohorts shared the same response to such knots as the 1930s, one can still seek to make sense of why some did. I cannot pretend to chart a "quantitative description of dated occurrences" that correlates with a statistically based cohort, but it remains possible to examine a political generation nevertheless.[3] Some growing up in the thirties were minimally affected by the Crash and went about their business oblivious to political events. Others found ways to integrate special experiences and social trauma into already established liberal or conservative frames. A much larger group, deeply affected by the trauma of economic dislocation, carried through the rest of their lives a sense of scarcity and the preciousness of food, clothing and shelter. A few within this affected group were "struck by the event as by lightning."[4] Most of those so affected were politicized by the Roosevelt Revolution, the banner of the New Deal. Among the politicized, however, were some who turned against the system itself, rejecting capitalism as inherently unstable and unjust and proclaiming socialism as a viable and inspiring alternative. Most such radicals found the American Communist Party to be the most compelling voice articulating their values, ideas, and visions. Those who joined the Communist Party in the Depression years are hardly typical or representative, but they are nevertheless a significant variation within both their own generation and the history of radicalism.[5]

To begin to examine what they found attractive in the Communist Party, one must consider initially how that party addressed the social issues and problems of the 1930s.

■ *cpusa, 1919–1935*

Those who joined the Party prior to the Great Crash well understood adversity; in fact, one can view the entire first decade of the Party's existence in the United States as one of crisis. What became the Communist Party, U.S.A., emerged out of a painful and destructive split in the Socialist Party that left all the groups involved weaker and smaller. Then, following a Soviet-directed strategy, American Communists went underground. When they re-emerged, their numbers were slight and their composition was disproportionately foreign-born.[6]

In the late twenties the Party became a more fully integrated member of the Soviet-dominated Comintern and began to establish some semblance of a stable identity after the purges of Trotskyists and Lovestonites. Earl Browder and William Z. Foster emerged as the dominant figures of a now "Bolshevized"—in fact, Stalinized—Party.[7]

Initially Finns were the dominant national group in the Party, but with the elimination of the autonomy of the foreign-language federations, Eastern European Jews, more assimilated and Americanized and centered in New York City and other urban areas, became the dominant minority.[8] Sam Darcy, born in the Ukraine in 1905, brought to the United States at the age of two by working-class parents, raised in the Yiddish-socialist subculture of New York City, a Young Communist League leader in the twenties and a national figure by 1929, is fairly typical of the first group of Party cadres. They lived by a Bolshevik code of behavior culled from the classics of Lenin: *What is To Be Done?, Imperialism: The Highest Stage of Capitalism, Materialism and Empirio-Criticism, State and Revolution, The Proletarian Revolution and the Renegade Kautsky,* and *"Left-wing" Communism: An Infantile Disorder.*[9] They believed that they knew what was to be done, these survivors of the origins of the Party, some of whom, like Browder and Foster, had roots in the old Socialist or Wobbly tradition.

In the late twenties the Party, under Comintern direction, entered what was called the "Third Period," a severely militant, abrasive strategy that anticipated worldwide depression. Communists at this time argued that reformers and social democrats, by suggesting ameliorative solutions to capitalist crisis, played into the hands of the rising reactionary and fascist forces. They were, indeed, "social fascists" and consequently more devious adversaries than the open enemies of the workers. On these grounds Communists, in the United States and elsewhere, eschewed alliances with liberals and socialists. In Germany, it was a tragic period in which Communists cried, "After Hitler, us."[10]

At the same time, Communists were able to win respect for themselves in the United States, especially after October 1929, as the most militant and uncompromising fighters for the rights of workers, blacks, and other oppressed groups. Communists fought against mortgage foreclosures and tenant evictions and for union recognition, better wages and working conditions, rights for the unemployed, and civil rights for black people in mines, mills, factories, and neighborhoods.[11] They formed the idealistic John Reed Clubs, called for "proletarian literature," and strongly condemned Hoover, Roosevelt, and the early New Deal. In 1932 many intellectuals rallied to Foster and Ford, the Party standard-bearers; membership, despite incredible turnover, rose from 7,500 in 1930 to 20,593 in 1933.[12]

■ *the popular front, 1935-1939*
Beginning with the national leaders, particularly in France and to some extent in the United States, Communists began to recognize the disastrous consequences of Third Period ultraleftism. The rise of Hitler and Nazism forced a change in strategy that reflected the already growing sense among many locally based Communists that an alliance against fascism, the primary and most dangerous adversary, was imperative. In the United States, signs of practical cooperation with "social fascists" predate Dimitrov's United Front speech of 1935.[13]

Georgi Dimitrov's manifesto called for a United Front, an alliance of all socialist and Communist forces representing the working class, and a Popular (or People's) Front Against Fascism, a coalition of all progressive, antifascist workers, intellectuals, liberals, and middle-class elements. It marked a new path for the world Communist movement.[14]

Under the banner of the Popular Front, the adage "All not for us are against us" was transformed into "All not against us are for us." It was an inclusive strategy, seeking to unite all of what came to be called "progressive" forces behind the Soviet Union's primary goal of forging an alliance with the Western powers against the aggressions of Nazi Germany and its allies, Japan and Italy. The former "imperialist powers" became "the democracies," and Roosevelt the "fascist" became a "progressive," if still criticized, chief executive.[15] The Party's role in the rise of organized labor during the CIO campaigns of 1936 through 1939 made it a minor but important factor in American politics. Between 1936 and 1939 (and again between 1941 and 1947), American Communists sought and often built alliances and coalitions with non-Communists in a struggle against domestic reaction and international fascism.[16]

It is significant that most of the interviewed Philadelphia Communists joined the Party between 1936 and 1938. One must imagine the political and moral universe facing a twenty-year-old in 1936, the beginning year of the Popular Front.

Such American-born, disproportionately Jewish recruits were not fired primarily by the memories of Tsarist oppression, Cossacks, or the Bolshevik Revolution itself. There are two generations within the Communist Party experience. The Popular Front generation, often assimilated Jews, lacked the first-hand experience of Old World oppression that marked the foreign language–based 1905ers, that is, those who came to the United States following the defeat of the 1905 Russian Revolution, and their 1920s progeny.[17] The thirties generation had only read about the early Bolshevik struggles in the era of War Communism and the New Economic Policy. They gloried in Soviet accomplishment, but were one step removed.

Depression-generation Communists were propelled by indigenous images of Hoovervilles, apple-sellers, breadlines, unemployed councils, and the militant strikes of 1934 in San Francisco, Toledo, and Minneapolis; they responded to the more progressive reforms of the New Deal and its patrician president and to the threats represented by the Liberty League, Father Charles Coughlin, and Huey Long. Their international issues, while very compelling indeed, were a part of Popular Front imagery: Five Year Plans, hydroelectric plants, Moscow subways, Stakhanovite altruism, all in contrast with American and Western capitalist stagnation and callousness. Most important was the struggle against fascism, a relatively new concept and reality but often the emotional and moral center of radicalization. The Popular Front persuasively called for a struggle against Hitler, anti-Semitism, concentration camps, book burnings, xenophobia, Italian aggressions against Ethiopia, and, finally, the fascist challenge in Spain.[18] Harry Freedman places Nazi Germany and fascism at the top of the sources of his radicalization: "First and foremost, I was a Jew and saw in the Party and in the Soviet Union a model," the only instruments fighting reaction on all fronts. Next in importance, he places the Spanish Civil War. Finally, Freedman lists the effects of the Depression, including the massive unemployment and the rising labor struggles.

Otto Kramer views his involvement as "comparatively simple. . . . just as the civil rights movement of the sixties fired up another generation, so the Spanish Civil War set off a rocket in my behalf." The Spanish Civil War inspired the chief international metaphor of all progressive and democratic peoples: "*No pasarán,*" they shall not pass.[19] Along with Dimitrov, the most articulate spokesman for the Popular Front theme of collective security was the Soviet diplomat Maxim Litvinov, whose impassioned speeches at the League of Nations brought many Americans to accept the USSR as the most consistent opponent of fascism.

As the historian Robert Rosenstone suggests, Spain was the issue that brought the most recruits into the Party and the catalyst that led many into the Popular Front movement.[20] Johnny Tisa, already a labor organizer, heard a Spanish Republican woman speak at a trade-union convention and immediately volunteered to go to Spain. Others put most of their political time into support work and relief drives in aid of the Republic. To most thirties Communists, it was the dress rehearsal for the coming confrontation with fascism.

The Depression generation of Communists also responded to the revival of Americana that the Popular Front both fostered and celebrated. Perhaps more than "The Internationale," thirties

Communists sang Woody Guthrie's "This Land is Your Land," enveloped in images evoked by John Steinbeck and Clifford Odets and emotionally close to, if sometimes uncomfortable with, Browder's disingenuous slogan "Communism is Twentieth Century Americanism." Communists of the Depression generation read more of Stalin and Lenin than of Marx and were perhaps equally influenced by Charles Beard and Vernon Louis Parrington; their new pantheon of heroes included Tom Paine, Jefferson, Lincoln, and Frederick Douglass.[21]

In a very special sense, the Popular Front allowed Communists to combine two sometimes contradictory beliefs and sets of images: a kind of populist patriotism and an international sense of solidarity that was ultimately attached to Soviet interests. American Communists were able to balance, at least until 1939, attacks on "Tories" and "Copperheads" in the name of a crusading New Deal, efforts to create an alliance of all democracies against fascist aggression in Spain, and defenses of the Soviet Union against "Trotskyite" and "fascist" slander and counter-revolutionary plots. As second-generation Americans, sensitive about being indigenous, thirties Communists could attack convention while remaining true to their nation. One Old Leftist speaks of feeling that she was "going with the mainstream" in this period. Others refer emotionally and respectfully, though always critically, to Roosevelt and the New Deal. Mort Levitt calls this period "the zenith" and refers to Eleanor Roosevelt as "the greatest First Lady the United States ever had." Others agree that it was "a golden era."

The historian Richard H. Pells argues that "in a curious way the Communists appeared more comfortable when they could regard themselves as integral members of the larger society rather than when they were forced to act as its critical conscience."[22] Popular Front Communists, like all activists of the period except the merely rebellious, chose to combine a rootedness in the American experience with a militant assault on social injustices. This preference sometimes approached the grotesque as people overcompensated for Soviet idolatry. Indeed, there were conformist and conservative aspects to the Popular Front ethos, as many observers have stressed.[23]

However, the desire for an intimate connection with the American experience is also in part a result of the relative tenuousness of Communist ethnic identity. That tenuousness, in Philadelphia within a district that might be 75 percent Jewish and 75 percent second-generation, was likely to respond to the Party's manipulative use of native symbols. The American Communist volunteers in Spain formed the Lincoln, not the Debs, Brigade. The accomplishments of that era within the CIO and the labor movement in general sustained and deepened certain indigenous associations, even among experienced cadres. John L. Lewis was a genuine folk hero to many Communists, including those fully aware of his past and his political perspective. They were pleased to follow a large May Day rally with a July 4th celebration that featured banners proclaiming "Life, Liberty, and the Pursuit of Happiness" along with "Communism—Twentieth Century Americanism."[24] They wanted, perhaps too deeply, an indigenous radical tradition.

Arthur Liebman suggests that the Left, from the turn of the century through the thirties, was "in large part dependent on the support it received from persons and institutions imbedded in an ethnic subculture—that of the Jews." He describes a world familiar to all twenty-three of the Jewish Party members interviewed, and to several non-Jewish ones raised in northeastern cities: a Yiddish-socialist subculture of *landmanschaften,* fraternal orders, Jewish trade unions, especially in the garment industry, progressive *schules,* and summer camps. This constellation that Liebman calls "contra-culture" made Communism, if not the norm, certainly a commonplace in urban areas like Philadelphia.[25]

Whether Jewish members had conventionally religious or more secular upbringings, all grew up within what Liebman aptly calls a subculture of a subculture that allowed political activism and Marxist ideas to become familiar phenomena. If one's parents were not left-wing, it is likely that one's uncle or cousin or neighbor was. Thus, the theme of continuity is particularly strong among Jewish Communists.

I found little evidence of generational rebellion or of a psychosociological motif of alienation and frustration. There was one case of a cruel and insensitive father whose chronic belittling gestures still rankle after forty-five years, and in another instance, Fred Garst was disowned by an embarrassed and hostile family who blamed him for the strike facing their business. On the whole, however, Philadelphia Communists seem to have had relatively normal upbringings and conventionally loving relationships with their parents.

In a time of political turbulence and moral crisis, like the thirties, a certain proportion of young people, especially those with some higher education, will be attracted to idealistic causes, impressed with the integrity of encountered radicals, and driven by the injustices they observe and soon experience directly. Most begin to investigate radical groups tentatively, sometimes out of curiosity, sometimes pushed by circumstances. Few share one former Communist's feeling that the initial involvement with the Party "changed my whole personality." As with contemporary religious cults and therapeutic cure-alls, such transformations involve a problematic trade-off of rigidity, dogmatism, and detachment from important reservoirs from one's own past.

Most Communists speak of significant changes in their lives, especially in the discovery of a new meaning to life, but essential personality seems to have remained constant. Few members castigated their pre-Party lives or gave any indication that their political choices led them to deny their roots. I recognize the softening of older tensions, the mellowing of family hurts, the moderating of political passions, that come with the years. In addition, it is important to be careful about the retrospective whitewashing of events and experiences. But the telltale signs of this process—rigidity, hyperbole, memory blocks, fumblings— rarely appeared in my interviews. Old Leftists spoke at times of childhood and adolescent pains, of youthful excesses, of limitations in their own characters. But most managed to grow up without breaking all links with their families. These Philadelphia Communists experienced considerable continuity within a context: the continuity of the Jewish left-wing subculture in northeastern cities like Philadelphia within the context of the thirties.

□ *sammy cohen*

Sammy Cohen was raised within that Jewish left-wing subculture. His father was a skilled craftsman, a socialist, and a self-educated intellectual, who arrived in America from the Ukraine in 1906. His mother, who arrived in 1910, was a seamstress. The father, a militant and idealistic immigrant worker, took his small family West to Utah to participate in an agrarian socialist community and later, after being fired for his radicalism from a local shop, gave farming in Bucks County a short fling. Eventually, however, they settled in the Strawberry Mansion section of Philadelphia, a working-class and lower-middle-class Jewish neighborhood, where, as Sammy Cohen says, his father was alternately fired for his politics and rehired for his skill.

The elder Cohen was sympathetic to the old Socialist Party and apparently had met Debs, Big Bill Haywood, and Elizabeth Gurley Flynn. He decided not to join the Communists in 1919 but remained friendly with them in his Jewish local of the carpenters' union.

Sammy's parents, caught between the antagonisms of Socialist and Communist networks, at first did not send him either to the Workmen's Circle or to the International Workers Order *schule*; instead, the independent carpenter taught his son himself. Later the parents relented, and in 1934, at age eleven, Sammy was sent to the Communist Party–related IWO *schule* and soon allowed to join the Young Pioneers, the Party youth group.

Sammy's mother, while sharing her husband's political values, felt that he "trusted too many non-Jews" and crossed over to the Gentile world without sufficient caution. Like many Jews within her Jewish-socialist subculture, she was more comfortable with her Jewish bourgeois neighbors than with her husband's radical but "*goyische*" comrades.

The elder Cohen was widely read in both the Yiddish and English language press. He admired the scientific and technical institutions, like the Massachusetts Institute of Technology, that represented the best of a bourgeois culture and the achievements that had to be absorbed by the proletariat, but he believed that an education in the humanities should come from experience and self-education, removed from the ideological distortions of bourgeois instruction. He believed that the working-class revolutionary did not need college to learn philosophy or to be enriched through literature and the arts. Although he enjoyed, and encouraged his children to participate in, athletics, Sammy Cohen's father was disturbed by an American popular culture in which spectatorship and professionalization seemed to be turning sports and entertainment into a mere opiate.

Sammy moved very smoothly into Communist activity while in high school in the late 1930s. It was the heyday of the Popular Front's mobilization. As a young member of both the American Student Union (ASU) and the Young Communist League (YCL), Sammy, a student at Central High School, worked with students from about half a dozen other senior high schools in the area. His transition into the Communist Party network seemed smooth and natural, and he officially joined the Party in 1938 at the age of fifteen. He was indeed his father's son.

□ *sam katz*

Sam Katz's parents were Bundists from the Ukraine who became supporters of the new American Communist Party in the 1920s. They were both tailors struggling to earn a living in the Strawberry Mansion section. By age twelve, Sam was being sent to Young Pioneer meetings by his father to hear speakers evoke the new Russia, the future China, and the present struggles of the labor movement. He quickly became an activist, brawling with the football team over his activities in high school, fighting for a free lunch program, and getting expelled (he had called upon Party longshoremen and seamen to combat the varsity). He recalls that his mother successfully pleaded for his readmission; immigrant parents, Bolshevik or bourgeois, wanted their children to get the benefit of an education.

During the 1928 presidential campaign, young Sam, fourteen, spoke for the Party's Foster and Gitlow ticket on a West Philadelphia street corner, only to be met by taunting American Legionnaires. Once again, Party prols came to the rescue. When the police came to break up the brawl, Sam was arrested for inciting a riot and spent a week in jail. Local papers headlined the story, "Boy Red Incites Riot."

Sam was not particularly interested in school, spending most of his time on YCL activities or listening to the intriguing stories of international adventure told to him by the Communist seamen. Finally he quit school to go to work in a factory, despite his parents' disapproval. He was soon selected to become a "colonizer" in Reading, that is, to enter a garment factory and attempt to organize the workers. He spent his time there "under conditions of privation," living in an attic, hidden from a sympathizer's own household, never receiving promised Party funds, often hungry, and thanks to the Depression, unable to get a job. Returning to Philadelphia with a sense "of personal defeat," he turned seventeen.

Home was tough; his parents found little steady work, and Sam survived on odd jobs. Most of his energy went into the earliest efforts to organize unemployed councils. He recalls being "impressed with the size of the demonstrations" in Washington and especially with the estimated 100,000 who rallied at Rayburn Plaza in Philadelphia. Sam was living, eating, and drinking Party activity, only coming home to sleep, if that. His home base was Party headquarters, then at 5th and Spring Garden Streets.[26]

In the mid-thirties, with the Depression showing some signs of lifting, Sam began to get "a little tired of poverty" and found a full-time job in one of the state-run liquor stores. There he proceeded to help organize a local that eventually joined the State, County and Municipal Workers Union (CIO). He moved up to districtwide leadership, became involved with the Philadelphia CIO Council, and was now "a full-fledged trade unionist" and a Party leader in union affairs.

Sam Katz became a Party functionary, remaining at the district level of activity for the next fifteen years. While his early life had been filled with rebellion against authority, it was not a generational rebellion in any sense. He was pursuing the core values he absorbed from his family; he was a "red-diaper" baby. Such a family background, while not typical, was hardly unique. While only four of the Old Leftists I interviewed are the children of Communist Party members, fourteen (39 percent) experienced some variety of progressive political upbringing. The other twenty-two (61 percent) either had conservative or reactionary parents or, more often, had no discernible political background at all.

Of the fourteen from progressive political homes, six had fathers active in labor unions, five came from socialist milieux, and several had parents who belonged to the Workmen's Circle or the International Workers Order. A few had parents with Old World loyalties to the Jewish Bund or to such left-wing Zionist groups as the Farband. For such young people, as Nathan Glazer notes, "it was neither eccentric nor exceptional to become a Communist."[27]

Ruth Shapiro speaks of growing up "smelling the clannishness," the sense of community, within the Jewish Left. As her father experienced upward mobility in America, becoming "a somebody," he became a more moderate leader within the Workmen's Circle and an active Zionist. Ruth's more radical mother, on the other hand, opted for the IWO. Ruth describes the intense Jewish radicalism of both her parents as a "political religion," with all of the heat, passion, and intolerance that the term implies. She says that "when Palestine became a crisis, our house became a crisis." Al Schwartz's father was a Communist Party organizer, blacklisted from local shops but comfortable within the Yiddish-speaking world of garment workers and machinists.

More characteristic Jewish subjects felt political radicalism "all around" them rather than within their immediate families. Meyer Weiner's parents were nonpracticing Jews, poor and politically uninvolved, but several of his older brothers became union activists and organizers. He also remembers that a close friend's father was a militant socialist and that his neighborhood had "a fairly strong socialist-communist composition." Several Philadelphia Communists had brothers or sisters, sometimes cousins, who joined the left-wing movement.

Milt Goldberg's father, working in the garment industry, shifted his allegiance from Eugene Debs to Franklin Roosevelt in the 1930s. Like several others, his family experienced an Americanization that touched politics as well as everyday life. Otto Kramer describes his Russian-born parents as highly Americanized, apolitical and "religious only to a certain extent." Kramer feels that "the new culture almost immediately took them over."

Some Jewish Communists, like Mort Levitt, were raised outside the Jewish subculture, in Gentile neighborhoods, "the only Jews on the street in a working-class area." And a few, like Tessie Kramer, describe their parents as "illiterate," with no books in the house and a total absence of any cultural stimulation. As with all stereotypes, that of the vibrant Jewish-Left subculture must be tempered by significant exceptions.

Working-class backgrounds predominate among the Old Leftists, Jewish and Gentile. Twenty (56 percent) come from working-class homes, while another four (11 percent) have lower-middle-class backgrounds. Few parents, however, were engaged in the mass production or heavy industrial work emphasized by Marxists in defining the proletariat. Most were skilled or semiskilled workers: barbers, tailors, cabinetmakers, jewelers, or garment workers; some owned small businesses. The remainder

(33 percent) includes one upper-class and seven middle-class backgrounds, with the professions and commerce predominating.[28]

Twenty-four of those interviewed were raised in the greater Philadelphia area; twelve migrated to Philadelphia during their adult lives, from metropolitan northeastern cities (eight), from smaller industrial towns (two), or from the rural South (two). Of the Philadelphia-raised Old Leftists, all grew up in ethnic, primarily Jewish, neighborhoods such as West Philadelphia (seven), South Philadelphia (five), and Strawberry Mansion (three). Such neighborhoods were left-wing strongholds until the "red scare" of 1947–1954 weakened the Party and, simultaneously, suburbanization undermined inner-city ethnic areas.[29]

The Gentile life stories reveal more discontinuity. In the radical pockets within the Southern and Eastern European Catholic immigrant communities, however, the process of radicalization followed similar lines.

□ *angie repice*

Angie Repice's parents came to North Philadelphia in the years before the Great War. Her mother was "a charming, quiet lady," deeply religious, and deferential to Angie's father, a railroad worker. Mr. Repice had become militantly anticlerical because of what he saw as the hypocrisies of priests. Initially "pretty much of an anarchist," he was called "the Bolshevik" by fellow immigrants because of his outspoken support for the Russian Revolution.

It was a poor household but a loving one. The family spoke Italian at home, and Angie's father was active in Italian fraternal organizations. She remembers the devastating influenza epidemic of 1918/1919, during which her infant brother died. The local priest wanted money to perform the last sacraments; her struggling, proud father saw this as "the last straw" and forbade all church-going within the family.

Angie did piecework in the garment industry while attending public school; it was a family effort in which she labored before and after classes and during her lunch break. The Depression made things worse, as her father's construction business collapsed. There were six children to support.

Angie "was furious" that she could not continue her schooling after graduating from elementary school—that was sufficient for girls, she was informed—but accepted her fate. She entered the full-time work world in a period when unemployment was approaching one-third of the labor force. This "very aggressive little girl," still a teen-ager, got factory work and discovered the class struggle. "Who knew from strikes?" she recalls with wry amusement. With her father's approval—the union leadership came to the house to gain it—she became an activist with the Textile Workers Union.

Angie's education, now mostly from the school of experience, expanded when she was invited to attend the eight-week summer sessions of the Affiliated Schools, a Bryn Mawr College program influenced by radical YMCA-YWCA staffers and specifically geared to working women. There she studied economics, labor history, and literature. Such training gave her a context within which to assess her experience.

Angie Repice's road leftward had already been smoothed by a brother who was a YCL activist and, of course, by her father's lifelong radicalism. Her house had served as a center for Sacco-Vanzetti protest meetings, raucous, argumentative, laughing meetings that included such prominent figures as the Wobbly organizer Joe Ettor, who, Angie proudly proclaims, "wanted to adopt me." She wanted to enter that political universe, seemingly exclusive to men, and, with her brothers and sisters, would sneak as close as they could: "They were in the dining room eating; we were in the kitchen listening."

As Angie's activism burgeoned, she found herself filling all of her time with meetings, lectures, discussions, at all hours and late into the night. Her father, still the Old World patriarch, tried to limit her involvement, but she said, "Either you let me go or I'm not going to go to work." One of her activist friends, a socialist, came to the house and persuaded Mr. Repice to allow her to continue participating in radical and trade-union activities.

In 1934 she joined the YCL and became, as she stresses, "*the* activist of the family." She worked within the "Y," her "mass organization," and with the YCL and the American Youth Congress. She rose quickly to leadership in the youth activities of the Party, partly, as she admits, "because of my background," but also because of her energy, enthusiasm, and ability to work with a variety of groups. An Italian working-class woman was, of course, a valuable asset to the Communist Party.

Several subjects with Catholic working-class backgrounds recall that their fathers were union sympathizers or even militants. Tim Palen remembers his father's involvement in mining strikes in western Pennsylvania; Jack Ryan's father was simultaneously a Democratic Party precinct leader, a staunch trade unionist, and a noted local bootlegger.

None of the black Old Leftists had radical political upbringings. Ethel Paine's father was a Republican leader in his community. The other three blacks, however, had low-income parents who simply struggled to earn a living and lacked the time and the energy to provide a political education for their children.

Some young people came to the Communist Party from much less congenial environments. They came from politically conservative homes or unhappy ones, or simply conventional families that did not seem to speak to their disaffections and their dreams. And they found a new home, a new family, in the support network that was the Communist Party in the thirties.

□ *mark greenly*

Mark Greenly was introduced to the Communist Party in an almost comical fashion. While at Gratz High School, he found an ASU membership card decorated with the slogan "Stop the Hearst March Toward Fascism." He was curious about the group and finally made contact with a Gratz member who invited him to a meeting.

The meeting was across town in Strawberry Mansion, a section unfamiliar to Greenly. He arrived an hour early after walking across town and found what to him was an exotically Jewish, disheveled apartment, with broken-down furniture, the powerful smell of Jewish food, a little, dark girl with no underwear, and "a bushy-haired guy." As others began to drift in, "one guy wanted to put up a picture of Lenin on the wall." Others, however, argued that it was inappropriate (since ASU was a coalition of Communists, Socialists, and progressives and not formally a Marxist-Leninist group). Greenly, bewildered by the argument that ensued and dazed by the fury of the combat, the political terminology, and the plethora of initialed groups mentioned, sat and listened. The meeting finally began and ran very efficiently, covering electoral issues and the need to support New Deal candidates. During the question period Greenly innocently asked, "Is this a Communist organization?" He was immediately and furiously attacked by all parties: "That's red-baiting!" Greenly had no way at that point to know that within Popular Front groups like ASU it was considered provocative to bring to the surface the very sensitive issue of Communist domination.

Yet Greenly was not driven away by this minor trauma; he soon became heavily involved in his school's ASU chapter, rose to a leadership position, and helped to make it the largest in the city. What were the life experiences that permitted his radicalization despite an inauspicious beginning?

Mark Greenly is of Scandinavian descent. His parents were first-generation Americans. He was born in 1922 in the Midwest and came to Philadelphia with his family a few years later. His father was a mining engineer, a "near-genius" who spoke six languages but was "bigoted and intolerant," a man whose technical accomplishments got him listed in *Who's Who* but who nonetheless was never materially successful. Greenly's mother's family apparently included Socialists, but his father was "reactionary and anti-Semitic," although the household was essentially bereft of political discussion. The father traveled a great deal, and the marriage broke up in the early thirties. His mother, who experienced some emotional instability at this point, eventually remarried. Greenly describes his stepfather as a drunken "ignoramus" and "a real prick," who fought a great deal with his mother.

Greenly therefore sought comfort and support elsewhere. Initially, he found it with the father of a boyhood friend who discussed current events with him. Greenly recalls, "I didn't like what Hitler was doing," and the friend's father, a retired army officer, took him seriously enough to discuss such issues. He remembers a brief flirtation with religion at age fourteen but for the most part describes his teen years as somewhat lonely but filled with the typical pleasures of an urban neighborhood: hanging out, playing ball.

Greenly would practice the arguments he absorbed from his friend's father with people in the neighborhood. But another friend's parents "kept refuting all my arguments." He argued for Alf Landon; they countered with FDR. They were tolerant of his views, however, and gave him lots of literature to examine, including some about the Soviet Union.

Meanwhile, Greenly's schoolwork was "just enough to pass," and his stepfather advised him to enter a commercial program. Instead he took his married sister's advice and made a commitment to academic studies. During our interview, Greenly spoke warmly of his sister and her husband as family "who cared."

His schoolwork began to improve, and it was at this point, in tenth grade, that he found the ASU card. His integration into the student radical universe came quickly as he began to clash with school authorities over their denial of permission to bring antifascist speakers to school assemblies. He was soon arrested for illegal leafletting on school grounds, which only served to deepen his growing radicalism.

Greenly's pattern of radicalization is almost the polar opposite of Sammy Cohen's. Greenly rebelled against the bigotry of his erratic and critical father and the instability and neglect of his unstable mother and alcoholic stepfather. He found a variety of resources to help him establish a sense of self and a mode of representation, political discourse, to express that self. Without psychologizing, it seems clear that Greenly's radicalization allowed him to express his resentment at the injustices of his own life within a political context that tempered rage with a sense of social justice and a belief in humanity. Greenly could have chosen another kind of conversion, but he chose one that allowed him to join with a political generation of Communists who felt that they were defending "the salt of the earth" against fascism.

In 1938 he attended an ASU national meeting in New York and was elected to its executive committee. He was one of only two high school students elected. Greenly, a Northern European Protestant, was much cherished by a Communist student movement deeply embarrassed by its predominantly Jewish membership. He was often chosen for leadership or to attend conferences because of his ethnic identity. Yet Greenly did not feel used but rather took advantage of his opportunities to become a citywide student leader. He does recall, interestingly, that whereas the Jewish student activists were hopeful about their futures, he was oblivious to his own, and more recklessly "militant."

The critical moment for Greenly, as for many other young militants, came in 1939 when the Soviets agreed to a Non-Aggression Pact with Nazi Germany. Greenly says, "I had to decide whose side I'm on, on the side of the working people, or with the other bastards." He stayed loyal, became a YCL leader, organizing a small group with "Bolshevik discipline," and looked forward to becoming a professional Communist, a full-time revolutionary. He also married a Jewish girl, a comrade. Greenly sprinkles his comments with Yiddishisms and notes that he is often mistaken for a Jew.

A few Gentiles, never mistaken for Jews or, for that matter, with being anything but White Anglo-Saxon Protestants, embraced the Party in the context of the traumatic events of the thirties. Typically, they were from affluent families, went to the best schools, and had some of their illusions shattered by the economic suffering and oppression of the American working class and the mounting ugliness of fascism.

☐ *sally turpin*

Sally Turpin was born in upstate New York during World War I. Her father was a prominent Republican officeholder with Mayflower credentials, but her mother, who Sally asserts was the greater influence, was of immigrant, working-class stock. "My mother was much more political and analytic than my father, who was a sweet but shallow man," she adds.

She attended a "small and snobbish" Quaker school, where she was, as she describes herself, "a very unpopular girl," physically unattractive, occasionally obstreperous, and very bright.

At a prestigious Main Line college, Sally "busted out in culture all over the place," attended concerts, read voraciously, and "fell in with a bohemian bunch, largely Jewish." It was the heart of the Depression, but her family was untouched. In 1936 her father financed a European trip on which she was escorted by "a lively, unconventional" art professor.

Visiting galleries and cathedrals, Sally found herself in a France racked with labor conflict, with "people in the streets. . . . I had never experienced anything like that before." She remembers giving away all of her money to a struggling striker's family. The moment remains with her and marks a turning point in her life. They journeyed to Italy; meanwhile, "the war in Spain broke out under my nose." Sally recalls troop trains of Italians being sent out to Ethiopia and, at Padua, a heated argument with Italian Fascists during which, she says, "I found myself declaiming about liberty, fraternity, equality."

She had changed, but it was not yet clear in exactly what way. In 1936 she campaigned on campus for Roosevelt. That same year she read W. E. B. DuBois's *Black Reconstruction* and found herself angered at the lies she had been fed by her history professors. "A very exciting man," a Marxist classics professor, brought her into study groups, and the world of ideas seemed to explode. By early 1937, she had joined the YCL.

Such experiences and intellectual tutelage helped to ensure Sally Turpin's conversion to the Left. A multitude of activities brought her to total immersion and identification. She recalls attending massive rallies in Washington, having an affair with a fellow radical student, and being "up to my ears" in ambulance fund raising for Spain, the ASU, and local labor politics. After she graduated, this "convinced, committed, thoroughly organized Communist . . . wanted to go into the labor movement," but was instead assigned to head the high school section of the citywide ASU office.

Sally Turpin just immersed herself in a Communist Party milieu in which "everyone was so friendly—I cannot tell you how comradely the movement was then." She soon met a YCL organizer working out of Kensington, an intellectual of working-class origin. Their marriage cemented Sally Turpin's organizational commitments for the next fifteen years.

What kinds of children were these future Communists? What were their goals, their aspirations as adolescents? Were they high achievers, underachievers, chronic rebels, mediocrities? While there is much diversity, the predominant experience, at least among males, is that of the urban "street kid," with minor Jewish variations.

Although one working-class Catholic ran crap games on the streets and a Jewish Old Leftist was expelled from Hebrew school for punching the rabbi, there is little evidence in the Old Leftists' life stories of physical toughness or street-fighting experience. On the other hand, few seem to have been exclusively bookish. Ike Samuels recalls that he became "street-wise" early in life, hustling for money to help out his family, and Moe Levy describes his growing up in South Philadelphia as a period of "hanging around with the guys," playing ball, and being what he calls a "street kid." Most of the men had sports interests, including stickball, ping-pong, basketball, and other city games. Such Americanized behavior was linked with solid, often impressive, scholastic achievement. Harry Freedman, for example, speaks of being "active physically, a good ballplayer, a good student" who initially wanted to become a rabbi. Mort Levitt recalls that he was "a complete athlete who loved the outdoors" and "a pretty good student" as well. Several refer to themselves as high achievers and avid readers. Otto Kramer was an active Boy Scout and almost an Eagle before his political interests began to influence his extracurricular activities.

The women's childhood and adolescent experiences range from Angie Repice's sweatshops and piecework to Sally Turpin's upper-class private school. While the women were more studious in elementary and secondary school, they were not expected to proceed to college. One Jewish woman who, at her mother's urging, "went through the classics at age twelve," was encouraged by her father to attend normal school rather than seek a classical undergraduate education. She resisted and instead entered the job market. Tessie Kramer, on the other hand, says that she faced no battle at all about going to college and describes an active, stimulating high school period. She characterizes herself as "a very aesthetic and bright" adolescent, active in a wide variety of extracurricular activities. She adds, "I never really learned to cook an egg."

Ambitions and goals vary considerably in the life histories. In most cases one finds traditional attitudes toward work, although quite Americanized ones. The parents of the Depression generation often looked critically, at times angrily, and always quizzically, at their children's passion for sports, movies, and radio. Parents would exclaim, "What's a big boy like you, almost ready to get a full-time job, doing wasting his time with children's games like baseball?" These were decidedly American youth, more accomplished than the norm, more ambitious, perhaps even harder-working, yet very much products of the urban street society and of the new mass culture of ballparks and movie theaters. Even if they were "red-diaper babies" or raised within the Yiddish-socialist subculture, most still added popular culture heroes to their pantheon of socialist idols. It would be members of this generation who would see fit to proclaim mournfully "Babe Ruth Is Dead" on a *Daily Worker* front page headline.[30]

Only a few Philadelphia Communists share Ruth Shapiro's assertion that "we were very much immigrant children," envious of the social life of the public schools and feeling like outsiders in a milieu of proms, hops, and sports events. Nor do many relate to the more splendidly parochial remembrance of one national Party figure: "We were happy, unconflicted, suffered no identity crisis, saw no generation gaps. We lived in isolated security amongst our own kind. The goals and hopes of our parents were ours. We rejected those of society around us; ours was the dream of the future."[31] Such insularity may have been possible in environments like the New York City Coops, but in Philadelphia a fusion of left-wing and indigenous modes was more typical, at least among Jews of progressive backgrounds.[32]

All but four Philadelphia Communists attended urban public schools; two went to parochial and two to private schools. Only four did not complete high school, a measure of the value placed on education by Jewish culture in particular, but present among all groups considered. Many went on to college, and nearly half (seventeen) gained bachelor's degrees. Almost a third of the sample went on to attend graduate school. Philadelphia Depression-generation Communists were an impressively up-wardly mobile, educationally minded group.[33]

Most Communists stress the naturalness of their radicalization, giving support to Glazer's observation that "the Communists who joined the party in the course of a relatively common psychological development, far, far outnumber those who had exceptional and rare psychological reasons for joining." Few fit Gabriel Almond's assessment that American Communists, more middle class, more rebellious, more needy than continental European Communists, with weak fathers and dominating mothers, were casualties of "acculturative and socialization processes."[34]

Many simply stated that "the Depression molded our whole generation"; some tersely emphasize "the times," recalling the ever present news about Hitler, the New Deal, unemployment, the rising militancy of unemployed marches, rent strikes, and labor struggles.[35] Several Philadelphia Communists speak of entering the job market of the early and middle thirties, realizing how little was available, not despondent, still young, but forcefully made aware of the realities of the Depression.

A few Old Leftists remember being strongly anti-Communist at some point in their youth, although never actively so. One veteran had even joined a local fascist club, although primarily as a means of earning a scholarship. He adds that eventually he was "red-baited" out of the group for raising questions; at that point he hardly knew what communism was. Moe Levy recalls a "questioning period" during which he headed a Jewish high school discussion group. He invited one of the city's more prominent Jewish attorneys to speak and was amazed at the man's arrogance and insensitivity. Levy concludes that such experiences made him "disenchanted with this type of people." Those not from a left-wing milieu typically found themselves excited by the window on understanding that the Party provided. Stan Wax, for example, remembers the thrill of discovering Marxist literature, usually in pamphlet form, providing him with an alternative and more enlightening way to make sense of the world around him. Many subjects devoured Party literature, finding in it a key to knowledge in anything from the causes of the Depression to the nature of art. Tessie Kramer recalls feeling that "the whole world of literature fell into place . . . [through] dialectical materialism." Surprisingly few, however, had read the classics of Marxism before entering the Party. Pamphlets, mimeographs, leaflets, and speeches were the core of their early political reading.[36]

Stan Wax speaks euphorically about the lectures and rallies he attended in his youth. The speakers were always fiery and enthusiastic and the crowds were attentive and responsive. He reflects that such experiences led him to believe that "there was something beautiful in this socialism."

The Communist movement on campus attracted many to Party-initiated activities. Ike Samuels, after having dropped out of school for a year because of the Depression pinch, returned to join the pre–Popular Front National Student League. He began to learn about the causes of the economic crisis from his new comrades and soon was vigorously arguing in the classroom with an economics professor over what now seemed to be callous reflections on the laws of supply and demand. Several collegians were swept up by student strikes that provided them with intense and pleasurable contact with already radical students.

The campus Communists impressed many neophytes with their dedication and intelligence. As Arthur Liebman states: "Those who were attracted and became involved with the Left, especially those who rose to leadership positions as student leftists, were not the campus oddballs. They were generally the brightest, most precocious, and most dedicated students."[37] Neophyte Communists wanted to spend time with the campus radical leaders. Tessie Kramer speaks of the ASU and YCL leaders on her campus as "the most wonderful, the most creative, the most intelligent . . . they were the brightest." It is clear that those who joined the Communist movement were particularly impressed by the quality of its adherents.

Milt Goldberg casually replies, "I read a couple of books," when asked to explain his radicalization. He adds, however, that he found intellectual and moral stimulation at a Society of Friends center that he attended regularly, helping out with the arrangements for guest lecturers. Finally some radical students from Swarthmore took him aside and suggested that he was "too advanced" for Quaker activities. He had never met a Communist before and was intrigued by their confidence and their apparent knowledge. Moreover, he was very much flattered by their attention. He joined a clandestine Party club and became active. "I respected Party people; they were able, talented people," he concludes.

Soon he found himself in the midst of a strike at his workplace. The strike failed, but Goldberg discovered that most of the strike leaders, all fired and blacklisted, were Communists. Goldberg stresses that such discoveries were typical of the thirties, cementing recruits' belief in the integrity and dedication of Party people.

Thus, the process of radicalization for many began with contact with radical "significant others" who stimulated some tentative involvement. The recruit next experienced excitement and a sense of community through ongoing activity. Constituted authority then confirmed the emerging radicalization through acts of suppression, confirming the validity of radical categories and metaphors and providing the recruit with an intense experience of himself or herself as part of "the movement." All of a sudden, one was part of a new "we" whose very existence presupposed a "they" in a thoroughly visceral sense.[38]

In a common variation of this pattern, many were introduced to and recruited into the Communist Party by a single significant other, a dynamic and convincing politico who came to personify the movement to the neophyte. This person was characteristically a mentor rather than a guru, a teacher who influenced, not a prophet who mesmerized. Henry and Laura Blum joined their neighborhood Party club under the influence of "this very brilliant guy" who would "stand out when someone would bait him." This "wise-guy New Yorker" helped them slide smoothly into Party activities. They regard those early years as "the best years of our lives," mixing with Communists who were "brighter, more interested in the important things" than previous friends. They became socially close to their mentor and his wife, sharing meals, talking politics, and generally joining together in Party activities.

One Communist speaks of a YCL "older guy," maybe eighteen or nineteen (he himself was fifteen at the time) who "played a helluva game" of ball and who started a political group: "he was a very good and gentle person," the veteran remembers, not at all manipulative or cynical. Tim Palen was influenced by a Party functionary, Betty Gannett, who told him "the truth" about the new Soviet experience and predicted the Crash in mid-1929. Ethel Paine, a black Communist, speaks of being deeply impressed and influenced by Eslanda Robeson (Mrs. Paul Robeson) during the period of the Progressive Party.

Harry Freedman's brother's wife was his "significant other," while Fred Gerst had a "Damon and Pythias" relationship with a close friend who had a "mentor influence." Jack Ryan recalls a socialist "who couldn't read or write until he was twenty-three," whom he met while working in a knitting mill. This self-educated socialist worker told Ryan of his labor experiences and explained socialism to him in simple, clear, and attractive ways.

Why did not any within the sample opt for other left-wing groups, such as the Socialist Party, A. J. Muste's Workers Party, the Trotskyist Socialist Workers Party, or one of the many single-issue groups? Why did they not find satisfaction with Franklin Roosevelt's New Deal?

In the context of the thirties, the Communist Party seemed to these young people to be the most active, most militant, and most impressive organization around. It basked in the reflected light of the still young Soviet Union, identified in many minds with enlightened planning, the absence of any forms of discrimination, full employment, and a fierce opposition to fascism. New recruits were often inspired with the idea of "uniting scattered but kindred peoples into a whole of international solidarity."[39]

Some did explore other left-wing groups. Johnny Tisa initially joined the Young People's Socialist League (YPSL), a Socialist Party youth group. He was sent to their labor school for training but recalls that he was already becoming disenchanted with what he perceived as their excessive factionalism. At the school he met Communists who persuaded him to join what seemed to be a more effective and serious outfit. Many young radicals shared John Gates's conclusion: "It seemed that the Socialists only talked, while the Communists acted."[40]

Other political groups also recruited and organized, but apparently never had the drawing power of the American branch of the Communist International. There are no data, unfortunately, on the number of people who joined other radical groups, shifted from one to another, or dropped out of radical politics upon entering the work world. Harvey Klehr suggests, possibly with some exaggeration, that as many as 750,000 people may have joined the Communist Party at one time or another. The turnover was continuous and high. Many recruits left within a short time, making the CPUSA and, one suspects, other radical groups, revolving doors of the naive and the disillusioned.[41]

Some, however, stayed for several decades, during which they gained remarkable organizing experiences, contributed to key progressive achievements, lost all too many battles, fought against demoralization, married and had families, went off to war, sought to make ends meet, and participated in the organization and subculture that was the Communist Party, U.S.A. The following chapter will examine that organizational and cultural context.

three

organization and subculture

Many scholarly analyses, influenced by the Cold War, have considered membership in the CPUSA in highly abstract ways, relying on Party manuals, formal doctrine, Party media, and the often jaundiced reports of former adherents.[1] Fortunately, more astute scholars recognize the existence of national variation, especially in the wake of the Yugoslav, the Chinese, and now the Euro-Communist divergences.[2] In addition, several studies consider sequential variations—the ways in which national Party histories and historical circumstances in general color particular generations within the Communist movement.[3]

Local realities and variations of the Communist experience are as critical in making sense of national variation, as recent, more localized studies make clear.[4] There is not yet a systematic analysis of Communist organizing activity at the local level that looks beyond political analysis to how Communists at all levels of importance and rank lived, worked, and coped within a particular environment. After all, the "colonizing cadre" working in a steel mill in Bethlehem or an electrical equipment factory in Southwest Philadelphia responded to national and international crises like the Nazi-Soviet Non-Aggression Pact through the filters of his social and personal life. Leadership, his fellow cadres and co-workers, his support network within and possibly outside the Party, and his family situation all influenced him. Consequently, to answer the often posed question of why Communist Party members remained loyal under duress and toed the Party line, one must examine the social context within which members lived. Perhaps it is a bias of intellectuals, including academics, to consider behavior exclusively in terms of ideas and ethics; most people, including the majority of Communists, respond to more mundane influences, such as loyalty, tradition, and habit. Harvey Klehr, in his study of the Party's national leadership, notes, "Surprisingly little information is available detailing Party activities at the local level throughout the country."[5] As Mark Naison, probably the most incisive recent researcher on American Communism, suggests, "Historians who base their evaluation of the Party solely on Comintern resolutions or writings in the *Communist* are open to grave errors of interpretation." He correctly adds that "party life at the grass roots could be alive and vital even if it were rigid at the top."[6] Naison's studies of Party activity in Harlem apply such insights, but primarily to political activity.

While affirming the need for more political studies at the local level, one may add that such efforts ignore certain factors in the Communist experience. What has been missing is not primarily the "emotional and spiritual context" emphasized by Vivian Gornick,[7] but rather the texture of everyday life as shaped by formal and informal organization.

The formal aspect is institutional and bureaucratic. The informal is social and interpersonal.[8] Each contributes to the sense of identity and, consequently, the loyalty of a group member. In the literature on the Communist Party, the formal organization has been too often examined exclusively at the national level.

While such analysis remains essential, given the Party's highly centralized command structure, scholars need to pay more attention to the subordinate structures where national policies were implemented according to unique, local circumstances and milieux. The differences between the Communist Party in northeastern cities, the midwestern industrial heartland, and the South are striking enough to require more comparative, empirical study.

■ *organization*

There are no available official records concerning the Eastern Pennsylvania and Delaware District (District Three) of the CPUSA. The present national Party headquarters in New York does not make such records available, to the extent that they exist at all, and the veterans of the district Party organization know of nothing extant. Information gathered from a variety of old Party sources, however, provides a relatively clear and detailed historical picture of the district. A few key participants who worked at district levels of leadership, a number of items of district literature now in a personal collection, and a judicious culling of information from the national Party press contributed to the following picture.[9]

The CPUSA, from about 1929 through the late fifties at least, was organized and subdivided into districts, sections, branches, and clubs. In 1929 there were sixteen districts; by 1946 there were twenty-six. The largest district, by a wide margin, was New York State, which, centered in New York City, contained one-half of the total national membership and the major Party media. California, eventually divided into a northern and southern district, was next in importance, having its own regional Party organ. Other important districts were Massachusetts, Ohio, Michigan, New Jersey, Western Pennsylvania, Minnesota, and Washington. The Eastern Pennsylvania and Delaware District was sometimes combined with Western Pennsylvania, parts of New Jersey, and Washington, D.C., but its center was always the greater Philadelphia area.[10]

District Three was one of the most important Party regions by virtue of its large membership and therefore its contributions to Party fundraising and literature distribution. Five percent of national goals in fundraising and subscription quotas, for example, fell to District Three, at least in the period immediately after World War II.

In most nationwide efforts, District Three ranked second to fifth in importance. Within the national Party press, however, Philadelphia events received significantly less coverage than a half-dozen smaller districts. The Party emphasized the heavy industry districts, especially those of the Midwest; consequently, greater Philadelphia, with its lighter and smaller industry, received less attention.[11]

The district structure followed closely that of the national organization. At the top was a district committee consisting of between twenty and thirty members. This formally directive body had a cabinet or secretariat that ran the day-to-day operations of the district. It usually included minor functionaries, such as the circulation manager of the Party media, a literature director, an education director (often combined with the literature post), and a treasurer. At the apex of leadership within the committee and the political bureau that determined policy were the organizational secretary (OrgSec), the district organizer (D.O.), and the district chairman. Least important was the chairman, usually an elderly, august figure revered within the Party for past services and reputation but not particularly powerful in decision making.

The OrgSec was responsible for increasing membership within the district. In addition, he worked to increase *Daily Worker* and *Sunday Worker* circulation, to organize the distribution of Party literature, and to stay on top of all fundraising efforts. In brief, he supervised all cabinet work.

The D.O. was the most important member of the committee and of all decision-making bodies. For one thing, D.O.s were always appointed by the national office and thus carried policy from the national to the district level. They were usually outsiders, unlike most of the other committeemen. Basically the D.O. was the political leader of the district and the public face of the Party in its dealings with allies and with the non-Party world.

Because the Party operated electorally, there was also a state and a city structure that the district leadership used when convenient. For example, the D.O. in the late thirties and early forties, Sam Darcy, was also the Pennsylvania state secretary.

The district committee included other, often influential members with particular responsibilities, such as Negro work, industrial work, youth work, and professional work. The remainder of the committee reflected the geographical subdivisions of the district.

The sections within the city of Philadelphia were based on electoral, usually congressional, districts. In 1951, for example, Philadelphia had seven sections of varying strength:

the First Congressional District (C.D.) Section in South Philadelphia, an old immigrant section of Italians, Jews, Poles, and blacks

the Second C.D. Section in West and Southwest Philadelphia, including an area of Party strength in the Jewish fifty-second and forty-sixth wards

the Third C.D. Section in Center City, parts of North Philadelphia, and some of the so-called working-class river wards

the Fourth C.D. Section in North Philadelphia and a part of West Philadelphia, including Party strongholds in the Jewish twenty-eighth and thirty-second wards of Strawberry Mansion

the Twenty-fourth Ward Section in the Parkside area of West Philadelphia, another Party center, again mostly Jewish

the Fifth C.D. Section in Northeast Philadelphia, running from working-class neighborhoods to new lower-middle and middle-class suburbs in the Far Northeast. A Party focus developed in the thirty-fifth ward (Oxford Circle) among Jews moving out from older inner-city neighborhoods

the Sixth C.D. Section in Northwest Philadelphia, with some Party strength in wards fifty, forty-nine, and twenty-two, middle-class Jewish areas for the most part.

Outside Philadelphia, the district included sections in Camden, Delaware County, Southeast Pennsylvania, Lehigh Valley (Allentown, Bethlehem, Easton), the Scranton, Wilkes-Barre anthracite area, Harrisburg-York, Bucks County, and Delaware. Finally, there was a professional section (clandestine) and possibly two industrial sections. By various indices, West Philadelphia, particularly the twenty-fourth ward, the Strawberry Mansion neighborhood in North Philadelphia, some Jewish pockets in South Philadelphia, and some downtown areas were the center of Party membership and support. All of these areas were disproportionately Jewish. The focus of attention, however, was more often in areas and sections containing those groups the Party most desired to recruit and generally failed to reach—that is, blue-collar working-class whites and working-class and poor blacks (see ward map of Philadelphia.)[12]

Each section had a section organizer in charge, a section committee, and other subdivisions analogous to those of larger units. Sections were of great importance. Their role was to stimulate recruitment, organization, and activity at middle and lower levels. The section organizers usually were young and motivated activists, or cadres, sifted from the rank-and-file branch members, committed to Party growth, and often looking to further their Party stature and careers with sectionwide successes.[13]

Each section was divided into branches and clubs. There is some confusion about the difference between the two; the terms are used sometimes interchangeably and sometimes distinctively. A branch was generally a geographically defined unit of fifteen to thirty members. A club could be geographically defined but was sometimes organized according to interests as well. For example, the Party had clubs for nature study, hiking, singing, sports, and dance and a host of youth-oriented activities. A strong district built a rich web of branches and clubs, the smallest units, permeating the neighborhoods, the leisure-time interests, and the vocations of working people. The Coops, the Communist

Areas of Left-Wing Strength as Indicated by 1948 Progressive Party Election Returns

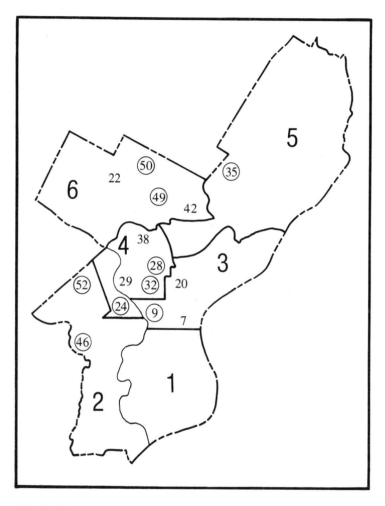

The circled wards (9, 32, 28, 46, 52, 24, 50, 49, 35) indicate areas of Progressive Party strength in the 1948 presidential election. Wallace also had some support (400 votes or more) in wards 7, 20, 22, 29, 38, and 42. Wallace received 20,745 votes in Philadelphia, about 2.5 percent of the total. (Philadelphia *Bulletin Almanac* [Philadelphia: Philadelphia Bulletin, 1949], pp. 36, 38.)

cooperative apartments in the Bronx so movingly described by Vivian Gornick, are, perhaps, the densest subculture the American Communist Party generated. However, such neighborhood-based units, in their insularity and parochialism, could limit rather than nurture districtwide growth.[14]

Before considering district membership, it is useful to examine national figures longitudinally. Most accounts show the Communist Party rising from a low of perhaps 6,000 in 1923 to as many as 100,000 members in the period immediately after World War II, if one includes the YCL. Party membership was chronically unstable; nevertheless, it charts an upward trajectory from the time of the Crash until the late 1930s, especially during the Popular Front period of 1935–1939. The Nazi-Soviet Non-Aggression Pact cut into membership to some extent, but with the Soviet entry into World War II as an American ally, a revived Popular Front produced membership growth during and immediately after the war. The beginning of the Cold War and the McCarthyite repression during the Truman and Eisenhower administrations cut sharply into membership. By 1953 membership had dropped to 24,796, and by 1955 to 22,663. The Party was down but not quite out. Support networks and a central core of cadres still remained, including national and district leaders either released from prison or finally exonerated by higher courts. The final collapse for all intents and purposes came with the traumatic events of 1956—Nikita Khrushchev's Twentieth Party Congress revelations about Stalin's crimes, and the crushing of the Hungarian uprising by Soviet troops. By 1958 the CPUSA had dwindled to a few thousand loyalists without influence or prospects.[15]

A similar process took place at the district level. The membership of District Three, for example, which numbered in the hundreds in the twenties, rose to perhaps 3,500 by 1938.[16] Some members resigned after the Pact, although most sources indicate that losses were relatively slight and mostly among intellectuals. The war period and its immediate aftermath saw district membership range from as low as 2,000 to as high as 3,800. My impression, based on many sources, is that in its heyday—that is, the period from 1936 to 1948—the district averaged approximately 3,000 members.[17]

In the late 1940s and early 1950s, membership fell off for several reasons, all related to the rising political repression. Some members were dropped from the rolls for failure to fulfill Party chores, including the payment of dues. Others were expelled or dropped for security reasons, on suspicion of being government agents or for ideological causes, such as charges of "white chauvinism" or "Titoism." The Party in this period of retrenchment followed Lenin's line of "better fewer, but better." Purges in Philadelphia, however, were relatively mild.

In fact, the major purge in District Three came in 1944–1945, when Sam Darcy, the D.O. and a nationally respected leader, publicly opposed Earl Browder's replacement of the Party with the Communist Political Association. When Darcy was expelled for his intransigence, an undetermined number of district members joined him. Darcy claims that a significant number of members— working-class members—resigned, but all other sources suggest that perhaps thirty to thirty-five close Darcy loyalists, mostly professional people, resigned or drifted away.[18]

Most of those who left the Party during the McCarthy period were rank-and-file members who stopped attending meetings and failed to renew their membership, frightened by the mounting assault on radicals and other dissenters. In addition, a significant number of members resigned for practical purposes while retaining their Party loyalties. For example, many faced with loyalty oaths and non-Communist membership strictures in the labor movement or public employment resigned from the Party but remained active. As a result, the Party, although weakened by the Cold War attacks on its members and leaders, retained a hard core of cadres and functionaries as it faced the crisis of the mid-fifties. That cataclysm of soul-searching, reflection, disillusion, and, remarkably, hope ultimately decimated the district.

How was the membership within the district distributed? One former leader put it succinctly and bluntly: "The Jews dominated the district." All sources and interviewees agree that approximately 75 percent of the district membership was Jewish. This striking fact will be extensively analyzed in Chapter Four.[19] Black membership was estimated at 10 percent "at best," according to one well-placed authority. The membership included a smattering of white Protestants, a small group of Eastern and Southern European white Catholic workers, and remnants of the foreign-language federations. By the late 1930s, the foreign-language federations had long been transformed into fraternal organizations within the International Workers Order.[20] The IWO included a wide range of ethnic affiliates; the most significant nationally and in Philadelphia was the Jewish Peoples Fraternal Order (JPFO), but there were also Greek, German, Russian, Ukrainian, and Italian groups. The IWO usually had a district committee representative, and possibly as many as 800 of the 6,000 fraternal members were in the Party in 1938–1939. Such "1905ers" were the parents of the "red-diaper babies" within the sample.

District Three ran Communist Party candidates for public office without success. Occasionally it established a front party at the local level to try to defeat a particularly noxious Democratic Party candidate.[21] In the post–World War II period through the early fifties, the district leaders supported Progressive Party candidates. For much of the time between 1935 and 1958, however, especially in Popular Front periods of coalition and reform, Philadelphia Communists worked in and around the Democratic Party.

Philadelphia was a Republican stronghold until the late 1940s and early 1950s, when liberal reformers headed by Joseph Clark and Richardson Dilworth led a Democratic sweep. The Communist Party of District Three, in the late thirties and early forties, used a Popular Front strategy of working with the minority Democrats in support of New Deal policies and labor legislation and for shared foreign policy objectives. The Party had significant influence in approximately eight out of fifty-one Democratic wards during this period. Most of these wards were in the Jewish and/or black areas of North, West, and South Philadelphia and in Center City, the neighborhoods where the Party had section-level strength. District leaders had ongoing communications, circumspect but not clandestine, with Democratic Party leaders and elected officials. In one period, the chief counsel for the local Democratic Party was, in fact, close to the Communist leadership.[22] After the war, with the rise of the Cold War followed by the disaster of the Progressive Party campaign, the district lost the small but strategic influence it had had.[23]

The large membership of the Amalgamated Clothing Workers (22,000 members) under Charley Weinstein and the Textile Workers (9,000) under Bill Leeder, both old social democrats, ensured that the city CIO Council was never dominated by the Communists. But the Party was a significant force in such unions as the United Electrical, Radio and Machine Workers of America (UE), especially within Local 155, a machine shop local led by business manager Dave Davis, a Party district leader, Westinghouse Local 107, R.C.A. Local 103, and G.E. Local 119. Communists also played significant roles in the Food, Tobacco and Agricultural Workers Union at Campbell's Soup in Camden, in the Transport Workers Union, in the State, County and Municipal Workers Union, the Philadelphia Teachers Union, and among retail and wholesale workers and such skilled craftsmen as jewelers, painters, and paperhangers.

Thus, the Party district was a moderately powerful force that seemed to be growing, albeit slowly. If the Democrats wanted to turn out a big crowd for a visiting New Dealer with progressive credentials, they often called on the Communist district leadership to bring out the troops. And the evidence suggests that the district could, indeed, deliver troops in the thousands for such occasions. Within the labor movement, the Party had a presence, open in some instances, covert in others; it could achieve goals through strategic alliances and was, at least until the late 1940s, a force to be reckoned with.

Finally, the Party made its presence felt through its almost jerry-built structure of front groups. Front groups were created to allow for more mass participation under non- but not anti-Communist auspices in areas supported by the Party. These groups included foreign policy fronts like the American Peace Mobilization, the North American Committee for Spanish Democracy, the American League for Peace and Democracy (at one time the American League Against War and Fascism), civil liberties fronts like the International Labor Defense, the Civil Rights Congress, and support groups for such victims of injustice as the Trenton Six and Willie McGee (Willie McGee was a Mississippi black executed for raping a white woman, despite significant doubts about the fairness of his trial. The Trenton Six case involved black men charged with the murder of a New Jersey furniture dealer in 1948. After years of appeal, four were released from prison and acquitted in 1955; one had died in prison, and the last was sentenced.) There were also civil rights fronts, like the National Negro Congress, and specialty fronts, like the Slav Congress and American Youth for Democracy. Party members organized and usually directed such fronts, sometimes in alliance with non-Communist, progressive groups, often disingenuously, trying to make them appear to be autonomous. By 1948, however, the Cold War had mandated that the new form of Popular Frontism was to be Senator Vandenberg's bipartisan alliance of Democrats and Republicans, liberals and conservatives, against the alleged threat of foreign and domestic Communism. At that point, Party fronts became increasingly skeletal.

In the period between the mid-thirties and the late forties, the greater Philadelphia Communist Party organization was a small but important part of a small but important national movement. Its numerical strength was impressive, although weakened by its ethnic imbalance i.e., it was a force in the labor movement, and it played a role in local New Deal and Popular Front electoral politics. To new recruits, the district organization seemed to be a viable and vital entity, providing them with innumerable activities, both political and social. They were part of an impressively structured district organization that was bureaucratically and ideologically linked to a national and, most critically, an international movement.

■ *subculture*

Most analyses of the American Communist Party limit themselves to its structural, political, and ideological aspects or, alternatively, study the social or psychological dynamics of its membership. Some recent efforts, however—for example, that of Vivian Gornick—help students of the Party recognize that it generated its own subculture, not simply as a means of entrapment, as so many earlier studies argue, but as a means of both survival and enrichment.[24]

The Communist Party subculture rested on an institutional framework that included the district, the section, and particularly the branch and club units. In the heyday of the Party, few weeks went by without lectures, classes, parties, concerts, socials, and rallies sponsored by Party units.[25] Many Philadelphia Communists speak of particular loyalties to the Party people in their immediate units; these were their closest comrades, their fellow workers, their friends. Abe Shapiro remembers going to meetings every night and "three times on Sunday." On Saturdays he and his wife would go to an early evening Party meeting or session, and then, when it was over, join a few close Party friends for a late movie. Others note that they lacked the money for movies but tell of social get-togethers for cards and food. One woman speaks warmly of weekly pinochle games over hot tea and freshly baked hot bread. Others gathered at favorite spots like the Center City Horn & Hardhart's restaurant known as the "Heel," where they met to chat and eat. Conversation was always the spice of political life, and members cherished the amiable if heated discourse of such occasions. For young, unmarried, or childless radicals, Party social events were lively and fulfilling in the thirties and forties. The comrades seemed the best of people, activity was meaningful and promised success, and energy was at extremely high levels thanks to the adrenalin of youthful idealism and camaraderie.

Stan Wax, as a young YCLer just out of college, organized a chapter of the American League Against War and Fascism with a few neighborhood friends. "I was a street-corner speaker," he brags, describing his successes over the first six months of effort. His world at age twenty-two was one of "total activity" in a "social, fantastic organization" that integrated all aspects of the lives of those involved. The League had a newsweekly, held dances at least once a month, ran various cultural programs including a hiking group, a chorus, and a theater group, and engaged in ongoing protests over anything from an eviction to Italian aggression in Ethiopia. During this energetic period Wax met and courted his wife within a round of Party activities that included informal bull sessions on street corners, on porches, and at kitchen tables. Party activists laughed as well as did their political work together. As Wax indicates, it did not even matter who was and who was not actually a Party member; all came within the compelling orbit of Party-sponsored and Party-staffed activities and their spin-offs.

These social and cultural interactions, these extensive and intensive acquaintanceships and friendships, these social networks of aid, comfort, and warmth, were the core strength of the local Party. The Party's informal organization has too long been underestimated and ignored.[26] Who stopped over at one's house after dinner to play cards, listen to a ball game, sit on the porch drinking a beer, discussing the news, imagining the future? Whom could one depend on to take care of the kids, lend one money, go shopping? Who knew of a politically reliable lawyer? With whom did one create a tradition of attending summer concerts in the park? Certainly non-Party neighbors were often friendly and sociable, at least until the McCarthy period, and some Party colonizers mixed smoothly and comfortably with working-class people. But even colonizers off in distant towns were sustained by a Party social network. They would have contact with a few Party people in nearby areas; they would correspond with Party friends back in their old neighborhoods. Many Philadelphia Communists proclaim that they still can go anywhere in the country and be welcomed by Party friends they have made over the years. "It's like family," Edith Samuels concludes proudly.[27]

The Party social network acted as a job referral agency for many. Formally, the Party placed some cadres and even rank-and-filers in Party-influenced positions with unions, fronts, and sympathetic political organizations. In addition, Party members found jobs for the faithful in companies owned or managed by sympathizers or members. There are countless stories of such sympathizers coming through with money or employment to help out those giving more time to the Party. In the early and middle fifties, such informal placement salvaged the situation for many Party cadres isolated and injured by political repression and blacklisting. Many were enabled to start new careers through employment assistance rooted in the Party social network.

The organizational density of the Party in the United States and in Greater Philadelphia did not approach that established by the massively supported German and Austrian Social Democrats of the pre-Nazi period and or by contemporary Communist parties in Italy and France.[28] The American Party, however, with its IWO fraternal groups among ethnic minorities, its choral groups, sports clubs, nature clubs, lecture clubs, dance and art classes and performances, picnics, and summer camps, established a cluster of activities for locally based members that was, indeed, a subculture.

For example, a Philadelphia Communist, or anyone operating with the Party network, remembered the 1938 May Day picnic at State Chairwoman Mother Bloor's farm near Allentown that celebrated the 35,000 people who marched in Philadelphia carrying caricature placards of Hitler, Mussolini, and Tojo down

Broad Street across Chestnut and, finally, to Independence Hall. Some veterans recall a caricature of Neville Chamberlain with an umbrella ten feet high. State Secretary and D.O. Sam Darcy headed a speakers list that included labor representatives (electrical, meat cutters, maritime), ethnic leaders (Czechs and Slovaks, Negro women, IWO), the Workers Alliance, the American League Against War and Fascism, Spanish Republic support groups, and Popular Front student groups. The march was headed by Abraham Lincoln Brigade veterans in uniform. The 1938 May Day Committee included two hundred organizations.

Such impressive outpourings were indeed special—and soon to dissolve with the coming of the Nazi-Soviet Non-Aggression Pact—but they were not rare. The months were packed with activities. In this same period, the spring of 1939, one could go to a fundraising party for Spanish refugees sponsored by the Spanish Popular Front in South Philadelphia on 30 April, attend "Marching Song" at the left-wing New Theatre downtown, stop in at "Philly's First Progressive Flying Club Music Center," or attend the progressive Camp Ridgedale's conference on 2 May, and then, on 6 May, frolic at a dance party featuring the Merle Hirsch Dancers at the Artists Union Studios on Walnut Street.[29] There were lectures sponsored by the New World Bookshop Forum and the National Negro Congress, a Retail Clerks' Artist Union, lectures at the People's Forum, and even jitterbug contests at a YCL dance. The Philadelphia Workers School gave a broad range of courses in addition to sponsoring a "Dude Ranch and Amateur Show." There were always *Workers* to sell, quotas to fill, branch and section meetings to attend, and, in that heyday of Popular Front efforts against a rising fascism, Spanish Civil War support efforts: relief ships to fund, orphans to save, recently returned visitors to welcome. The Philadelphia Communist subculture offered much more than mere ideology and bureaucratic organization to its members.

Vivian Gornick quotes a former Party member who reveals the subtle force and warmth of that subculture.

> You know, it's funny. In the old days of the Party, I never had "personal relationships." Now I have personal relationships. Everybody's in analysis, everybody's confessing their lives to each other day and night, and there are an awful lot of people about whom I just *know* an awful lot of personal stuff. And they know an awful lot about me. And yet, it really is odd. I don't feel intimate with any of these people. And I know I never will. And with the people from the Party, I felt intimate. I couldn't tell them anything about what we call my "personal life," but I felt an intimacy with them I also know I'll never feel again with anyone else.[30]

The sociologist Richard Sennett argues that contemporary life, by blurring and merging public and private spheres, eliminates the possibility for people to play roles and establish a space within which they can explore and create; thus, it destroys the qualities of intimacy rooted in family and friendship by vulgarly universalizing them.[31] The Communist subculture, at the same time as it interfered with certain aspects of one's personal life through its rich and enveloping milieu, accepted and respected the fundamental distinction between public and private spheres. There were sometimes gross violations—for example, the shunning of expelled members, the use of personal attacks against members for "white chauvinism" or "male supremacy" to settle personal scores. But such essentially totalitarian interventions were characteristic of the Party apparatus, not of the subculture. There, tenuous balance between political responsibilities and personal and private life was more the norm. The Party's total environment allowed for primary group intimacy and personal discretion.

Some members, of course, suffered from blocking personal feelings, as Gornick argues;[32] others, however, were saved from aggressive intrusions into their affairs by such discretion. They were raised to withhold personal feelings, especially in public;

failure to do so was not considered to be proper and indicated a certain lack of character. Within the subculture, respect for privacy was the rule.[33]

Clearly Communists were and are not "psychological men" or "protean" in any way.[34] They are, especially the men, singularly naive about the subleties of personal behavior. Party culture always eschewed psychological explanation, seeing it as a bourgeois smokescreen obfuscating the realities of the material and objective world. As a result, Communists often seem to have a poorly developed sense of dynamics of individual behavior that is not at the level of the rational, the material, or the political. This is not to suggest that they are bereft of common sense, merely that they are strikingly rationalistic.

These are not cold or austere people; indeed, the stereotype of the humorless Communist fits only a very few within the sample. Most seem quite unremarkable in their ability to laugh, kid, sing, enjoy, and reflect on life. Many Communists were raised in immigrant households filled with storytelling traditions, boisterous table talk, and a sense of humor that necessarily included oneself as a target. Fred Garst, in the middle of our interview, mischievously asked me, "What's a Shmarxist?" I replied, like a good straight man, "I don't know," anticipating his Yiddishist response; "A shmuck who believes in Marx." Of course, a loosening up and a certain mellowness come with aging and removal from the intensity and intolerances of Party life. But it would be a great error to describe these Old Leftists as characteristically repressed or humorless.

Many speak of youthful friendships established through politics, that have continued to the present. Abe Shapiro met his closest friends while in his first year in college. They would meet every day in the gym locker room to talk about current events, politics, Marxism, sports—seven to ten guys beginning their involvement in campus radicalism. One died in the war, another got divorced and left town, a few others have moved elsewhere, and one is very ill and incapacitated, but Abe still maintains contact with all of them who are still living. His friendship with those who have stayed in Philadelphia covers forty-five years. When Abe gets together with Mario Russo and Sammy Cohen, the conversations and, more subtly, the gestures, the signals, the raised eyebrows and momentary glances, evoke the sense of familiarity one associates with a well-worn, loving, but utterly human—that is, slightly irascible—married couple.

One finds surprisingly little bitterness. Although there are indeed instances of permanent ideological separations between old friends, one also finds former Communists with sharply diverse views still maintaining their friendship today.

In his memoirs, George Charney stresses that among his reasons for joining the Party, "not the least important was the fact that I was in the company of my dearest friends."[35] And Jessica Mitford reflects that she was "struck by the instant friendship based on mutual loyalties and shared dangers that one developed with fellow Communists, the total welcome and acceptance by complete strangers once one had established one's comradely credentials."[36] One local Communist tells of an out-of-town friend who is constantly astounded by how often she runs into old Party friends and acquaintances. Ike and Edith Samuels constantly talk about their nationwide circle of old Party friends. When they visit the West Coast, they stop in to see old comrades they worked and lived with in another city; at a senior citizen conference Edith runs into someone she worked with for a half-dozen years in New York State; and when old Party friends travel East, they stop in and stay with the Samuels. Although the Party is gone for people like the Samuels, the network based on shared lifelong experiences remains and flourishes.[37]

Not all Party members ignored friendships with outsiders.[38] Professionals in particular were able to uphold social relations with non-Party peers, although usually ideological tolerance or sympathy was a necessary ingredient. The Katzes had a rich and varied social life in their early married years. They went to ball games with a non-Party sports crowd and to the theater with a non-Party circle. By the early fifties, however, their social network and friendships were totally left-wing. Sam Katz views this as a "loss" but feels that under the circumstances of political repression it was inevitable. Those Party people working in the trade-union movement, and able to go on doing so during the fifties, sustained associations and friendships outside Party circles. In fact, in the case of one trade-union leader, non-Party support was critical in that era.

This activist was one of the few to sustain friendships with old neighborhood friends over many decades, totally separate from Party involvements. Many old Leftists look back nostalgically to their old ethnic neighborhoods, but few maintained significant ties, partly because most of those neighborhoods collapsed and were transformed in the period following World War II. Several feel that the stability of their own upbringings contributed to their ability to sustain work, family, friendship, and a special social network of old comrades. They experienced and understood the value of stable relations and rooted lives and sought to replicate them in the unique context of the Party.

A few old Leftists found Philadelphia to provide a less intimate and cohesive radical subculture than districts elsewhere. One couple lived in an apartment building in Washington with "the greatest concentration of leftist people I've ever experienced." Ike Samuels describes extensive political activities, "surrounded by all these magnificent people"; it was, he says, "the happiest time of our life." He stresses that "these were not depressed people, somber people, none; they didn't have any hang-ups." Dozens of young couples with children created daycare and babysitting cooperatives and shared vacations. Another local Communist describes Baltimore as "unusual" in that it had a Party organization that was not stratified and bureaucratic but was instead, filled with "genuine friendships."

Some found Philadelphia at first "a very strange city" containing a segmented Party with "a certain amount of exclusiveness." Others note lower levels of intimacy in Philadelphia as compared with other, smaller, Eastern cities. The unfavorable contrast may derive in part from the fact that such subjects moved to Philadelphia at the outset of the McCarthy period and may have romanticized their previous residences as a result. On the other hand, Philadelphia, as the third largest city in the nation, with a sizable Party operation, may have been less warm and supportive than smaller urban centers. Only comparative empirical research can settle such matters.[39]

Vivian Gornick says of Communists, "They were like everybody else, only more so."[40] Part of the extra ingredient was the radical subculture with its extensive social networks. Joseph Starobin, a historian and former Communist, concludes of the American Communist Party that though it was "not intended to be a family but a quasi-military elite, forged for stern tasks, it was in fact a family to many."[41]

Like most families, it had expressive functions that were intertwined with the more instrumental operations of the Party's formal organizational structure. The district Party was simultaneously a political instrument, an employment network, a social organization, and a circle of friends, whom Communists called comrades. One of Gornick's subjects sums it up best:

> It was a total world, from the schools to which I sent my children to family mores to social life to the quality of our friendships to the doctor, the dentist, and the cleaner. We had community. We had integration. We had that civilizing sense of connectedness, it's the heart and soul of all civilized life. It wasn't just good wine in our veins, that life, it was ambrosia.[42]

four

ethnicity

An analysis of the ethnic dynamics within the American Communist Party is absolutely essential to an assessment of its effectiveness as an organizing agency. Although there is a certain faddism to the contemporary interest in ethnicity, it remains clear that the problem of group identity in an immigrant society and culture such as that of United States merits serious and sustained attention.[1] Ethnically, the CPUSA appears to be a four-cornered playing board of Jews, blacks, white Southern and Eastern European Catholics, and white Anglo-Saxon Protestants.[2] It was an organization that had been disproportionately foreign-born and that became native-born and second-generational in the late thirties.

Vivian Gornick's *The Romance of American Communism* properly focuses on the Party as a passionate community of believers; yet it oddly minimizes the uniqueness of the ethnic composition within the Party—that is, its disproportionately

Jewish membership.[3] Arthur Liebman, on the other hand, conclusively demonstrates that the American Communist Party, growing out of a Yiddish-socialist subculture transplanted from Eastern Europe, was 40 to 50 percent Jewish in the 1930s.[4] The Jewish dominance was especially pronounced in northeastern urban areas such as Philadelphia.

Fully 72.2 percent of Philadelphia's Communists were the children of immigrants who came to the United States in the late nineteenth and early twentieth century. Of the twenty-seven second-generation Americans, twenty-two have parents of Eastern or Central European Jewish origins; one Jewish-American had a foreign-born father and an American-born mother. Of the remaining four, three have Southern European Catholic backgrounds and one has an ethnically mixed Catholic background including an American-born father. Of the nine of native-born parentage, four are black Protestants, two Northern European white Catholics, and only three are Northern European Protestants. The sample is 64 percent Jewish, 19 percent Protestant, and 17 percent Catholic; it is 89 percent white and 11 percent black. Although the sample does not in the least reflect the Depression generation at larger or within greater Philadelphia, it does represent the distribution of Depression-generation Communists within the Philadelphia area (see table).

FAMILY BACKGROUNDS OF THIRTY-SIX PHILADELPHIA COMMUNISTS

Origin of Parents	Number	Percentage
Foreign-born (52)		72.2
White E. C. European Jewish	45	
White S. European Catholic	6	
White mixed European Catholic	1	
Native-born (20)		27.8
Black Protestant	8	
White N. European Protestant	6	
White N. European Catholic	5	
White E. European Jewish	1	

Even the three foreign-born local Communists arrived in the United States before the age of five. It was the thirties generation of Communists who brought the Party in October 1936, to the point where it became more than one-half native-born. The Philadelphia district, according to Nathan Glazer had only fifty native-born members, out of a total of 481, in early 1929.[5] As late as June 1933, the national organization was still 70 percent foreign-born.[6]

It is of critical importance, consequently, to keep in mind that Philadelphia Communists were not only heavily Jewish but also the first American-born generation within their respective families. This is relevant not only to the distinctly Jewish response to the rise of Nazi anti-Semitism, but also to the Party's Popular Front efforts to root itself in native soil, to become thoroughly American.[7]

To join the Party after 1935 was to enter a potpourri of Americana: celebrations of Lincoln, Jefferson, Douglass, Debs; calls for the revival of indigenous cultural traditions; paeans to folk art. However disingenuously these themes were manipulated at the command level, in many ways Communism became more than the 100 percent Americanism proclaimed by Earl Browder. This was a particularly attractive stance to members unusually sensitive to charges of being aliens. Communists who grew up in homes speaking Yiddish or Italian found great attraction in a Party that proclaimed, "This Land Is Your Land."[8]

The Jewishness of the American Communist Party is a sensitive issue, both to former and present participants and to liberal and radical scholars.[9] Political reactionaries traditionally have attacked leftists along anti-Semitic lines, finding Jewish conspiracies at all turns. The Party in Philadelphia had Jewish membership of at least 75 percent. What were the consequences of this predominance? Scholars need to know how Communists felt about their ethnicity, how potential constituents responded to Jewish organizers, and how Gentile Communists reacted to the Jewish aspects of their organization. The significance of the ethnicity of activists and organizers in an ethnically sensitive culture remains virtually unexplored.

Fred Garst describes the Communist Party as "a Jewish organization with a *goyishe cup* [Gentile head] and a token Negro." He feels that Communism is simply "a Jewish heresy," involving Jews who avoided their own ethnic identity and who never stopped to discuss seriously the Jewishness of their party. Others indicate that discussions of Jewishness were rare and that most members simply avoided or were oblivious to the issue.[10]

There is a wide range of responses to Jewish identity. Milt Goldberg admits that he had "very negative feelings toward the Jewish people" and was "anti-Zionist" and "offended by Yiddish." He concludes, "I guess I felt it wasn't American." At the opposite pole, Sammy Cohen comments on his lifelong ethnic identification: "I like being Jewish; my dad was a Jewish Socialist."

Between the above poles of disdain and self-affirmation, one finds a pattern of second-generational adaptation indicating a very substantial Jewishness encased within an encompassing Americanization. Most Jewish Communists wear their Jewishness very casually but experience it deeply. It is not a religious or even an institutional Jewishness for most; nevertheless, it is rooted in a subculture of identity, style, language, and social network. These are "secular Jews." In many ways, the words of Sol Davis—Jewishness "has never been a factor in my life—"speak for all of them. In fact, this second-generation Jewishness was antiethnic and yet the height of ethnicity. The emperor believed that he was clothed in transethnic, American garb, but Gentiles saw the nuances and details of his naked ethnicity.[11]

Within the Communist movement, most Jews were fervently anti-Zionist (at least until the post–World War II period, when it became acceptable to express sympathy for a Jewish homeland). Jewishness was to be submerged and transcended within the international brotherhood of the proletariat. The Popular Front re-established the value of ethnicity, including Jewishness, but most Jewish Communists of the thirties generation did not choose to identify themselves with specifically Jewish left-wing activities. Some who did were motivated more by the desire to work within a mass organization than by any ethnic identification.[12]

Indeed, even the Popular Front validation of ethnicity remained essentially instrumental, if not manipulative.[13] The Marxist vision was a universalistic one that anticipated the replacement of national with class loyalties. Parochial identifications were being obliterated by market forces generating a universal class with nothing to lose. As Harry Boyte shrewdly notes, "From the pinnacles of 'advanced thinking,' voluntary associations like the family, the church, and ethnic traditions tend to appear as backwaters of culture."[14] Most Communists, whatever their feelings about their own ethnic identities, accepted a historical projection biased toward universalism.

Sarah Levy declares, "I don't think that our generation thought consciously of ourselves as Jewish." Her husband, however, adds, "We knew we were Jewish; we felt comfortable among ourselves." Evidence of the importance of ethnicity in general and Jewishness in particular permeates the available record. Many Communists, for example, state that they could never have married a spouse who was not a leftist. When Jews were asked if they could have married Gentiles, many hesitated, surprised by the question, and found it difficult to answer. Upon reflection, many concluded that they had always taken marriage to someone Jewish for granted. The alternative was never really considered, particularly among Jewish men.

The Socialist Party incorporated a Yiddish-socialist left-wing subculture, while the Communists, using a centralized model, sought to reduce the strength of the ethnically rooted foreign-language federations, of which the Yiddish federation was one of the most powerful.[15] Jewish Communisits of the pre-Depression era, 1905ers and those who joined in the twenties, usually foreign-born, sometimes flaunted their disdain for organized Judaism, eating at big feasts on Yom Kippur and mocking religious customs in front of synagogues. On one almost legendary occasion in Philadelphia, one Chickie Katz, later a Party leader, intentionally and provocatively ate ham in front of the local synagogue.[16]

The Jews of the second generation, on the other hand, few of whom could speak fluent Yiddish, many of whom had little or no Jewish education, carried no passionate hostility toward Judaism—only indifference. Nevertheless these acculturated Jews did behave in decidedly "Jewish" ways.

The secondary evidence is contradictory. Mark Naison, a student of Party history in Harlem, implies, in part by omission, that white, usually Jewish Communists felt quite comfortable and competent organizing in black Harlem, despite moments of tension and misunderstanding.[17] George Charney, a participant in Harlem organizing, on the other hand, argues that there was considerable self-consciousness and agony about being an alien in a sea of blacks.

> I could never walk the streets of Harlem in a leisurely fashion, as though it were my community or stand on the outskirts of a meeting as another member of the throng, even in the company of Negro comrades. I could speak from a platform with passion and feel momentarily a part of the people, but once the meeting was over the sense of unease returned.[18]

He says he felt guilty about his fears of being attacked but "could never discuss this problem with anyone."[19]

Many Jewish Communists Anglicized their names. It seemed less risky to work in plants or organize Eastern and Southern European Catholic workers, Southern white Protestant workers, black workers or ghetto unemployed as John Gates, for example, than as Sol Regenstreif.[20] Such a practice was not peculiar to Jewish Communists, but given their predominance and the Party's obvious sensitivity to its ethnic composition, one is forced to examine it. Changing one's name for security reasons, a practice quite common in revolutionary movements, does not require a shift in ethnic identity. A Sam Cohen can become an Ira Gold, rather than a Joe Smith. Was this Anglicizing of names a symbolic and unconscious rejection, at least in part, of their own roots? Local Communists disagree about the motives for it, some agreeing that it suggests a certain self-hatred, others arguing that an Anglicized name was simply a ticket to enter industrial America. Sam Katz remembers A. W. Mills (formerly Sam Milgram), the district's D.O. in the early thirties, casually suggesting to Jewish members that perhaps "shorter" names, that were "more American," would be more useful to them. This advice was not policy and had no force behind it; Katz prefers to call such practices "folkways." Gentile subjects were much more likely to see Jewish self-contempt in name changes.[21]

At the national level, it was an open secret that the top leadership of the Party had to be Gentile. After the late twenties purge of Jay Lovestone, the leaders were Foster, Browder, and Dennis. Did Jewish members resent this? There is no evidence that Jewish Communists saw anything but the practicality of such a policy. After all, many Jews served the Party in prominent posts; they did not seem to be at all disadvantaged. Moreover, the strong opposition of Communists and of the Soviet Union to anti-Semitism and Nazism made Jewish activists tolerant of what appeared to be a practical and superficial form of discrimination.[22]

The heart of the Party's ethnic problem can best be examined through the relations between the Party's most notable minorities: Jews and blacks. The sociologist and former Communist Harold Cruse claims that Jews dominated the Party and double-binded blacks by furthering their own ethnic domination while denying blacks the right to a distinct identity. He argues that assimilated Jews in leadership positions accepted the existence of Jewish Party institutions—in particular a press and an ethnic organization— while charging similar black efforts with "bourgeois nationalism."[23] Cruse particularly resents the way assimilated Jews became the spokesmen on black issues.

> Jewish Communists, during the 1930's and 1940's, were able to
> compete with the Negro Marxist theoretician in the inter-

pretation of the Negro question. As late as the late 1930's the top Communist leader—the section organizer—in the Harlem Communist Party was Jewish. Needless to say, no one in the Communist Party spoke theoretically for Jews but other Jews.[24]

Morris U. Schappes, a former Communist Party member and the editor of *Jewish Currents*, on the other hand, argues that Jewish Communists were forced to deny their own ethnicity within the universalistic framework of Party positions on nationalism and nationality. He finds that the Party ignored the fact that proletarian internationalism presupposes the legitimate existence of national identities. Schappes sees nationality work, that is, Party efforts within the IWO, as "pragmatic" and "tactical," and consequently assimilationist at root.[25]

The Philadelphia experience offers some ways of relating the seemingly opposite views of Cruse and Schappes. A number of Jewish Communists speak of race relations as a primary cause of their radicalization and of the Party's antiracism as one of its primary attractions. Harry Freedman, for example, says "there was nothing like the early Party" in terms of interracial harmony. Many old Leftists felt particularly good about the Party socials, which seemed to demonstrate the possibilities of racial integration. For many, the Party provided their first experience working or socializing with black people. Communists were often deeply moved by such progressive experiences in a still Jim Crow society. After all, in Connie Mack's lily-white Philadelphia as late as the early 1950s, black professional baseball players were not welcome to join the Athletics, nor were they allowed to use the best hotels while in town with visiting squads.

There was also an undercurrent of anxiety about social interaction, particularly dating and sexual relations. Black men, never before able to openly mix with white women, were caught up in a cultural and psychological matrix of attraction and hostility. Interracial dating almost always involved black men and white women, and the women were almost always Jewish.[26] Several black Communist men married Jewish women, causing considerable resentment on the part of other blacks. Such patterns and feelings were taboo subjects within the Party.[27]

A central part of the debate on Party racism concerns the alleged patronizing of black recruits and members. More than a few Communist veterans, all white, mostly Jewish, argue that blacks were brought into the Party without the proper consideration of their political development and allowed to remain in the Party without fulfilling conventional obligations, such as dues payment and regular attendance at meetings. Abe Shapiro remembers a black recruit "who didn't have the faintest idea about the Party." He says that the more experienced Party members "died" when the Party allowed such practices but were afraid to speak out in fear of being labeled "white chauvinists." The postwar period, the era of the Progressive Party movement, seems to have been the time of most alleged abuses: the charge is that young blacks came into the Progressive Party organizations—fronts and mass organizations—attracted by civil rights and integrationist efforts and then were recruited into the Party simply to increase the black composition. The charge is supported by the extraordinary turnover among the black membership.[28] One black activist confirms that the Party hesitated to give black recruits material on socialism, preferring to limit itself to black-oriented and liberal subjects. But, he adds, the more receptive and experienced black members advanced to serious discussions about nationality, class, and more general Marxist issues.

George Paine denies that black turnover was unusually high but agrees that recruitment was often careless. All black veterans of the local Party movement charge that the Party was indeed racist or at least insensitive to black people. Paine argues that "there was a great deal of chauvinism" and that "they [the leaders] were still white" and "wanted to edit what you did."

Yet several blacks speak with pride about the Party's advocacy of a separate black identity through the Black Belt thesis—that is, the right of blacks to self-determination in Southern areas with black majorities. Although evidence exists that the Party subordinated the Black Belt thesis to day-to-day civil rights issues, many blacks found it a powerful and compelling symbol, especially when linked with the Soviet Union's much publicized treatment of its own less advanced minorities.[29] In all instances, blacks affirm the Party as the vanguard for racial justice in that era. They agree with Mark Naison's conclusion: "No racial organization in twentieth century America had greater success in uniting black and white working people around common ends or in mobilizing white workers to fight racial discrimination."[30]

Areas of bitterness and anger remain, however, Blacks typically experienced more job discrimination than whites, including Communists. Whereas Jewish people faced limits in the white-collar corporate world, blacks, less educated and less skilled in urban life, faced discrimination in all areas of work. One black Old Leftist, college-educated and experienced, could not find work commensurate with his training and finally was forced to take a factory job. Another educated black applied for a managerial job, only to be informed by the personnel director that he was qualified to be an elevator operator.[31]

Black Communists also had to deal with the small but emblematic contradictions of white and particularly Jewish Party members. Some Jewish members had black maids; even if they treated them with respect and friendship, this was an obvious source of unease to black members.[32] Some Jewish Communists were also able to enjoy summer vacations at Jersey or Pocono resorts and sometimes winter vacations at Miami Beach, all of which were racially restricted.[33]

Another source of contention is the charge that the Party exploited the black community by selling its literature there while ignoring the allegedly less hospitable white working-class areas. Moe Levy attacked Party leaders for avoiding this issue. Another Jewish rank-and-filer feels that his comrades avoided selling the Party papers in their own neighborhoods because "they lived in fear of exposure." Consequently, they went into the contiguous black neighborhoods.

While many Jewish members resisted going into tough working-class areas like Kensington to sell the paper, there is considerable evidence of resistance and grumbling over going into black neighborhoods like North Philadelphia as well. Moe Levy claims that in North Philadelphia distributors got "respect but not acceptance," whereas in Kensington they were afraid "to get their asses kicked." Others recall many incidents of rank-and-filers from the Jewish West Philadelphia branches objecting to Sunday forays into black neighborhoods. In one striking case, an affluent woman would drive to the edge of the ghetto, park her expensive car, take off her fur coat and put it into the trunk, and, with great and obvious repugnance, take her quota of *Workers* into the public housing projects.

It seems likely that rank-and-filers, living in their own ethnic enclaves and less fully integrated into the Party social network and behavioral ideal, experienced more ambivalence about race relations and were sometimes insensitive to black feelings. Party cadres, more likely to live in ethnically mixed neighborhoods, with more opportunity to transcend their own ethnic parochialism, were more consistently supportive of efforts to achieve racial equality and were more comfortable around black people.

One experienced cadre believes in an "unspoken negativism" of Jewish members toward blacks, captured in the expression "we'll have to teach them," a decidedly missionary and patronizing attitude. Indeed, one finds similar allegations concerning the treatment of white Gentile working-class constituents.[34] As was noted above, some working-class Gentiles also experienced condescension from Jewish party members:

> Jewish attitudes, styles and modes of expression did not encourage Gentiles to interact and communicate with them, especially in the context of a tight-knit group that placed so high an evaluation on intellectual sharpness. There was a style of argument, debate, and writing within the Left that had a distinctive Jewish tone and style. It was aggressive, polemical, highly critical, and often personally derogatory to even comradely opponents.[35]

The ethnic dynamics within the Party went beyond Jewish-black relations to incorporate white Gentiles, particularly immigrant Catholic and Southern Protestant working-class people. Every effort was made to promote non-Jewish cadres into leadership. As Nathan Glazer put it:

> Members in the categories the party favored—the English-speaking, the industrial workers, Negroes—were given every incentive to enter the party. They were pushed into party jobs, where these were available, they were flattered. They were urged to come in when their understanding and commitment were weak. Under the circumstances, they flowed out almost as fast as they entered.[36]

Many white Gentile men were attracted to the more verbal and assertive Jewish women they met in the Party. Sally Turpin asserts that she always "felt completely comfortable" among Jews. Other Gentiles agree. But Mark Greenly adds that working-class Gentiles did feel they were especially recruited to diversify the Party's ethnic composition. And several Gentile working-class members believe that they were quickly raised to leadership positions, as Glazer suggests, because of their backgrounds. Greenly, who believes he was favored for this reason, tells a revealing story about being sent as a student representative to a national ASU convention. He says that it became increasingly apparent to most participants that virtually all of the speakers were Jewish New Yorkers. Speakers with thick New York accents would identify themselves as "the delegate from the Lower East Side" or "the comrade from Brownsville." Finally the national leadership called a recess to discuss what was becoming an embarrassment. How could a supposedly national student organization be so totally dominated by New York Jews? Finally, they resolved to intervene and remedy the situation by asking the New York caucus to give "out-of-towners" a chance to speak. The convention was held in Wisconsin.

During the anti-white-chauvinism campaigns of the late forties, spearheaded by black leaders,[37] there was great unease and an undercurrent of defensive countercharges. Whites resented the promotion of inexperienced blacks to leadership and considered most of the charges of white chauvinism to be irresponsible and demagogic. In Philadelphia the problem seems to have been moderated, in part, through the leadership role of Ed Strong, a much admired black functionary who at one point served as D.O. On the other hand, some whites, while admiring Strong's abilities, viewed him as too color-conscious and nationalistic. One veteran found Strong's anti–white chauvinism efforts "abhorrent," especially the patronization of blacks, which he describes as "a pathetic grasping of straws in trying to develop black cadres." Black Communists greatly admired Strong and found him sensitive to their needs.[38]

Jewish and black Communists also clashed over residential problems. Jewish Communists tended to live in urban Jewish neighborhoods, like Strawberry Mansion and West Philadelphia's Parkside, where battles were being fought over black penetration. Blacks followed Jewish residential patterns, in part because other white ethnic groups resisted the black influx with vigilantism, discrimination of the part of real-estate interests, and overt hostility. Jews were more mobile; that is, they moved quickly into middle-class status and were more prone, for historical reasons, to flee rather than resist. Consequently, Jews faced the bulk of black migration and began the flight to Wynnefield, Overbrook Park, the suburbs, and, most often, the Northeast, a postwar quasi-suburb that became the city's section of Jewish concentration.[39]

Jewish Communists faced a painful dilemma in which their political vaiues often clashed with their personal and familially perceived interests. One describes the struggle in Strawberry Mansion in the early fifties during which Communists fought blockbusting and Jewish flight, built block organizations, and became extensively and vigorously involved in Home and School Associations in order to keep classrooms integrated. Yet the neighborhood changed from Jewish to black and signs of ghettoization appeared—subdivided apartments, abandoned housing, rising crime, racial conflict, and the deterioration of the schools.

Jewish Communists express anguish and pain about this experience. One describes it as "traumatic," arguing that the Communists were "the last ones to leave." She speaks of being "the only white family in the school," with a daughter who was "fairly terrified" by racial antagonism and threats. "The boys were better off; they had black friends," she adds. Another veteran of the Strawberry Mansion struggles, repeating a tale I heard from many, describes the suffering her children experienced in inferior schools, taunted by black children angry at their own plight and taking it out on the only available targets.

The commitment to racial integration was a vital part of the intellectual and behavioral baggage of Communists. One couple specifically joined a racially integrated planned community to uphold such principles. Unfortunately, many Jewish Communists seemed to catch the worst of both worlds, experiencing guilt about deserting the cause of integration and also a final reluctance to impose the consequences of staying on their children. As one put it, "If I had to do it again, I wouldn't permit my children to go to deteriorating schools." Many struggled with this problem, finally finding their own compromises by moving to integrated neighborhoods in Oak Lane, Germantown, and Mount Airy, where they could enroll their children in public schools and continue the fight for an integrated neighborhood.

Others removed themselves from the such struggles by moving into such thoroughly white and Jewish Northeast neighborhoods as Oxford Circle. Given the problems of the period, including McCarthyist harassment, such a flight is not altogether incomprehensible.[40] A few Old Leftists, however, speak bitterly about comrades who abandoned the cause by moving precipitantly and far away. Mike Caldwell feels that many Jewish Communists abandoned their integrated neighborhoods too soon. The majority, in fact, seem to have first struggled to remain and then, reluctantly, moved to other promising—that is, integrated— neighborhoods.

From the vantage point of black Communists, the above-mentioned anguish is suspect. Blacks feel another kind of abandonment; after all, they rarely had the luxury of choosing to move out of ghettoized neighborhoods. In addition, while some maintained firm community roots through church affiliations, Paul Jackson found that "we didn't fit into the black community" and were marginal to the Communist subculture as well. And they worried about their children. Would they be able to sustain them? One black says that his neighbors and non-Party friends would ask, "Why do you do something with no future and so many risks, given your skills? Look at so-and-so; he was once like you, but he found a way to get ahead." When the Party began to collapse in the fifties, such blacks were left without any support system. Another black concludes that "Jews don't know anything about black people." Although the black sample is quite small, it expresses attitudes consistent with Cruse's hypothesis and, strangely, with Schappes's as well. After all, while there could be a non-Jewish Jew, it was not possible for there to be a non-black black.[41]

The problem of ethnicity within the American Communist Party rests on the multiethnic nature of our society and the universalistic biases of the Communist movement. While the working class of the thirties was finally an English-speaking entity for the first time since the flood of immigration in the last quarter of the nineteenth century, it was still an ethnically rooted constituency. Industrial work was often defined by ethnicity; "What are you?" remained a significant question in the shops, factories, and mines of Depression and post-Depression America.[42] Jack Ryan got a job at one of the Philadelphia area's largest plants through his father, a local Irish politician who had worked there for a few years. He adds that all of the job areas were ethnically defined.

Several Catholic Communists regret not being more effectively used by the Party. They were never sent into either their own ethnic neighborhoods or areas with their ethnic identity. Mario Russo, for example, born and bred in Italian South Philadelphia, was never sent into either his old neighborhood or other Italian communities, and his experience seems to have been typical.

One of the most successful organizers in the district, Johnny Tisa, was exceptional in that he was able to take advantage of his ethnic and residential ties in his work. Being a South Camden Italian Catholic made a difference in the effort to organize the Campbell's Soup Company. Other Eastern or Southern European Catholic radicals, however, feel that they could not have worked effectively in their own communities. They speak of their estrangement from the parochial and conservative neighborhoods that once choked their imaginations and ridiculed their heresies. They were the rebels, the intellectuals; when they fled, they extinguished any desire ever to return. Angie Repice recalls, "Very few people could you get to make the break with their families, neighbors." She feels that she may have been mistaken in abandoning her ethnic community but ponders, "I wanted to get out; we were the only ones [radicals]. What would we have in common with them; you don't get in, they're clannish."

For a Party with such an ethnic imbalance and such insensitivity to ethnic matters, Communists did remarkably well in reaching outward. Many Jewish Communist organizers were quite success-ful in reaching white Gentile and black constituents. They had a gift for communicating their idealism and their genuine sense of internationalism, and, most of all, they could deliver services. But the Party bias against what it called "nationalism"—which in fact was ethnic identity—damaged its ability to reach beyond an essentially Jewish-American constituency. When services could no longer be delivered, even the most effective organizers were rejected by constituents—working-class Catholic, black, Ap-palachian white—hardly touched by the Party's ultimate vision of socialism.[43]

A series of double-binds confronted the Party. Secularized Jewish Communists could experience "chosenness" as they congregated, shared cultural mores and means of expression, and were sent out into the Gentile world as colonizers, and yet still feel some resentment at the Party's discrimination against them in terms of advancement and national leadership positions. Relations between Jews and blacks were vastly superior within the Party—after all, the idealism, the sharing, the generosity, the racial harmony, were real—and yet fraught with taboos and racist patterns. It simply was not possible to talk about the attraction of some black men to white women or the insensitivity of many Jews to their own cultural arrogance. There was no ideological room to discuss, openly and fully, the sending of Jewish members into black areas to sell subscriptions to *the Worker* or the tenuousness of sending Jewish colonizers into factories where there were ethnic traditions of anti-Semitism.

It is a fair assumption that the Party, by playing down the role of ethnicity, made it more difficult for Party organizers of all backgrounds to become more sensitive to their own roots and, consequently, to develop greater empathy for possible constituents, all of whom experienced in full the realities of a multiethnic society.

five

marriage, family, and sex roles

It is only recently, under the impetus of the women's movement, that scholars have begun to examine systematically the domestic and familial aspects of political life.[1] Although the political is not quite "the personal," nor vice versa, personal and domestic life act upon one's political behavior in definite and particular ways. It is therefore essential to examine domestic and personal life and their political consequences among thirties-generation Communists: courtship, decisions about marriage itself, the role of the Communist Party in marriage, the family, and sex roles, decisions about having and raising children, family dynamics, the particular choices women faced regarding marriage, family, and career, political or otherwise, and the kinds of lives—the lifestyles, to use contemporary jargon—established by Communists.

Although the proportion of women in the CPUSA rose from 26 percent in 1936 to 46 percent in 1944 and to approximately one-half in the postwar period, their status and power never matched their numbers.[2] The Party was male-oriented and male-dominated. Since a woman typically worked within the Party as a part of a married unit, the sample includes seven paired couples among the twenty-six men and ten women interviewed. Communist men married at an average age of twenty-four, whereas Communist women wed at approximately twenty-two (22.2).[3] How did young Communists decide to marry and what factors were considered in choosing a mate?

The vast majority, male and female, married fellow radicals—in fact, fellow members of the Communist Party. In most other instances, the nonmember (usually female) was soon brought into the Party by the member (usually male). In only a few cases did a couple consist of a Party member (male) and an uninvolved nonmember (female), not to speak of an anti-Communist. Most typically, young Communist men and women met in the midst of political activities—marches, demonstrations, meetings, club or branch socials, campus activities, and dances.

Harry Freedman met his wife at a YCL meeting and came to know her through American Youth for Democracy (AYD) activities. He agrees that it would have been "inconceivable" to marry a non-Leftist. One veteran Communist describes his wife as having been "antiboss" when they met; she was just getting involved in union activity at the time. Otto and Tessie Kramer, one of the sample's seven couples in "progressive marriages," met while working in support of Spanish Republican forces during the Civil War. In a number of cases, the man was the mentor, the woman the novice. Several Party marriages began through such teacher-student, organizer-organized relationships. Both Ike Samuels and Johnny Tisa met their future wives when Party headquarters assigned the women to do trade-union office work for them. I found no instance of a woman playing the mentor role with a man as neophyte.

Courtship was often brief, although several Communists delayed marriage because of such problems as unemployment and inadequate wages. Family pressures seem rarely to have intervened in the marriage decisions, although a number of left-wing couples married in religious ceremonies, usually Jewish ones, to placate and pacify traditionally minded parents.

Most were young and hopeful. Stan Wax met his wife, "a working girl who came to League functions," already "socialist-minded from her family," in the neighborhood in which both had grown up. Despite the Depression, "we were not really afraid to get married; we would make it." Radicals in their twenties like Wax and his wife lived on politics and political community.

Moe and Ruth Levy married in the late 1940s. He was twenty-three; she was twenty-one. Ruth came out of a Workmen's Circle background and was working with AYD at the time. Moe affirms that he had to marry a fellow Communist: "it couldn't be any other way." Sam Katz married a mild sympathizer. He was already a functionary and felt "a little uncomfortable" having a non-Party wife. But she became involved with union organizing, got much more active, and moved from sympathy toward full involvement and Party membership in a short time.

Sam Darcy married a woman, Emma, whose grandfather and father came out of the German workers' movement and were old Socialists. Sam and Emma Darcy met at a Farmer-Labor convention in the early 1920s. Later, while he was looking up material at Party headquarters in New York, they met again and began to court. She was secretary to the Party's Central Committee at the time. Sam Darcy remembers that her father gave them a special edition of *Capital* as a wedding present.

Few others were so immersed in the movement as the Darcys, but Meyer Weiner remembers that his YCL-involved wife brought him the collected works of Lenin as a wedding present, "which I proceeded to read."

Communist tradition, rooted in the historical experience of clandestine activity and recognizing the instability and mobility of revolutionary life, allowed for honorable but informal sexual relations. Bolsheviks, like all revolutionaries in Tsarist Russia, eschewed "bourgeois marriage" as a male-supremacist property arrangement and an empty formality. Affairs were not only allowed but required by the unpredictability of everyday life. But lechery, "womanizing," and all forms of deceit were considered behavior unbecoming a revolutionary.

Young Communists achieving maturity during the 1930s, under the cultural hegemony of the Popular Front, were torn between two unstated models of marital and familial behavior: conventional and Bolshevik marriage. The Bolshevik model viewed marriage as a mere form and stressed companionship and sharing.[4] One woman had been dating a very active and ambitious YCLer who told her he wanted his wife to be a "Krupskaya," a Bolshevik companion like Lenin's wife. She blanched at the offer: "I was afraid I couldn't meet his bill." Consequently they broke up. She finally married a "raw, unsophisticated guy" who was "friendly and relaxed" and offered "a certain stability." He was also, she adds, "attracted to me," and she "slipped into it." Both were YCL activists at the time. She had opted for the more conventional model of monogamous marriage, family stability, and child rearing.

Settling down, even within a patriarchal structure, was to many more attractive than a Bolshevik model that more often than not left the women at home base caring for the children while the cadre husband moved about serving the Party. In her autobiography Peggy Dennis recalls telling her mother, "an intense feminist," about her pregnancy. Her mother advised her to have an abortion and said, when she refused, "The pity of it is it will change your life, not his." Gene Dennis, her husband and a top Party functionary who served the Comintern throughout the world during the first years of their marriage, embodied the Bolshevik model.[5]

Both models are patriarchal, although the Bolshevik model offered women, at least in theory, the same opportunity as men to enter the field to make a revolution. Communist women had available such models of activism as Rosa Luxemburg, Emma Goldman, and Elizabeth Gurley Flynn, and yet none of the ten interviewed opted for such a life. Some sought a partnership of activists along Bolshevik lines but usually settled for a junior partnership—a "progressive" but fairly conventional marriage and family life that included children. The early age at marriage of Communist men and women suggests that the period of courtship and premarital sexual relations, including sharing a home, was relatively brief. In a society in which underground activity was generally dysfunctional and in a period when the Communist Party was seeking to present itself as nonthreatening and familiar, Communists generally chose to marry and have children. As James Weinstein notes, "The struggle against male supremacy in the party conflicted with its emphasis on party members living like 'ordinary workers' and also with the Victorian standards that prevailed among the rank-and-file members."[6]

When Mark Greenly married, he believed that his wife "supported . . . [his] perspective of being a professional Communist." He expected her to follow him in his revolutionary travels, but she resisted, preferring a Party office job. "I was slightly disappointed," he says. "I wanted a working-class wife." The Party, however, persuaded him that she was needed in the office.

Before their marriage Greenly had said to her, "I want two boys and two girls," and imagined, romantically, that it would be "us and the movement against the world." The marriage broke up after many unhappy and rocky years; he wanted to become a full-time field organizer, and she always warned him, "If you do, there will not be any children; there is no discussion." "I walked out," he concludes, after years of resentfully yielding to her pressure.

Greenly's dilemma is not necessarily typical of Party marriages, but it does reveal the confusion about the nature of Communist marriage that was characteristic of Communist men. Greenly's wife was asked to be a Krupskaya and a housewife simultaneously—a revolutionary comrade and a full-time mother. Under such circumstances, a more conventional marriage appeared to be an attractive alternative.

In many instances marriage—at least before the children came—had little effect on the ability of Communist women to remain fully active. One couple describes going off to work together, sharing in the making of dinner, attending meetings and various political events, and then, late at night, sharing their experiences and thoughts over tea. The men usually expected women to perform such traditional duties as cooking, house cleaning, and bed making. In a fair number of cases, however, women report that such household chores were shared. The Samuelses say that throughout their marriage, Edith has cooked dinner, and Ike has set the table and washed and put away the dishes.

Many Old Leftists speak of a high degree of shared interest. The better marriages are more "companionate," joint and complementary, similar to the arrangement Michael Young and Peter Willmot call "the symmetrical family."[7] The marriages are not egalitarian, since the husband's work is still considered primary and the wife performs the more expressive role. Many Party couples, however, experienced such marriages as relatively egalitarian because of the shared interests and relationships that grew out of their involvement in the Party subculture. This experience provides a counter example to sociologist Elizabeth Bott's thesis that only segregated conjugal roles are consistent with close social networks.[8] Many married couples shared and still share interests in politics, theater, and the arts and do so within the social network forged by the old Party.

The words most typically used to describe Communist family life, repeated many times by both men and women within the sample, are "partnership" and "teamwork." Many state, "We have always been a team; he [or she] is my partner." The Communist husband-father was not a tyrannical "king of the castle," nor was the wife typically a simple homemaker devoted to children, household chores, and supermarket shopping. Communist marriage was a variation on a theme; the theme was always patriarchal, but the music allowed greater play for the women. The men seem to have accepted the idea of active women, supporting them politically and vocationally within the limits already noted.

They were not always consistent, and there were underlying tensions that occasionally broke through. One case may shed better light on the dynamics of Communist marriage.

□ *ruth shapiro*
Ruth Shapiro compares her husband, Abe, with other Party husbands and pronounces him "much healthier, more stable, a husband-companion." She complains, however, that his patriarchial values imposed traditional child-rearing and housekeeping functions upon her. She was the one, Ruth emphasizes, who took care of the children. Early in their marriage, Ruth took a one-day-a-week job, leaving her youngest child with her mother. Abe expressed concern and suggested that she did not have to work, that he could support the family. She continued to work, however, sporadically and part-time until the children were older. Even then, she claims that her career possibilities were limited by her inability to put in any evening or weekend work. Ruth resignedly accepted the reality that "the male was the chief breadwinner." She could not hope to match a man's salary; consequently, her income was always supplementary.

Sometimes the hectic pace of political involvement got to her: "I felt it consumed our lives. I wanted to feel like a bride and we had all these meetings." At one point, she tried to put her foot down and exploded, "Is this a marriage . . . ?" But they continued to double up their lives with work, family, and politics. Ruth's seemed tripled up.

Ruth angrily asserts that "few women were sent to training schools," and even women in key posts were "treated differently." She believes that for a woman to make it to the top of the Party leadership, she had to have "an exceptionally strong personality."

"Behind the scenes" is the story of Ruth Shapiro's political life. "I'm a good organizer, a good administrator," she states. But because she was not an intellectual, she has always felt inferior to male leaders, including her husband. She recalls a discussion group in which the women were assigned the task of generating and leading discussion. "On the one hand we would lash out; on the other hand, we wouldn't try it; we'd be afraid to try it." Acculturated to deferring to men in public arenas, inexperienced at public speaking, and discouraged from organizing women to overcome such disabilities, most Communist women allowed their men to dominate all public forums, limiting their influence to the traditional behind-the-scenes conversations. The hostess might have inordinate influence over the host, but she still was expected to serve the coffee and cake.[9]

Ruth's attitude toward her husband is a mixture of admiration, love, and a touch of bitterness. She says of him, "He's a political animal, better than the rest," noting his basic kindness, his decency, and his helpfulness around the house, "I respect him; look up to him." But she resents always being identified with and through him. "If I said something, I would be asked, 'Is that what Abe thinks?'" Such encounters caused Ruth considerable self-doubt. She would ask herself, "What did I have going for me?" When other party wives told her how fortunate she was to have such a decent, nonphilandering spouse, Ruth wondered, "Why is this so great? Why should I be so grateful?"

Ruth intentionally worked apart from her husband to establish her own identity: "I felt more secure doing political work apart from him." Yet even in such quests for autonomy, she found herself reminded of the connection. After a speech and dinner for a prominent progressive, Ruth approached a female friend—a staunch feminist, she adds—desiring to discuss the speaker's main points. Her friend ignored Ruth's query, "What did you think?" and demanded "Would you tell Abe to look at such and such article, because I'd like to know how he feels about X, Y and Z." Ruth was deeply hurt. The story speaks to a lifetime of frustration and ambivalence about Communist men.

A few Communists married nonradicals or less involved "progressive" women, with differing results. One working-class radical's wife was "so politically uninvolved that she'd walk out when political discussions started." Another radical, also working-class and Gentile, married a local girl he describes as "quiet"; she has stayed quite distant from his activities, though supportive of them. Yet such a sexual division of political labor is quite atypical, and it is revealing that neither of those men was deeply part of the Party's social network and subculture. If they had been, the abstinence of their wives would have stood out and evoked some kind of subtle pressure. More typical and apparently more acceptable within Party mores were marginally involved wives. Fred Garst describes his wife as "only political because I was," while another man concludes his description of his marriage with "we didn't discuss politics much." In this type of marriage, the form clearly outweighed the substance of engagement.

The Communist Party involved itself in many ways in marital affairs. For example, Sammy Cohen married a woman "who never had a political thought" while attending school. He explained his political life and experiences to her before proposing. The district leadership opposed the marriage and initially fought it. "They wanted to meet her," he adds. Meetings took place and, as a result, the leadership approved the marriage. What would have happened if they had not remains unclear. She was judged a "progressive," that is, a non-Communist ideologically in tune with Popular Front positions on race, foreign policy, and social justice. That was enough. She gracefully declined the Party's offer of membership. What mattered was that she was not a security risk or a reactionary; beyond such bottom-line considerations, the Party remained oblivious, implicitly upholding patriarchy.[10]

Sam Katz emphatically asserts that the Party was male-chauvinist, like the rest of society, and that "women were still considered subordinate." He shrewdly adds that "the fact that a person is politically advanced doesn't mean that he's advanced in other ways, that he's personally a good guy; some people who are good politically are lousy bastards otherwise." In describing his own conventional marriage, he concludes, "We were intellectually bourgeois."

On the other hand, Sally Turpin, a cadre married to a working-class radical, stresses that "he had an attitude toward women that was unusual in its age, not feminist but conscious of the abilities of women." She feels that the Party had "a more conscious and theoretical approach" to what was usually called male supremacy, relying extensively on Engels's study of the family. Typically, however, practice lagged far behind theory.

Party literature occasionally provides a glimpse of the contradiction. The *Worker* Sunday supplement often carried pieces on marriage, family, child psychology, and sex roles. The tone of all such articles was sexually egalitarian, upholding a formally democratic approach to family decision making:

> Children, father and mother all must make decisions together, whether of money, of discipline, or anything else indeed. . . .
>
> A family, to be healthy, must be democratic. Women and men are equal. Children and parents are equal.[11]

But the emphatic words suggest uneven practice. As one woman wrote

> My husband could give an excellent lecture on the necessity to emancipate women. . . . If I have time to read the editorial in the *Daily Worker* I am lucky. I can jump up from a meal a dozen times, but my husband will pass the knife for me to cut him a slice of bread. . . . He's not the only one—I've met dozens like him.[12]

Mark Tarail, the child psychology columnist, emphasized that Communism included the "way of treating your wife, your husband, your children" and concluded,

> You can't be a nine-to-fiver, a true Communist in your shop and in your Party branch, and a reactionary in your own home. . . . Let us not have bossism in our homes.[13]

But the very existence of a supplementary section on the family directed toward women (it included fashion tips) marks the tension within Communist attitudes toward women and marriage. Typical of articles is one entitled "How Housewives Aid the British Communist Party," a very conventional piece that assumed that women, even Communist women, have their primary place in the home.[14]

Edith Samuels and her husband lived for some time in a working-class area. He was organizing heavy industry, and occasionally union leaders would exhibit what she calls "sexual looseness" or "carousing." The wives would call Edith's house asking for their husbands, and she would be uncomfortably aware that the men were likely to be involved in extramarital liaisons. She also speaks of being shocked and dismayed by the behavior at some Party socials where "they were practically screwing each other on the front steps." Exhibitionism was as distasteful to many old Leftists as infidelity.

Edith Samuels believes that in too many cases women rose within the Party because of the men they slept with but adds that she came to see this only in retrospect. Peggy Dennis, in her memoirs, gives some personal confirmation of this hypothesis. Upon returning from Party work abroad and finding her with a new, prestigious Party job, her husband angrily demanded, "How many nights with whom did all this cost you?"[15] Edith Samuels believes that the worst examples of such immoral and manipulative behavior occurred in the large urban areas and "at the highest levels." For the most part, as Peggy Dennis concludes, not without a certain contempt, "burgher-like stability" was the norm.[16] I myself heard many allegations concerning one district leader's sexual peccadillos, but little else.

Many old Leftists understandably prefer not to discuss the most private sexual matters. It would appear, however, that most young Communists stood somewhere between repressed Victorian and modern, "liberated" attitudes toward sex.[17] Several men speak of having been very inexperienced with women prior to marriage; one says that his wife was "my first experience with a woman." While some males, particularly those of working-class and Gentile backgrounds, seem to have had extensive dating and sexual experience as adolescents, many more from lower-middle- or middle-class and Jewish families were virginal and chaste prior to marriage. One woman describes her (Gentile) husband as shy and backward sexually: "He never kissed me until he proposed to me." It seems as if the majority of Communist men had little or no sexual experience before meeting their spouses and anticipated no extramarital activities in their futures. One woman recalls that although she was not a part of the conventional adolescent subculture, she had conventional views about marriage—she would meet the right guy, and they would fall in love, become engaged, marry in a proper ceremony, and then proceed to raise a family.

On the other hand, Communist youth were hardly Victorian in their sexual behavior. Although old Leftists inevitably colored their recollections about their sexual views and experiences in terms of their contemporary beliefs and several were critical of the sexual practices of others, both inside and outside the Party, few were self-righteous.

Ike Samuels says that initially he was uncomfortable with Party women and continued to date outside Party circles in the belief that Communist women "had a halo." Such a view is in significant contrast with the mythology of Bolshevik debauchery at socials and vacation retreats. Samuels finally broke up with his non-Party girl friend when she did not develop a "class-conscious" viewpoint. He was ready to take a chance with the more "angelic" women in the movement.

Another male Communist speaks of living with his future wife, a fellow radical, for several years prior to marriage. A variety of sources indicate that Communist morality upheld such arrangements. Monogamy was primary, in or out of marriage. There was a slight touch of the bohemian in some young Communists; they enjoyed life and all its pleasures, including sex, but, on the other hand, they were decidedly wary of hedonism. Gabriel Almond argues that there was "a real effort to eliminate the bohemian atmosphere after 1935" with the coming of the Popular Front. A number of sources concur, but within the sample, there is no indication that "faithlessness" was ever in favor. The attitude toward the substance of relationships—that is, fidelity and honesty—remained constant. The attitude toward the form—that is, marriage and the family—tended to become more conventional as couples settled down.[18]

Most old Communists are quite earthy and matter-of-fact in discussing sex.[19] They are neither bohemians nor philistines; instead, they uphold what came to be a strict Communist morality within both models of marital relationships. Communists always had to behave like a vanguard and were consequently under some pressure to show the way. Although this did not usually lead them to egalitarianism in marriage, it did induce most to affirm marital fidelity. In a sense, their viewpoint is a variation of "old-fashioned" behavior, Communist-style.[20]

This old-fashioned morality was often accompanied by a strong dose of egalitarianism and feminism. Edith Samuels recalls sharing an apartment with a very distinguished Party leader and his wife, also cadre. The leader would dictate his day's calendar and activities over breakfast to his devoted wife. The wife seemed comfortable in her secretarial role, but Edith Samuels found the routine abhorrent. She finally blew up and charged him with male supremacy. The leader took Edith aside, "What am I doing?" he implored, genuinely shocked by her criticism. He was a rather courtly and cultured man and had never thought to question the appropriateness of his wife's servicing his needs. But it all reminded Edith Samuels of how her own partriarchal Jewish father had behaved toward her mother: "I couldn't stand the way she was a second-hand citizen." Such Old World behavior patterns had no place in twentieth-century America.

She also recalls trying to organize a women's auxiliary to her husband's union. The workers came to Ike Samuels to complain about his wife's "agitation." They implored, "Tell Mrs. Samuels to leave them alone." These militant unionists even refused to give their wives carfare to come to Edith's meetings. Neither of the Samuelses felt that it would be worthwhile to directly combat such sentiment, particularly since the wives involved quickly and timidly retreated.

Communist women located in working-class communities seem to have had a harder time in achieving a modicum of equality with men. A Communist colonizer was under great pressure to conform to working-class mores in order to gain credibility in the community. Women in such situations had to either hold their tongues or ask out. Laura Blum remembers getting a job with the maritime union during the war and then being fired when the men returned. When she protested that there was still a need for her efforts, she was told that the NMU was "a man's union." Many women tolerated the prevailing codes and continued to do organizing work, often with greater success than their spouses. With Bolshevik self-discipline, they worked with the available material. Many successfully organized the kind of union auxiliary that Edith Samuels tried to form, and others managed human service organizations for neighborhood people—for example, helping elderly people get the federal and local benefits to which they were entitled.

Sally Turpin tried to do a study of Communist women in industry after World War II to find out how many had drifted back to family or to less physically demanding work after the war. She discovered significant declines in the employment of Communist women in plants, but Party officials did not give her any encouragement to follow up her study or publish it under Party auspices.

The operating assumption within the Party was conventional: as in Ruth Shapiro's case, the man's career came first, while the woman had the responsibility of raising the children. Interestingly, the men more frequently than the women resisted having children. Ike Samuels opposed the idea while his wife pressed him. Finally she exclaimed, "If Earl Browder had children, you can have children!" She also argued that "having children was part of what I was fighting for." (At this point in the interview Ike added, "She was more human than me.") Asked about the Party's role in such decisions, one Communist wryly answered, "There were some things about which we didn't consult officials."

There were occasions when the Party discouraged young cadres from having children, recognizing that family life limited mobility and commitment. One woman, married to a restless and very mobile activist and raising several children, saw her marriage fall apart: "I wanted to settle down, take care of the kids." He resisted and finally departed. Another couple emphasizes how Party work competed with child rearing. Members were often called on to attend meetings in the evenings, never having enough time to give to their children. One woman, speaking as a child-rearer, saw herself "in competition with an invisible movement." Several Communist parents blame themselves for neglecting their children during their years of activism and fear that psychological problems resulted.

In most cases, including those of cadres and functionaries, as family responsibilities became weighty, Communists became less mobile and more sensitive to family needs. Usually the wife took the lead here, at times imposing familial realities upon her spouse. In two cases, women drew the line by refusing to move to another area. Ike Samuels was asked to shift to another Party-oriented post after spending about ten years on the road. Edith Samuels, with several children nearing school age, emphatically refused, feeling that her children needed some stability in their lives. Consequently, they did not move. In another instance, after many years of living in one place, the husband was asked to move South. His wife refused, both because she felt settled into her neighborhood and because she did not want to raise her children in a conservative, Jim Crow region.

Was it problematic for Communists to have children? For some participants, the decision was automatic and made without any thought at all. One man simply notes that "you get to a certain age, your friends are having children," and therefore you do too. Another says that the first children just "came along." Others, however, gave more thought to the decision. Ethel Paine remembers discussions with her husband in which they asked, "Should we bring children into such a world?" But even in the anxious years of fascist triumphs, few Communists came so near to despair about the future. One woman recalls that her husband was going into the service and she was afraid of being left with nothing if he was killed; so she told him, "I must have a baby."

More typically, couples assumed that they would eventually have children but that in the short run it was wiser to wait, either for financial reasons or simply so that they could be fully engaged in political acitivites without such responsibilities. It was always assumed that the mother would play the decisive role in nurturing and raising the children, and current child-rearing theories stressed the importance of the mother's attention during the early years of life. One couple said, "We felt strongly at least for the first few years, the mother should be home."[21] In this instance, the wife left her job for several years. A male Communist says that his wife did not work "while waiting for the kids to grow up"; she did, however, get involved in her children's schools, organizing parents for progressive causes.

Many, in fact, most of the child-rearing women cut back on their political activities for anywhere from three to ten years and stopped working full-time, but nevertheless continued to be as active politically as their maternal tasks allowed. One continued working at her Party-related job through eight months of pregnancy and then resumed part-time work within several months of childbirth. Edith Samuels had her first child while her husband was in the midst of a critical strike. They lived in an immigrant, working-class neighborhood made up of the kind of workers he was trying to organize. Edith, nursing her baby, became part of the community by serving as a de facto social worker to neighboring wives and mothers. She helped the sick find medical services, aided parents in getting their children into summer camp, and made sure that an invalid woman's house was regularly cleaned. She also worked in electoral campaigns. To balance motherhood and politics, she tried to have as many meetings as possible at her home, but, as she admits, the situation became "hair-raising and very difficult." She persisted as activist and mother but now worries that "the children were the ones affected."

All of the women interviewed stress that child-care facilities simply did not exist in those years and that this lack severely limited their options. A few admit neglecting their children, running off to meetings, leaving children with babysitters or neighbors, or sometimes alone. Ben Green recalls the strains placed on families when the men ran off to evening activities, leaving their wives at home with the children. I heard of only one babysitting co-operative, and that was in another city.

Whereas activists rarely took their children to meetings, they did bring them to Party-sponsored socials and rallies. Tim Palen asserts that he sometimes dragged his children to important political events despite their resistance because "it was necessary" for their political education. No other interviewed parents, however, mentioned imposing political responsibilities on their children. The pressures were more subtle and indirect. Harry Freedman recalls that his child became such an enthusiastic and persistent supporter that the neighbors began to refer to him as "little Stalin." Certainly parents rewarded precocious radicalism with approval, but fairly normal leeway was granted for friendship and such childhood activities as play, schoolwork, and summer camp. Communist parents, like their nonradical upwardly mobile and well-educated peers, were achievement-oriented. They wanted the best for their children and saw academic achievement as the most promising path.

Several men speak self-critically of their behavior as husbands and fathers. Sam Katz views himself as "the outsider who was never home" to his children. He describes his wife as much more intimate with the children, then and now. "I laid problems on her," he adds; for example, he sacrificed his Party income for others in greater need. Katz feels that patriarchy was built into the times and concludes that, now that his children are grown and he is retired, "I can afford the luxury of anti–male chauvinism." Meyer Weiner acknowledges that he always dominated his wife politically: "She both accepted and rebelled against that situation." He never wanted children and admits, "I wasn't the best father." Characteristically, he exalts his wife's role: "She made up for my deficiencies." The Communist sex-role pattern of female expressiveness and male instrumentalism indicates no variation from conventional norms.[22]

One Party veteran claims that the organization made considerable efforts to push women into leadership. Harvey Klehr, a political scientist, presents evidence that beginning in the 1930s, women moved ahead faster than men within the national committee. But Klehr suggests that this was only true of Gentile women, white or black.[23] Peggy Dennis claims that the leaders of the Party's Women's Commission in the early 1950s were "without political career-women, husbands and children."[24] In some instances, the woman's status depended on her husband. Speaking of the French Communist Party in this period, Annie Kriegel observes: "If a woman wishes to acquire any kind of status within the party, she will find that it is not enough to play a role in the economic and social life of her community. It is more important for her to be married and a mother—married to a militant fellow-Communist, of course." She adds that seven of the nine women on the French Communist Party's Central Committee of 1966 were the wives of other committee members.[25] In District Three, other than Mother Bloor, the figurehead chairwoman of the district, no woman played a major role in decision making, although several were influential in front operations.

Communist marital and familial behavior must be labeled sexist, even though it is undeniable that Party women had considerably more leeway to achieve and produce and more support in the home and the work world than more conventionally situated women. What remains after countless stories of anguish, pain, bitterness, and, indeed, joy, sharing, and harmony are two intertwined and contradictory strands rooted in the unstated Party models of matrimony and the changing sex roles of twentieth-century America.

While some Communist couples felt the pull of the romantic, clandestine model of Bolshevik partnership, most settled for the more stable child-rearing model, some reluctantly, others more comfortably. They all assumed children, although some, particularly the men, tried to delay this for a number of years. When children came, the wives accepted their mothering duties, and most maintained political involvement on a part-time basis. Clearly, as in most American households, the man's career came first. As James Weinstein pointedly concludes, "as party members aged, married, and went to work their lives became more and more like everyone else's"[26] Ruth Shapiro concurs: "Our everyday lives were just like everyone else's; we lived one life and thought another."

Yet with this pull toward conventional social norms, there was a push toward the Party ideal of egalitarianism and the weaker hold of conformist morality on all political radicals.[27] In fact, they were not like everyone else; they were urban, mostly Jewish radicals with formal commitments to equality and with unconventional experiences that induced and sometimes encouraged men to work with women as comrades. As Edith Samuels says of her husband, "Ike always made it possible for me to function."

At their worst, Communist marriages match the most painful of conventional ones. One veteran guesses that almost half of the marriages within her social circle dissolved in the 1950s. The tensions and frustrations generated by the McCarthy period made it particularly difficult for less than ideal marriages to survive. For some, political visions faltered, hopes soured, suppressed personal ambitions re-emerged, friendships collapsed. "Real incompatibility" that had been covered by political agreement emerged and festered. Significantly, in all the cases noted the man initiated the split and the divorce. Several women stress that in their era "separation was unthinkable while you were raising the kids." Once the children were older, the man, feeling less responsibility, initiated the break.

One Communist man, an exception, bitterly reflects, "I was the woman's libber in the family," calling on his wife to share and participate, offering his aid. He claims that she did not want equality. While that may have been true in this particular case, too much evidence exists about the barriers facing Party women despite formal and verbal encouragement.

Party members, men as well as women, had no way to express their emotional problems. One Old Leftist delayed seeking psychiatric help for many years because of the Party taboo. Some members, of course, ignored the Party's hostility to psychotherapy, but all members were affected by the damper placed on any serious consideration of the ways in which personal life relates to political efficacy. Men and women often misunderstood one another and misinterpreted each other's behavior. Communist men, often sincerely, bemoan the silence of Party women, asking, "Why can't they take advantage of the opportunities for expression, leadership, responsibility?"

As Tessie Kramer suggests, Communist women "were not docile, cowed, inarticulate. However, they catered to their men in the areas of nurturing, food, orderliness, and cleanliness." And the men implicitly demanded such nurturing.

In brief, Communist women, with various degrees of reluctance, helped to sustain an environment that allowed the men to pursue their political and vocational careers. The men assumed the senior partnership role, mothered by their wives and congratulating themselves for the support they gave them in their lesser activities. The women accepted the junior partnership role, partly living through their husbands but investing enough in their own activities to feel fulfilled as wives, mothers, and activists. They too were part of the larger culture. And as a part of the Communist subculture, they could engage in activities beyond the dreams and experience of most American women, with the partial if not enthusiastic support of their husbands. As a result, Communist marriages at their best have a special strength and integrity.[28]

In some ways, Communist women patronized their husbands. The men blustered and pontificated, while the women sat back, exchanging knowing glances, realizing that "boys will be boys." Vera Schwartz sees herself as a strong, independent woman, but one who never wanted to operate politically like her husband, Al, who played a public role in the Party. She emphatically wanted to be a mother, raise her children, and be active in her own way. She is a feminist but not "liberated" and, in fact, associates the concept with sexual obsession, selfishness, and irresponsibility. On the other hand, she is hardly passive or docile. Like many Communist women, Vera Schwartz believes in marriage and the family, accepts motherhood wholeheartedly, and operates within a framework that values interdependence and responsibility to family and friends. She identifies with her own mother, a fiercely independent artist who believed in hard work, loyalty to one's own, and social justice.

Vera Schwartz in a sense both elevates and denigrates her husband, allowing him to occupy center stage but almost like a little boy who needs attention. She has taken care of the children with a sense of competence and continues to do the essential political work of mailings, phone calls, letter writing that later radicals would contemptuously call "shit-work"—in other words, women's work, which is never done.

Some Communist couples, having spent decades together, ideologically attuned, sharing a rich variety of experience, surviving crises like the McCarthy period, seem ideal, if patriarchal, pairs. While generally neat, few are fetishistic about housework. In fact, the juggling of child rearing and political involvement was often aided by the sacrifice of some house-cleaning chores. Tessie Kramer says that her mother, an immigrant Jew, would visit her home, scared to death about her politics, warning her, "You're going to bring the Cossacks on your head." But she respected her daughter's idealism; what bothered her most was the sloppy housekeeping, which she struggled to tolerate. In a mixture of frustration and confusion and some pride, she would conclude, "In my daughter's house, everything is different."

And it was different; most Party women were activists, involved in innumerable meetings, developing skills and impressive

six

the communist as organizer

In the period between the Great Crash and the McCarthy era the CPUSA was the most effective organizing agency within the American experience.[1] In this most politically stable of societies, radicals have usually battered their heads against the stone wall of affluence, rising expectations, and Democratic Party loyalty. Within the narrow space of agitation allowed by the political order, Communist Party activists built a small but influential organization devoted to organizing constituencies for social change. According to even the most unsympathetic accounts, Communist activists played important roles in organizing the unemployed, evicted tenants, minorities, and workers in a wide variety of fields. They were central in the emergence of the CIO and thus in the organizing of workers in heavy industry and mass production; they spearheaded the defense of the right of black people to equality before the law and social and economic opportunity; and they participated in virtually all of the national efforts to establish humane social services and eliminate hunger, disease, and neglect from our communities.[2]

Many analysts question the motives of Communist Party activists, and there certainly is controversy about the extent of their organizing successes. Nevertheless, Communist organizing merits serious and objective consideration. For a period of approximately thirty years, Communist Party activists and organizers sought out constituents in the mines, plants, and neighborhoods of the United States. Other left-wing groups, such as the Socialist Party, the Trotskyist Socialist Workers Party, and A. J. Muste's Workers Party, also deserve study, but the CPUSA offers students the best opportunity to examine the dynamics of organizing sponsored and directed by a radical political group.[3]

The organizers under consideration came to political maturity during the 1930s, mostly in an era associated with the Popular Front, and remained within the Party until at least the mid-Fifties. Indeed, many remained active organizers and participants after leaving the organizational framework of the Communist Party. In the thirties and forties, they modified their Bolshevik rhetoric and participated in antifascist alliances, worked for modest short-term successes within the fledgling CIO, and provided support and manpower for a diverse group of radical and progressive political movements and leaders, including Democrats, Farmer-Laborites, the American Labor Party in New York, and Communist Party councilmen in New York City, all under an essentially New Deal banner.[4]

Organizers operating in the greater Philadelphia district had important trade-union successes and played a key role in organizing unemployed councils, electoral efforts, tenant rights, and peace, professional lobbying, civil liberties, ethnically based, and neighborhood groups. For a period of approximately ten years, from 1936 to perhaps 1947, the Communist Party of Eastern Pennsylvania and Delaware, District Three, played an important if modest role in the political life of the area, generating ideas, programs, and visions that later became the commonplaces of social policy.

The Party offered its membership several roles. One could remain at the rank-and-file level, become a cadre, or rise to functionary. One could engage in mass work within one of the Party fronts or a non-Party organization (e.g., the YMCA) or one could become a "colonizer," engaging in industrial organizing at the beck and call of the Party. In addition, one could work within the professional section, providing the Party with such services as legal counsel.[5]

■ *rank and file*

At the lowest level of Party membership were the rank and file, the proverbial "Jimmy Higginses" who worked within Party clubs and branches, paid their dues, went to a variety of meetings, and joined the mass organizations and fronts, often focusing on a specific issue like Spain, civil rights, or Scottsboro. Such rank-and-filers were at the heart of everyday activities and what Gornick calls "grinding ordinariness."[6] There was an extraordinary turnover among such members, who often became weary of meetings, *Daily Worker* solicitations, and office chores.

Many rank-and-filers began their activism while in college or sometimes high school. The Philadelphia high school movement was quite sizable, including ASU and YCL chapters in at least eight schools. High school activists ranged throughout the city, meeting radical peers, socializing, and developing their own circle of comrades. For those who entered college either already active or about to be radicalized, there was an almost dizzying flow of activities, including demonstrations, marches, sit-downs, leaflettings, fundraisers, dances, parties, socials, lectures, speeches—and meetings. Always, there were meetings, one for every night of the week, often more.[7] Enthusiastic, recently converted Communists, like their spiritual children in the 1960s, had unbounded energy for political work. Most speak of being aroused and inspired by their sense of the significance of their efforts, the quality of their comrades, and the grandeur and power of their movement. Abe Shapiro recalls being engrossed at one time in the following activities: formal YCL meetings, ASU leadership, a university antiwar council (of which he was director), Spanish civil war relief efforts, a variety of antifascist activities, a student-run bookstore cooperative, and support work for assorted civil liberties and civil rights causes. Some activists found schoolwork boring under the circumstances and devoted all of their time to politics. A few became "colonizers." In most cases, however, Communist students completed their degree work, and if they dropped out of school, it was often for financial reasons. For most, the excitement of campus politics held their attention and their interest.

Some found Party youth work a path toward leadership, becoming citywide or national ASU or YCL leaders. Others on leaving campus became YCL branch or section organizers in different parts of the district.

Many who did not attend college did neighborhood work with the YCL, often focusing their mass organizational efforts through the American League for Peace and Democracy. To many youthful rank-and-filers, "the YCL became. . . Marxist-Leninist theory all mixed up with baseball, screwing, dancing, selling the *Daily Worker*, bullshitting, and living the American-Jewish street life."[8] Certainly the first flush of radicalism, the emotional high of purposeful activity, the sense of accomplishment and of sacrifice for the good of humanity, the work with fine and noble comrades, the love affairs with those sharing a common vision, the expectation that the future was indeed theirs, created a honeymoon effect for most young Communists.

For some, the fad of radicalism passed upon graduation or thereabouts. Others simply maintained a regular but distant "fellow-traveling" role as they entered the work world. And many were disillusioned by the Party's dogmatism or the great purge trials, the attacks on Trotsky, or the Non-Aggression Pact of 1939. Others, including those interviewed, remained in the Party. The shortest stay was six years, and most remained loyal for twenty years or more. For all of those who stayed, the Party and its small subculture became their lives.

Those working at the branch, club, and section levels were rarely on the Party payroll and had to find work to support themselves. For single people problems were few and life could be lived at a double-time pace, working hard all day and then organizing and holding meetings every night.

Some young Communists drifted for a time after school, doing Party work but not settling into anything. Ben Green lived in Strawberry Mansion, a lower-middle- and working-class Jewish neighborhood filled with Party people at the time. He did some work with the American League Against War and Fascism, spoke on street corners occasionally, went to three to four meetings a week, and helped to start a union local of public employees at his Works Progress Administration (WPA) office. He remembers that the Party "made it a big thing" when he shifted from the YCL to adult membership, but he was still looking at his future with uncertainty.

Upon completing high school, George Paine felt that "sports were gone" from his life except for an occasional neighborhood basketball game. He kept in touch but saw less of old non-Party buddies and did standard political work, "hustling the paper," going to meetings, demonstrating. Finally he decided to go to college, suspending but not ending his Party ties.

One rank-and-filer was a skilled craftsman, "glad of the class I was born into." He belonged to a conservative craft union and limited his political work to mass work at the local YMCA. He never really got involved with a club or branch group but paid his dues, subscribed to the paper, and worked with comrades to move the "Y" in a more "progressive" direction. He was quite open about his views, which would eventually get him into trouble at his job: "I felt that since to me everything was so clear, they'd hug me."

Tim Palen, a farmer and skilled craftsman who lived in a rural suburb of Philadelphia, worked with the Farmers Union. A Party rank-and-filer, he helped farmers get low-interest loans through the union and sympathetic banks. Palen never involved himself with Party affairs in the city, and the highest office he held was dues secretary of his section.

Since the Communist Party did not formally label members according to their rank, it is not always clear who was a rank-and-filer and who was considered cadre. One former district leader defines cadres as the people in training for leadership, like officers in an army. The rank and file are, therefore, foot soldiers, less involved and more a part of their own neighborhood or plant, more likely to hold conventional jobs, and more subject to pressures from neighbors, family, and changing circumstances. Annie Kriegel, who analyzes the French Communist Party as a set of concentric circles, places fellow travelers who vote for the Party and read the Sunday Party press on the "outer circle" and "ordinary party members" in the "first circle."[9]

Many observers describe such rank-and-filers as less "Bolshevik"—that is, more likely to break Party discipline in everyday activity and closer to the behavior and sensibilities of their non-Party peers. Harvey Klehr puts it, "Many party members received no training of any kind, attendance at party meetings was often spotty, and members frequently ignored or failed to carry out assigned tasks."[10] Almond presents esoteric and exoteric models to distinguish rank-and-filer from cadre, suggesting that the Party daily press directed itself to the relatively idealistic and naive external members, while the Comintern, Cominform, and internal Party journals spoke to insiders and sophisticated activists.[11]

■ *cadre*

The cadre has a "personal commitment." He or she is a "true Bolshevik," internally Communized, with an almost priestly function and sense of specialness. The cadre is a "professional revolutionary" along Leninist lines.[12] Philip Selznick adds that cadres are "deployable personnel," available to the Party at all times.[13] Some observers use "cadre" interchangeably with "functionary," while others distinguish them. I interpret "functionary" as a more administrative and executive role, usually carrying more authority and generally associated with top district and national leadership.[14]

Cadres were field workers, organizers, sometimes on the payroll but often holding a non-Party job. Some more mobile cadres left their own neighborhoods, but most worked at least within their home districts. (Functionaries, on the other hand, could be home-grown and district-bound or at the service of the national, even international, office.)

Many studies exaggerate the distinction between inner core and outer rings because of their dependence on the abstractions of Party tracts. Almond, for example, claims that the "true Communist" was beyond any commitment to the Popular Front since he was presumably fully Bolshevized and aware of the duplicity and tactical nature of moderated rhetoric. Perhaps this is true of the national leadership, who had associations with Moscow, training at the Lenin School, and Comintern experience. At the district level, however, the patterns are not as clear and seem to be more sensitive to generational, class, and ethnic variables.[15]

Among informants, the word "cadre" connoted "hard-work-ing," "brave," "dogged," and "honorable"—someone who fol-lowed a Leninist model of behavior; "functionary," on the other hand, was often used negatively to imply that someone was "bureaucratic," "aloof," "abstract," and "remote from struggle"— in brief, the Stalinist *apparatchik*. Neither necessarily belonged to an inner core.

Fred Garst tells of the "process of indoctrination" he underwent as he entered into Party life, beginning with "the regularity of systematic participation"—dues, meetings, selling Party liter-ature. He says that the number of meetings began slowly to escalate to three, sometimes five a week: section and subsection meetings, executive meetings, front meetings. Next, Garst was asked to lead a discussion, then to take responsibility for organizing the distribution of literature. He started taking classes at a local Workers School in Marxist theory and labor history. His commitment grew, his experience deepened, and he soon became a section leader.

Some Philadelphia Communists moved from rank-and-file to cadre roles during important political campaigns like the

Progressive Party efforts of 1947–1948. One woman had been serving in a minor capacity—"not anything earth-shattering"— but was swept up by what Wallace referred to as "Gideon's Army." She became a full-time Progressive Party organizer at a district level, her "first real organizing"; from that point on, she was fully involved in Party work at a variety of levels.

Some cadres emphasized front and mass work, serving as leaders of IWO ethnic groups, youth groups, and defense groups. Such cadres were particularly likely to operate clandestinely, although many communicated their affilitation all but formally to constituents.

Cadres can be distinguished by their level of operation (club, branch, section, or district), by their funding (on the payroll or holding a regular job), by their relative mobility and willingness to do political work outside their own milieu, and, finally, by the type of organizing they did (mass or front work, electoral party work, industrial organizing). The most prestigious cadres were those who did full-time industrial organizing at the will of the Party leadership. Such organizers, whether of working-class origins or not and whether indigenous or colonizers, were the heart of Party operations, seeking to develop a proletarian constituency and a trade-union base.

□ *johnny tisa*

Johnny Tisa's history shows what an experienced organizer could accomplish. Tisa, a second-generation son of illiterate, working-class peasants, went to work at the Campbell's Soup plant in his own South Camden "Little Italy" after completing high school in the early 1930s. While working summers at the plant, he had been stimulated by street-corner radical speakers and had joined the Socialist Party, which had a presence at Campbell's Soup. The Socialists sent him to Brookwood Labor College, where he met young Communists who impressed him with their earnestness and apparent lack of factionalism, a problem he encountered among the Socialists. He returned to help organize the plant, starting with a small group of about a half-dozen Italian workers, none of them

Communists, whom he molded through a discussion group. His group received a federal charter from the American Federation of Labor and began to develop an underground, dues-paying membership.

Tisa tells of frustrating experiences within the conservative AFL. At the 1939 convention in Tampa, for example, he found himself accidently strolling into a local walk-out of Del Monte workers, just as the police were arresting the leader. He spoke to the angry workers and was himself threatened with arrest. The workers exclaimed, "You got Bo [the arrested leader] but you're not gonna get him," and made a ring to escort Tisa to a streetcar. That evening, at his suggestion, there was a union meeting, packed and excited. When Tisa tried to speak about this remarkable experience at the AFL convention, he was refused the floor. Finally he simply took over the podium and microphone. Later that day, he met with other militants, including Communists, to organize the CIO-affiliated Food, Tobacco and Agricultural Workers Union.

He took a detour, however, as events in Spain captured his energies and idealism. Tisa served two years in Spain with the Abraham Lincoln Brigade, gaining "a sense of internationalism that never escapes you." On his return, he immediately set out to organize Campbell's Soup.

At the time Tisa began to organize it, Campbell's Soup employed about 5,500 full-time workers, with another 5,000 part-timers who came in during the heavy season. At least half the workers were of Italian descent; there were few blacks until the late 1940s. About half the work force was female. There was a sexual division of labor based on physical strength. Tisa's organizing group consisted of eleven or twelve key workers, all leftists, mostly Italian. None were "colonizers." All were indigenous workers who, under Tisa's leadership, planned the unionization of Campbell's. Tisa recalls that the group would often go crabbing and then return to his home to eat, drink, and talk strategy. Tisa was the only member of the group on the national union's payroll; he made a bare ten or fifteen dollars a week.

The organizers distributed themselves through the plant, reaching out to obvious sympathizers and picking up useful information that they would relay to Tisa, who could not enter the plant. He would take names and visit workers in their homes, signing them up so that the union could hold a National Labor Relations Board (NLRB) election. He would also cull information about working conditions from his organizers and publish it in a union bulletin that they distributed clandestinely, each carrying five to ten copies.

As their numbers increased, they became bolder and distributed the much discussed bulletin openly. Campbell's Soup had Tisa arrested once, but when he was released, many workers came to greet him. He assured them that the law permitted them to organize a union. The company tried many tactics to block his efforts: they started a company union; they charged that he was a "Red" and had raped nuns and killed priests in Spain. But Tisa lived in an Italian neighborhood among plant workers and had a mother who had worked in the plant for many years (cheering his speeches, often at the wrong times, he wryly and lovingly notes); he could not be red-baited easily. He was an open Communist; his neighbors would say, "Johnny's a Communist, but he's all right." Despite the real barrier of the workers' traditional Catholicism, he produced traditional trade-union benefits for members and was popular enough locally, a neighbor, to remain in leadership until the CIO purges of the late forties and early fifties finally forced him out.

Tisa's experience highlights the importance of developing indigenous personnel in organizing activity. His efforts were certainly bolstered by support from the national union, by Communist Party training and aid, and by the relative benevolence of the federal government as expressed through the new NLRB. Yet the presence of local activists, something the Communist Party sought but did not often achieve, invariably made the task of organizing a plant or neighborhood that much easier.

Other organizers performed similar roles without formally entering the Party, preferring to remain independent although generally taking positions consistent with Party policy.

□ *jack ryan*
Jack Ryan's old man was "a union man," later a foreman, a local Democratic politician, and a bootlegger. As a teen-ager, and a high school drop-out, Ryan ran poker and crap games in the neighborhood with a group of friends, some of whom wound up in prison. He worked sporadically as a roofer, during which time he was influenced by a socialist "who couldn't read or write until he was twenty-three."

His father finally got him a job at a local plant, where he worked as a crane operator in the early Depression years until he was laid off in 1931. Over the next two years, he tried a small store and "managed to hang on," selling water ice and running crap games. In 1933 he went back to the plant just at the point when the local union was being formed. Ryan recalls that he was "sworn in in an elevator with the lights out in between the floors." Despite his emerging radical politics, Ryan remained on the margins at first. "I deliberately didn't get active," he says, indicating that life seemed too unpredictable to take chances. In fact, he entered into a real-estate business on the side, and it eventually provided him with the cushion that allowed him to become more active within the plant.

Initially he ran for the general committee, backed by the other crane operators because of his successful grievance work. Still cautious ("I kept my mouth shut," he notes), Ryan went along with the conservative local leadership while maintaining contact with the plant militants, several of whom were old Wobblies suspicious of any Communist Party leadership. Ryan worked primarily through his own crane operators' network within the plant. He played the trade-offs in union posts among the plant's crafts to become local president, an unpaid post, and finally business representative, the only salaried position within the local. Ryan remained close to the Party but never joined. "I was more radical than they were," he brags. He criticizes their twists and turns and suggests that "in the end you can't trust any of them" because of "the goddamn line." He adds that the *Daily Worker* was "written for a bunch of morons." On the other hand, Ryan admits that Party union members were often competent and successful organizers and that he agreed with most of their Popular Front stances, particularly their antifascism. On the Soviets, he says that he did not spend too much time thinking about them, but adds, "I don't blame them for having a treaty with the Germans."

Ryan is clearly concerned with the practical issues of trade unionism. In describing one of his national officers, he exclaims, "A dedicated Communist but a helluva guy." He praises John L. Lewis's efforts at industrial unionization: "him and the Commies put together the CIO; they were the smartest crowd." So Jack Ryan worked with but kept some distance from "the Commies": "they were a little bit nutty." His union was one of those expelled from the CIO in the late forties, and he remains bitter about the Party's role in the union's decline. He remained active, holding union office on and off until his retirement. Ryan proudly concludes that he was placed on Social Security while on strike for the last time in the early seventies.

Johnny Tisa and Jack Ryan were working-class organizers, with roots in their ethnic communities, able to establish a rapport with their peers and, at the same time, develop more sophisticated skills within a broader and more ideological movement in or around the Communist Party. Their failures were mostly exogenous, the results of Taft-Hartley oaths, CIO purges, and McCarthyism in general.

Others operated in less favorable terrain, without the decided advantages of an indigenous, working-class background. The most characteristic Party labor organizer was a young, educated, second-generation Jewish-American sent to "dig roots into the working-class." The efforts of such organizers were prodigious; their accomplishments, however, were more problematic.

□ *al schwartz*

Al Schwartz's father was a 1905er, a Party organizer in the garment industry who had to open a small shop after he was blacklisted. Al, a classic "red-diaper baby," went through all of the Party developmental steps, from Young Pioneers through YCL to full Party involvement. Most of all he wanted to be a radical journalist. For a few years he was able to work on the Pennsylvania supplement to the *Worker*, but when it folded, his journalism career seemed over. Over the next half-dozen years, Schwartz, now in his late twenties, went into the shops as a "colonizer." He remembers the sense of adventure and mission he felt working at a few of the larger heavy industrial plants in the area. Yet he also speaks of his sense of loss and defeat in having to abandon hopes of writing. Schwartz's response to colonizing was painfully ambivalent: a college graduate and a Jew, born and bred within the Yiddish-Left subculture, he both relished the contact with blue-collar workers and remained distant from them. They were not like him, he stresses; they were mired in back-breaking labor, poor educations, and plebian forms of leisure. For a time he enjoyed the camaraderie of the local taverns, but ultimately he was an outsider, a Jewish family man and a struggling intellectual. Schwartz most fondly recalls the hardness and fitness of his body, the feeling that he was young and strong and physically a worker. But the successes were few, and later the McCarthy period made such Party efforts even more marginal. Schwartz found himself a family man in his mid-thirties without a career or a profession; frustrated and drifting out of Party life without drama or flourish, he moved to reorganize his life. His political values held, but his colonizing days were over.

□ *sol davis*

Sol Davis grew up in a poor, working-class, immigrant household. He was a bright young boy, and like many other upwardly aspiring Jewish males, he flourished at the elite Central High School and began moving toward a professional career. At this point, in the early years of the Depression, he was swept off his feet, as he puts it, by the Communist Party. After completing his schooling, he worked lackadaisically at his profession while seeking an opportunity to go into the shops as a Communist Party organizer; he was "determined to be shop worker."

His first attempts allowed him to learn something about machinery, although in each instance he was fired for his inexperience and incompetence. Finally he caught on. "I was in my element," he asserts, describing the war years in heavy industry. For Davis, the good organizer had to have a commitment to "the principles of Communism," "a talent for leadership," and a willingness to listen. A confident speaker, whose words are clipped and terse, he worked twenty-nine years in the shops, twenty-six of them at one plant. Located within the city, the plant was staffed mostly by Catholic workers (Polish or Irish), initially few blacks, and even fewer Jews.

Davis's recollections are filled with bitter refrains about red-baiting and "turn-coat ex-CPers," sell-outs and "social democrats." He is proud of his successes, which include chairing the grievance committee and serving as shop steward during most of his union years. Davis presents his life as devoted to organizing in the shops; he never got involved in his neighborhood and tended to leave Party electoral work to others. A hard-line orthodox Communist still, Davis argues that those who abandoned the Party were "petty-bourgeois with petty-bourgeois ideas," whereas he "was nursed out of the trade-union movement." In the fifties, he admits, "life became unpleasant," both in his largely Jewish lower-middle-class neighborhood and in the shop, where "a certain resistance developed to my activity" among people he calls anti-Communist socialists.

Davis believes that most American workers have been bought off in "discrete and discernible fashion" by imperialist profits, manipulated by the mass media, and blinded by nationalism, religion, and racism. After spending almost thirty years in the industrial heartland, Davis remains "dedicated to an idea," an "unquestioned belief" in communism.

Yet when asked about his ability to convert workers to class consciousness, a saddened Sol Davis replies, "Never—the shop was a desert for me." He did not convert a single worker and was "in that respect an utter failure." The shops, to the stoical Davis, were "a cultural, political, and philosophical wasteland despite having made so many friends." Sol Davis has kept the faith since he was "baptized" in the movement; his singular lack of organizing success rests, in his mind, on factors beyond his control—repression, cowardice, self-interest. He is a confident man.

□ *mike caldwell*

Other colonizers had more mixed results. Mike Caldwell, a college graduate with a middle-class WASP heritage, recalls that in his initial colonizing effort, "I wasn't very smart and made a lot of stupid mistakes—talked to people, became known as a trouble-maker." He was fired. Fortunately for Caldwell, his firing made him a "celebrated case," and the predominantly Irish and Italian Catholic workers, and even the conservative union officials, rallied to his support. Caldwell says that whereas other Party organizers had their best contact in their own departments, he touched bases throughout the plant and often socialized at the local bar to maintain and develop relationships. "A fair number knew I was a Communist," he says. "I never denied it." But most did not. In most plants to admit membership in the Party meant probable firing and certain harassment. For organizers like Caldwell, discretion was the rule.

His efforts paid off against the union's local establishment. The national, a left-wing union, sent in an organizer to help fashion a local coalition to defeat the established group, and Caldwell worked with him as elections chairman. The progressive slate was successful.

Caldwell, a leader of a left-wing veterans' group, participated in the 1946 strike surge. When mounted police chased people onto porches in Southwest Philadelphia to break up injunction-defying demonstrations, the local CIO was able to bring out 25,000 workers to protest against police brutality in front of City Hall. But such Popular Front–style unified efforts were shattered by the developing Cold War consensus, which began to drive radicals, particularly Party members, out of the unions.

Caldwell shifted jobs in this period, finally taking a full-time organizing job in a nearby industrial town. The plant had some IWO members and a few Party members, but no organization. Caldwell, who observes that "it really became difficult after the Korean War" started, found some success in putting out a small paper and handing it out at the main gates. He worked to develop contacts mainly by distributing the Party paper, first for free, then by subscription. Caldwell remembers proudly that he won a district drive with eighty subscriptions in his area. Gains were modest: a Hungarian sympathizer sent him two black shop stewards; then a few Irish Catholics made contact. Caldwell recalls going into Philadelphia to see prize fights with the latter workers, mixing pleasure with discussions of possible articles about their area for the Party press.

But the times wrecked any chance Caldwell had of developing a Party group. The FBI scared off possible sympathizers; he was arrested for circulating antiwar petitions, and the venture finally ended in the heyday of the McCarthy period when Caldwell was sent to join the Party's underground.

Caldwell and Al Schwartz experienced the ebb of the progressive union movement in the late forties and early fifties. Most Party labor organizers and colonizers, however, joined the fray during the extraordinary upsurge of the late thirties that established industrial unionism through the CIO.

□ milt goldberg

Milt Goldberg, despite winning a Mayor's Scholarship, was unable to continue his education after graduating from Central High School. Instead, he scratched to make a living at odd jobs, gradually becoming interested in radical politics. While he was working a pre-Christmas job at Sears, the department store warehousemen went out on strike. Clerks refused to cross the picket lines. Goldberg recalls that the increasingly anxious owners persuaded the clerks to return to work with promises of improved conditions and wage increases that were never fulfilled; meanwhile, the warehousemen settled. In the aftermath, the strike leaders were all fired. Goldberg says that many of them were Communists and that he began to notice how often that was the case: "I respected the Party people; they were able, talented people."

Goldberg became an organizer for a white-collar union dominated by mobsters who made deals with management at the expense of the membership. He describes his early efforts as "naive, inexperienced." Goldberg played a key role in leading his membership out of the corrupt union into a new CIO local, whose Philadelphia office staff was dominated by Party organizers. In those days, the late thirties, the era of sit-downs and a crescendo of collective bargaining agreements, organizing was remarkably fluid. Goldberg says that charters were granted easily and with little need for substantiation or the apparatus of negotiation soon to appear under the NLRB. In those days, he asserts with some nostalgia, one could go in and organize a place in one or two days, present demands to the employer, and make a deal. Such rapid victories were, of course, exceptions; Goldberg also recalls the often brutal resistance of management, particularly in heavy industry.

After serving in the war, Goldberg returned to his union efforts, despite family advice that he try something more prestigious and lucrative. The union was his life, so he stayed. He never formally rejoined the Party, although he remained in close contact. The Taft-Harley anti-Communist oath soon reinforced this decision. Nevertheless, Goldberg and his small union were red-baited and constantly under McCarthyite attack.

How did he survive? Goldberg argues that he "was very close to the membership" and had solid support from his fellow leaders. He emphasizes that the union provided real benefits and services to membership and sustained their loyalty despite the attacks. In addition, he notes that by this time the small union did not have a Party group, only him. One of the more damaging policies of Party-dominated unions was what Goldberg calls "the resolution bit"—the passing of Party-sponsored resolutions on every issue from Scottsboro to Spain. Too many left-wing unions manipulated such resolutions without making any effort to educate the membership; all that mattered was that local such-and-such of the so-and-so workers sent a resolution attacking Franco's dictatorship in Spain. Goldberg dropped such tactics in the postwar period, instead working with his local's officers and servicing the practical needs of the membership. By the mid-fifties, still a socialist, Milt Goldberg had become estranged from the Communist Party.

As is true of most arts, the qualities that make for a successful organizer are uncertain and descriptions are inevitably cliche-ridden. As the experiences of Johnny Tisa and Jack Ryan indicate, having roots in the work force being organized gives one a decided advantage. But the Party could use only the troops it had available, and these were for the most part educated, urban, Jewish Americans, most of whom had no experience in the heavy industries that were their "colonies." Most of them experienced frustration; one cadre estimates that 95 percent of all Party colonizers failed. Too often colonizers were unable to operate in a sea of Gentile proletarians. Fred Garst, still angry at the Party for its insensitivity to context, charges that "the Left didn't have any organizing skills." But some organizers, remarkably, succeeded.

□ *ike samuels*
Ike Samuels still speaks with an accent that reveals the years he spent in Eastern Europe before his mother, taking the remains of the family silver, arrived in the United States. No red-diaper baby, Samuels describes his youth as "street-wise" and his ambition as making it in America. Like many others, however, "the whole thing burst into flame" when the Depression forced him to drop

out of school and hunger marches, bonus marches, and unemployed council protests acted on his emerging social conscience. Soon he was moving toward the Party and engaging in union organizing.

Samuels, a gruff, self-deprecating man who often refers to his "big mouth," rose to leadership within a small craft union and served on the city CIO council. His CIO union was dominated by a Popular Front coalition of the Party and a progressive Catholic group. The union president, a leader of the latter, was incompetent; on several occasions Samuels had to bail him out of collective-bargaining disasters. Finally the Catholic faction and the Party faction sought to replace the president with Samuels. The national Party leadership, however, afraid of upsetting the delicate coalition, said no. Samuels recalls that he "didn't even question" the decision, but he was frustrated and soon left the union to become an organizer for a larger, industrial union.

Samuels agrees with Milt Goldberg that it was relatively easy to be a good organizer in that period. Labor was in an upswing, workers were clamoring to be organized, NLRB cards were easy to accumulate. In heavy industry, Samuels stresses, the key was to seek out the pockets of old radical workers—not colonizers, he emphasizes—who had broken down the old ethnic barriers. Many such organizers were members of the IWO foreign-language federations. Next, one needed the "pie-cards," the full-time organizers supplied by the CIO itself, many of whom were veteran radicals. Along with and sometimes among the pie-cards were the younger Communists going into the shops, supported by a growing and confident Party organization. A "highly developed structure," Samuels recalls, was essential to organizing success. One had to develop shop committees and day-to-day contacts in each department.

The sense of strength provided by the union itself and, crucially, by its CIO sponsor, allowed workers to imagine that the employers could be successfully challenged. In the automobile, steel, rubber, mining, and electrical equipment industries, workers faced mammoth corporations willing to use any means necessary to throw back the unionist surge. The New Deal, by encouraging a more neutral judiciary and law enforcement role, made it easier for the coordinated CIO drives to gain concessions from corporate heads. Samuels suggests that the workers, some of whom had backed decades of unsuccessful rank-and-file efforts, needed the sense that they were a part of a powerful coalition. John L. Lewis appealed to this sense when he proclaimed, "The President want you to join a union." Such a coalition advanced unionization at the same time that it necessitated concessions and strictures that limited the leverage of the newly legitimized unions.[16]

Samuels argues that it was imperative for organizers to have knowledge of their industries. He deliberately worked in a craft shop to learn the trade and later carefully studied one heavy industry before going out to organize its workers. He was not typical. Hodee Edwards, a thirties organizer, stresses "our consistent failure to investigate the neighborhoods and factories where we tried to work, thus applying a generalized, sectarian plan usually incomprehensible to those we wanted to reach."[17] And Sam Katz suggests that the Party did not always recognize the tension between the leadership and the activist/organizer over the pace and nature of organizing. The functionaries often pushed for the most advanced positions, including the "resolutions bit," whereas the organizers focused on the issues that confronted their constituents. Conflict was inevitable between broad policy and local needs and variations, and between policy planners and functionaries and field organizers and the rank and file. It is clear that the Communist Party suffered chronically from top-heavy decision making, which often left local organizers and members with policy directives that made little sense in local circumstances.

In addition to organizational strength and preparation, Samuels feels that leadership ability and, at times, personal courage must be demonstrated. On several occasions he had to take risks or lose the confidence of his membership. In one local the workers affectionately referred to him as "R.R.J.B.," Red Russian Jew

Bastard. He tells of organizing workers in a small Georgia company town. Fifteen hundred were on strike, and the patriarchal owners were negotiating only under pressure from the NLRB. They were stalling, however, so Samuels called on the work force to increase the pressure by massing outside the building where the negotiations were taking place. The next day, in the midst of bargaining, Samuels noticed the face of the company's attorney turning an ash white as he glanced out the window. What he saw were about three hundred workers marching toward the building carrying a rope; lynching was on their agenda. Samuels went out and calmed them down, "modified" their demands, and then wrapped up negotiations. His early organizing days also included maritime struggles with gangster elements who were not beyond "bumping off" militants. Samuels implies that the Left elements fought back, sometimes resorting to their own brand of physical intimidation.[18]

Peggy Dennis describes the Bolshevik ideal as "soldiers in a revolutionary army at permanent war with a powerful class enemy." And "in permanent war, doubts or questions are treason."[19] Yet as Joseph Starobin asks, "How could the Leninist equilibrium be sustained in a country so different from Lenin's?"[20] In fact, it was sustained unevenly and at a price. In a society with a tradition of civil liberties (albeit inconsistently applied and occasionally suspended in moments of stress) and a remarkably resilient political democracy, the Leninist model, hardened and distorted by Stalinism, mixed uncomfortably with American realities.[21]

At its best the Leninist ideal encouraged the incredible levels of hard work and perseverance that even critics of Communism grant to its cadres; it also evoked such personal qualities as integrity, courage, honesty, and militancy. Yet the ideal seemed to degenerate too easily into a model of behavior appropriately labeled Stalinist. Communist cadres accepted deceptive tactics and strategies that inevitably backfired and undermined their integrity and reputations—for example, the front groups that "flip-flopped" at Party command after years of denying Party domination. The intolerance and viciousness with which Communists often attacked adversaries, including liberals, socialists, and their own heretics, remains inexcusable.[22] As organizers, Communist activists suffered from a tendency toward a special kind of elitism that often made them incapable of working with diverse groups sharing common goals. In some periods they turned this streak of inhumanity against themselves, engaging in ugly campaigns of smear and character assassination to eliminate "Titoists," "Browderites," "revisionists," "left-wing adventurists," or "white chauvinists."

Moreover, the secrecy within which Communists often operated, while sometimes justified by the danger of job loss or prosecution, served to undermine the Party's moral legitimacy. An organizer's relationship with his constituents depends on their belief in his integrity, and this is especially true when the organizer is an outsider. Too often, Communists undermined their own integrity by covering manipulative and cynical acts with the quite plausible explanation that survival required secrecy. The tendency of Communists to resort to First and Fifth Amendment protection during the McCarthy period falls under similar challenges. As Joseph Starobin asks:

> Should left-wingers and Communists have gone to jail in large numbers? Might they have been better off *politically*, in terms of their *image*, to assert their affiliations, to proclaim them instead of asserting their right to keep them private, to explain the issues as they saw them, and to take the consequences?[23]

Communist activists certainly did not lack courage or commitment to a protracted struggle. Many risked prison, and some served prison sentences; perhaps as many as one-third of the cadres painfully accepted assignments to go underground in the early fifties. Their Leninism had to navigate contradictory currents of Stalinism and Americanization, militancy and opportunism.

Local Communist activists often lived a somewhat schizo-
phrenic life, alternately internationalist and indigenous, Bolshevik
and "progressive," admiring the Leninist model of cadre and yet
falling into more settled, familial patterns of activism. There was a
clear if often ignored sexual division of labor: men were more
likely to be the cadres, women performed auxiliary clerical
functions and unnoticed but essential neighborhood organizing.

The Party was also divided between theorists and intellectuals
on the one hand and field workers and activists on the other. As
one field worker proclaimed, "I couldn't be spending hours on
ideological conflicts; I'm an activist, not an intellectual." Many
agree that the bulk of an organizer's time went into local actions
and much less went into discussions and considerations of
important theoretical or programmatic matters.[24] Only a small
proportion received the type of ideological and intellectual
training suggested by the Leninist ideal, an ideal that formally
sought the obliteration of the distinctions between thought and
action, intellectual and activist.

In fact, Party intellectuals faced chronic and ingrained
suspicion, even contempt, from Party leaders. Abe Shapiro
sardonically charges that the function of Party intellectuals was
"to sell the *Daily Worker* at the waterfront." He remembers
checking on a new Party document on the economy: "I actually
read the document. I wanted to know what the Hell it was." He
found it infantile and far below what well-trained but never used
Party intellectuals and social scientists could have produced. The
Party rarely, except for showcase purposes, relied on its trained
intellectual or academic members; instead, it called on Party
functionaries, often of very narrow training, to write about
complex sociological, economic, and scientific matters. Theory
suffered as a result, and the Party, particularly after 1939, included
very few intellectuals.

Until the mid-fifties crisis, the Party, strangled by Stalinist
dogma and intolerance, was closed to intellectual discourse. Abe
Shapiro finally left the Party because his intellectual training had

given him a commitment to intellectual honesty that he could not shake. Among organizers, Party arrogance cut off messages from the grass roots. Orders from what one veteran calls "the Cave of Winds"—Party headquarters in New York—often contradicted practical organizing experience.

The Party also suffered from insularity. Mark Greenly brought interested fellow workers to a Party-dominated union meeting. They were curious and "antiboss" but quite unsophisticated and not at all ready to make any commitments. Unfortunately, the Party organizer immediately started to discuss class struggle and a variety of abstract political matters. The workers were quickly alienated and frightened away, never to return. Ethel Paine recalls such "inappropriate behavior" as the sectarian conversations Party people would carry on in the presence of non-Communist acquaintances and neighbors. Although chronically secretive about membership, Communists could be remarkably insensitive to their audience in revealing ways. A successful organizer learned when and how to introduce more controversial ideas to nonmembers. Training, including the Party schools, helped to some extent, but most Communists agree with the veteran organizer who feels that such learning has to be done on the job, by trial and error. Many Communists, like Sam Katz and Mike Caldwell, tell painful if sometimes hilarious tales of their own and others' ineptitude as beginning organizers. Some discovered that they simply were not suited for the job and would never develop the personal qualities that make for a competent organizer. Several veterans insist that organizers are born, not made. Yet relatively introverted and socially awkward young people, inspired by the idealism and the comradeship of the Communist movement, did transform themselves into effective organizers. Vivian Gornick points out that such transformations did not always survive the collapse of association with the Party.[25] I did not, however, discover total or near total personality changes caused either by joining or abandoning the Party.

Although most of the literature about radical organizers deals with men, it is increasingly apparent that some of the most significant and consistently ignored organizing within the Communist Party involved women. The ten women interviewed performed a rich variety of Party tasks, but perhaps the most important were those not officially designated, like the informal neighborhood activities organized by Edith Samuels, described in Chapter Five.

Sarah Levy was also involved in such efforts. Sarah and her two children joined her colonizer husband, Moe, in leaving the comfortable Party concentration in the Strawberry Mansion section to live in a nearby industrial town. She refers to the next three and a half years as "not the easiest times and, yet to me, personally, one of the best growing experiences—and I have never regretted it." (Moe's wry rejoinder was "She didn't have to work the blast furnaces.")

There were only three Party families in the town, quite a difference from the thirty or forty Party friends they left behind in Strawberry Mansion. While Moe worked the furnaces and tried to develop contacts with plant workers, Sarah joined a folk dance group at the local "Y," where she got to know Greek, Yugoslav, Italian, and other immigrant women. Moe, limited in the plant to a small Party circle of colonizers and sympathizers, was able to socialize with the husbands of Sarah's folk dancing partners.

Colonizers often ended up working with a local Party apparatus while their wives, working through neighborhood networks, reached into the community through its women, older people, and children. As Angie Repice casually but proudly concluded about her work with a community center during the war years; "I am an organizer, so I organized a nursery." Her husband was in the service. Moving around to stay close to his base, she put her organizing abilities and political values to work. Such efforts remain an unwritten chapter in the history of radical organizing.[26]

■ *functionaries*

Few district functionaries other than Sam Darcy achieved any national stature or had much leverage outside the district. Dave Davis, the business manager of UE Local 155 and an important

Philadelphia-area labor leader, was often elected to the Party's national committee but never entered the inner decision-making group. Other district leaders—like Pat Toohey, Phil Bart, Phil Frankfeld, and Ed Strong—were D.O.s sent into the district and then moved out again to other assignments.

Most district functionaries played dominant roles within the district committee and ran such important Party operations as the local Progressive Party and the Civil Rights Congress. They drew meager salaries, which were sometimes supplemented by Party-related employment. The Party network, at least during the late thirties and forties, could place members in some union jobs.[27] Possibly several dozen members depended on the Party for their livelihood in this way.

■ *nonmembers*

One often encounters Communists who, for very specific reasons, were not formal Party members. One former Progressive Party leader never joined the Party but worked closely with district Communist leaders to map strategy and coordinate activity. Some union leaders stayed out of the Party to deny employers the red-baiting weapon, and a number dropped out after the Taft-Hartley Act made a union officer liable to prosecution for perjury if he lied about current Party membership.[28]

■ *professionals*

Some professionals who joined the Party operated at a rank-and-file level, belonging to a professional branch or club, attending meetings, and fulfilling subscription quotas. Several recall being highly impressed with the other professionals they met at Party functions. But such members—often doctors, dentists, and architects—were on the margins of Party life.

Many professionals, especially lawyers associated with Party causes, found membership problematic and chose not to formalize their relationships with the Party, though they might be members of a professional club. "I fought against loose tongues," one states.

"I never asked a soul whether they were Communists or not." Several left-wing attorneys stress that they did not want to be in a position to betray anyone or risk a perjury charge if questioned about their own affiliations and associations. The law in America is a conservative profession, and several Left lawyers paid a high price for their efforts.[29] Another consideration was that the Party sometimes pressured lawyers to use a particular legal strategy in Party-related cases, and such pressure was more effectively applied to members.[30] One attorney notes that the Party itself seemed ambivalent about requiring formal membership. A few district leaders pressured him to join, while others understood that it was not particularly useful or necessary.

Some lawyers, whether members or not, found their services very much in demand. They were needed in labor negotiations, electoral activities, and civil rights and civil liberties cases. In the late forties and early fifties, Party-affiliated lawyers found it less easy than it had been to earn a living through Party-based clients, such as left-wing unions. Instead they were called upon to deal with the titanic task of defending Party members indicted under the Smith Act and other pieces of repressive legislation. Thanks to this demand, as one attorney suggests, they received special treatment from the district leadership. They mixed with labor leaders, politicians, judges, and, at times, the national Party leadership. Several had more contact with the non-Communist local authorities than district functionaries had. One left-wing attorney recalls that he had the luxury of criticizing Party policies and decisions, within limits, because "I was needed, I was special, a lawyer."

More significant than membership was the degree of autonomy a member had, and this was based on his importance to the Party or his institutional leverage. A professional could get away with criticism of the Nazi-Soviet Pact that would not be tolerated from rank-and-filers or most cadres. A union leader could ignore Party instructions, aware that his own organization was his power base. A former Communist, George Charney, criticizes in his memoirs the "left-wing aristocracy of labor that rarely mingled with the herd of party members or the middle functionaries."[31] Such trade-unions "influentials" often had contempt for functionaries and would go over their heads to top leadership.

Those who entered the Party, at whatever level, in whatever role, operated within a well-defined organization and lived within a somewhat insular and often nurturing subculture that provided them with formal and informal relationships. These relationships eased the often lonely organizing work. One veteran unashamedly calls his fellow Communist organizers "the most dedicated, most selfless people in the struggle." Many would share Jessica Mitford's feelings:

> I had regarded joining the Party as one of the most important decisions of my adult life. I loved and admired the people in it, and was more than willing to accept the leadership of those far more experienced than I. Furthermore, the principle of democratic centralism seemed to me essential to the functioning of a revolutionary organization in a hostile world.[32]

Any tendency to romanticize such activists must be tempered by an awareness of their mistakes, limitations, and weaknesses, and it is true that many non-Communists made similar commitments to organizing the oppressed and the weak. They too merit consideration. These Philadelphia veterans of the Communist Party are very human actors who worked on a particular historical stage. Some conclude that their years of effort never really brought any of their factory and shop constituents into the movement. Like Sol Davis, they admit that they were utter failures in that "cultural, political, and philosophical wasteland" of blue-collar America. Others share the pride, perhaps the arrogance, of one of Vivian Gornick's subjects:

> We're everywhere, everywhere. We *saved* this fucking country. We went to Spain, and because we did America understood fascism. We made Vietnam come to an end, we're in there in

Watergate. We built the CIO, we got Roosevelt elected, we started black civil rights, we forced this shitty country into every piece of action and legislation it has ever taken. We did the dirty work and the Labor and Capital establishments got the rewards. The Party helped make democracy work.[33]

The road from Spain to Watergate is a long one. Communists, euphoric at their prospects in the heyday of CIO sit-downs and Popular Front triumphs, later needed remarkable inner resources to sustain political activity. They sensed the first tremors from the purge trials, received a severe jolt from the Nazi-Soviet Non-Aggression Pact of 1939, and in the postwar years faced first political repression and then, more painfully, internal disintegration and demoralization.

seven

problems and crises, 1939–1956

In the early summer of 1939, a Communist militant could look back with satisfaction on the previous four years of the Popular Front and anticipate a future of continuing growth. Certainly the dark war clouds of fascism were overhead and the New Deal reforms had been stalled by the 1938 congressional election setbacks, but the construction of an international coalition against fascism abroad and Hooverism at home seemed promising. Sorrow at the collapse of the Republican forces in Spain was tempered by pride in the valor of the international brigades and the support provided by the Soviet Union. Neither Orwell's reports of repression in Catalonia nor the Dewey Commission's assaults on Stalin's massive purge campaigns and trials could shake the loyalty of most of the Party faithful.

News that the Soviets had signed an agreement with the mortal Nazi enemy began a testing of Party commitments that was to last until the Party's effective demise in the mid-fifties. Many, particularly intellectuals, abandoned the Party, flailing at "the god that failed." Fortunes and hopes sometimes revived, as they did during and immediately after World War II, when the Popular Front seemed restored. But the restoration was more apparent than real: it occurred under the auspices of anti-Communist liberals and organizations like the Americans for Democratic Action. The CPUSA was in fact its victim.

Most studies of Communist behavior ignore the social and cultural context within which Party members responded to the flood of crises. Too often, scholars have been content to focus on psychology to explain why some remained loyal members. Others stress the social ostracism that faced prospective dissidents and renegades, without placing such social pressure within the context of everyday Party life, informal Party networks, and the Party subculture. Students too often ask the wrong questions in attempting to figure out how and why an apparently intelligent person remained loyal to a movement that seemed so patently dishonest, ignoble, even evil. To stomach Stalinism and mouth Comintern lies, one had to be a knave or a fool, an authoritarian personality, a true believer.

The fact is that Communists perceived information about purge trials or Soviet anti-Semitism through the prism of small-scale, local, and ongoing experience. They were often as concerned about what was happening in their own milieu, about what the comrades working alongside them did and thought, as they were about as the international issues that dominate most studies.

Just as many Communists were recruited into the Party by "significant others," many continued to be influenced by those with whom they worked most closely. This is especially true of nonintellectuals, whether cadres or rank and file, petty-bourgeois, or working class. If Communist cadres were working in a shop or as section organizers or working with a mass organization like the American League for Peace and Democracy, with people they respected and with whom they had shared difficulties and sometimes dangers, it is unlikely that they would break with comrades over a single, remote issue. First of all, Communists assumed that the press was biased against the Soviet Union and all working-class peoples; they experienced media deception and hypocrisy almost every day in their own work; lies about strikers, sensationalism about outside agitators, and selective reporting. It is understandable, therefore, that Communists mistrusted press reports and relied on their own Party media.

The unsettling problem was that of the liberal, "progressive" publications, such as the *New Republic* and the *Nation*, which often sided with the Left but which, on particular issues, criticized Party positions and behavior. Communists resolved any uneasiness caused by this criticism by falling back on old Bolshevik suspicions about intellectuals. And who read such journals but intellectuals anyway? Most Party members adopted or simply maintained an "us and them" attitude. As is true of most people, the majority of Party members chose a politics of loyalty over one of conscience; they opted for their own, "right or wrong."[1] Group loyalty allowed them to evade the issue.

In 1939 most Party members were too busy doing the demanding work that the Nazi-Soviet Pact made necessary to spend much time agonizing over it. They were *busy*; they felt contempt for the soft and fuzzy intellectuals wasting their time in morbid introspection. Radicals were used to attacks from other quarters. Ike Samuels proudly recalls Edith's reaction to an attack by Marines wielding Sam Browne belt buckles during an American Peace Mobilization march with the theme "The Yanks Are Not Coming."[2] She kicked them "where I knew it was going to hurt." Later they both participated in an antiwar demonstration in front of the Supreme Court in which police billy-clubbed demonstrators, setting off a panic and a frightening stampede for safety. In such circumstances, the loyalties of those who stayed solidified. The Bolshevik code, which visualized all struggles through military metaphors, argued that there are times when the revolutionary cadre has to simply maintain discipline and have faith that information will eventually be revealed to clarify seemingly compromising situations. Such moments were tests that comrades had to pass. After all, only bohemians, intellectuals, petty-bourgeois faddists, and lumpen elements expected class struggle to be easy. Most Communists—that is, those who remained within the Party through these crises—had such a perspective.

It would take almost two decades for such deeply loyal, committed activists to make the momentous decision to abandon not their values and visions, but the institution that they had for so long believed to be their embodiment.[3]

■ *the pact*

The signing of the Nazi-Soviet Pact in August 1939 ended the Communists' fusion of patriotic and internationalist beliefs and generated the first major trauma within the Party. The purge trials within the Soviet Union had generated some doubts, but most Communists were so convinced of "Trotskyite" venality and of the reality of imperialist sabotage that they fairly easily accepted Vyshinsky's fabrications.[4] But the Pact, with the accompanying handshakes between Molotov and Ribbentrop, shocked and upset many partisans of the Popular Front against fascism.

Most Communists supported the Soviet tactic.[5] One member argues that "the capitalist world was out to get the Soviet Union" and so "a pact with the Devil" was justifiable in the name of self-defense. He adds, "I had no doubts, then or now." Most Philadelphia Communists believe that the Soviet Union was a bastion against fascism in the thirties and was allowed to remain isolated by the West, an obvious target for fascist attack. Another argues that "Stalin was a very great man who had to do terrible things" to maintain the Revolution. Mark Greenly best explains the visceral quality of responses: "We were apologists for the Soviet Union." He says that the 1939 decision "still makes sense to me. I had to decide whose side I'm on, on the side of the working people, or with the other bastards." Deep loyalties rather than personality quirks determined the choice for most. And, of course,

Party training and self-discipline made it easier for "people who internalized the line," as Meyer Weiner puts it.

Weiner remembers only a few organizers who quit over the Pact. He spoke about the Pact with a Party veteran, a major influence on him, and discussed it at length with his wife: "We worked it through to our own satisfaction." Tessie Kramer says that she was "able to rationalize the decision after endless hours" of discussion and debate.

While some members affirmed the Party shift immediately, others needed an ideological and organizational boost. As Sally Turpin recalls, "The YCL did some smooth talking then." Another veteran was persuaded of the Pact's value by some well-known Communist artists at a Party summer camp. Eight of those interviewed recall "small qualms" but saw the move as fundamentally sound. As Sam Katz observes, "My mind triumphed over my heart." Otto Kramer, like several others, justified the Pact on defensive grounds but believes that the Soviet Union and the Communist movement went well beyond a defense of necessity to a proclamation of virtue. As so often happened, the Party felt the need to wrap all decisions in a banner of historical necessity and, paradoxically, absolutist morality.[6]

Stan Wax says that the Pact made him "disenchanted with the way in which the CP handled that thing," meaning the collapse of Popular Front groups he and others worked with. He could not discuss the matter with Party friends, "close friends, decent people," and survived by having "confidence that the Soviet Union was probably doing something right." Yet he was uncomfortable, exclaiming, "A Burton K. Wheeler on our side!"[7] The pact generated "the first defeatist feeling I had." Yet he stuck with the Party, convinced that this was a test of his moral fiber as a Communist. The fair-weather friends deserted the cause, he reflected, but the true of heart remained. All of one's friends seemed to stick. In any case, how could one admit doubt in the face of the taunts of the enemies, the Trotskyites, the social democrats, and the turncoat liberals? Better to continue with one's work, which was still in the interests of working people. So reasoned most Philadelphia Communists.

There was work to be done, grievances to pursue, meetings to attend, comrades to meet, adversaries to attack. Most comrades passed this first major test, but not without some jolt to their previously confident assumption of the historical inevitability of socialism, and not without feeling some twinge of pain as their Popular Front patriotism rubbed against their commitment to Soviet hegemony.

■ *world war two*

The period of the Pact ended with the German invasion of the Soviet Union on 22 June 1941. American Communists rejoiced in the realization that they could now re-fuse their American patriotism with their international loyalties. The Popular Front revived, despite significant attrition, the virtual end of all New Deal efforts, and deeply rooted bitterness on the part of anti-Communist Popular Fronters disenchanted with Party shifts and apparent deceptions. As FDR put it, Dr. New Deal became Dr. Win-the-War. Meanwhile, American Communists worried about the reports of German successes in the fall of 1941, hoping that the Red Army could stem the tide of fascism. Previous studies suggest that the war period allowed American Communists to break away from Party discipline and Party ideology; there is some evidence that many who served in the armed forces never rejoined the Party after they returned to civilian life.[8] The Philadelphia experience indicates a different pattern. In most cases the war reinforced rather than undermined Party loyalties. Members returned from the war energized to rebuild their lives and rejoin their movement.[9]

When the Soviet Union was invaded, many Communists became, in the words of one cadre, "Soviet patriots," listening to war bulletins, feeling "moments of despair," awaiting news of counterattack. Several Old Leftists recall awaiting Winston Churchill's speech following the beginning of Operation Barbarossa, the German invasion of the Soviet Union, actually fearing that he might opt for an anti-Communist alliance with the Axis. They expressed great relief and new confidence when Churchill chose to ally with his old enemy against a common foe.

When the United States was attacked at Pearl Harbor, the draft brought thirteen interviewed Old Leftists directly into the war. Only one agrees that Communists found relief in the service from tedious meetings and rigid ideology. Milt Goldberg says that "at first I was kind of happy in the Army"; it was "like a vacation" from Party chores. A Depression-era youth like Moe Levy, however, could describe the Army as "an adventure," but "not much different from South Philly." Most served willingly, seeing the war as a continuation of the antifascist struggle. Like George Charney, many felt relief: "Once again, I felt like an American, with different ideas perhaps than the others, but basically in harmony with them."[10] The Popular Front lived again.

All of those who served faced surveillance and a variety of restrictions and barriers because of their Party associations. Johnny Tisa, who had served in Spain for two years and had combat experience, was told by a sympathetic officer that he would never see combat or be sent overseas. He spent the war stationed with an infantry group in the South, bored and discouraged. Harry Freedman, sent from school to school while others were shipped out, says he was "the best-schooled and least-used person the Army ever had." Milt Goldberg remembers being questioned about the Soviet Union, Stalin, and the *Daily Worker* by Army intelligence.

Most of the thirteen eventually were shipped out to combat zones. They served in the D-Day invasion, across the Rhine, in the South Pacific, in Burma. Several became officers, others rose to sergeant, and a few received battle stars. Almost half (six) were made information or orientation leaders, indoctrinating troops about Nazism, teaching geography and history, even generating interest in Spanish Civil War songs. Because they were well prepared and knowledgeable about the history and nature of fascism, superior officers, often unaware of their Party membership, assigned them to such educational tasks. Party G.I.s upheld

Bolshevik work habits while in the service, doing a thorough and conscientious job in all such efforts. Even when military intelligence finally caught up with them and expressed horror at finding Communists teaching soldiers about current events, superior officers often protected them as long as possible. In this sense, Communists were able to maintain continuity with their Party ties, using organizing skills and sustaining their self-esteem as competent and valuable people. As one ex-G.I. notes, "I'm an organizer, so I organized."

Several Communists experienced some shock over the political attitudes of many of the G.I.s, especially Southerners. Eastern, mostly Jewish, urban radicals had rarely encountered "rednecks" before and "were appalled by the backwardness of the Army" and upset by its anti-Semitism, racism, and authoritarianism. Fred Garst "saw how America really was." Sammy Cohen, on the other hand, experienced persecution from some Southerners but feels that as a Communist he was more prepared than most Jews to cope with it. He cut through much antagonism by reading letters from home to semiliterate and illiterate Southerners. Most eventually came to respect and trust him, viewing him as different but "a good egg." Sam Katz encountered some organized hostility, "a little guerrilla warfare," from G.I. anti-Semites, but, he adds, "I was very aggressive about it" and met it head on when attacked.

Bigotry did not disillusion Communist G.I.s. Milt Goldberg, involved in European combat and occupation, emphasizes that his experiences left him amazed "at how strong human beings actually are" under stress. Moe Levy speaks of his reinforced hatred of authoritarianism; he refused to salute and was "busted" for insubordination. Several Jewish Communist G.I.s believe that the war made them more aware of their Jewishness. One found that he began to read about the Holocaust after returning home, asking, "Why the Jews?" He now expresses some shame about his youthful obliviousness to his own ethnic identity.

Bonds with the Party were tightened by the experiences several had with other Communists in Europe, Asia, and Australia. Henry Blum, knowing that in France "every fifth person is a

Communist," visited Party offices in Paris and "found a second home there." Mike Caldwell, who got to know the *Humanité* staff during his stay in France and met with Communist transport workers in England, recalls, "it gave me insight into how a mass Communist movement comes about and how it operates." Sammy Cohen made contact with Party members in Australia, while Mark Greenly discussed aiding Burmese guerrillas with Party comrades in Calcutta. Several developed friendships that remain in existence today. The idea of an international revolutionary movement was much strengthened by such experiences and by the very existence of the worldwide antifascist effort. Their relatively small party was part of an international movement that played a decisive role in defeating fascism.

Those who remained stateside engaged in the same support efforts—calling for a Second Front, promoting war bond sales, collecting needed war material—as many non-Communist Americans. Women with husbands overseas, like Sally Turpin, took jobs in heavy industry and helped to organize new workers, often women. Several Communist men and women working in plants succeeded in becoming rank-and-file union leaders, despite the Party's no-strike war pledge and its often hysterical attacks on "slackers," "wreckers," and "fifth columnists."[11] Many workers responded to the calls for national self-sacrifice emanating from virtually all trade unionists. Ike Samuels feels that some Party unionists developed dangerously close relations with employers under the wartime negotiations structures, but that many of them also found ways to "cheat" on the no-strike pledge, struggling for better conditions through other means of pressure, such as slow-downs and trade-offs.

The most explosive issue in Philadelphia during the war was the wildcat strike against the Philadelphia Transit Company, a response by Irish Catholic workers, led by the company union, to a ruling by the Federal Fair Employment Practices Commission that blacks should be hired as drivers and not simply be given janitorial jobs.[12] The Transport Workers Local 234 (CIO), led by progressives, won a representation election over the company union and fully supported the FEPC order. Left-wing and liberal groups in the city demanded government intervention to end the wildcat strike, arguing that the strikers were committing treason by holding up workers from reaching their war-related jobs and therefore causing G.I. deaths. Roosevelt finally sent in troops to operate the buses and trolleys; they left after a week when wildcatters, threatened with formal charges, backed off. It was a great victory for the kind of Popular Front alliance the Party would seek in the postwar period.[13]

The Party rebounded from its difficult and defensive position in the period of the Pact to again become a part of a Left-Center alliance in labor and party politics. There were less harmonious moments too—for example, when the Democrats nominated William C. Bullitt for mayor in 1943 despite Communist Party opposition. Sam Darcy, then D.O., strongly opposed Bullitt, at first trying to get other Democrats to run against him in the primary and then mounting an independent campaign against him. Although Bullitt was defeated by Republican Barney Samuel, there is little evidence that the Communists played a significant role in this result.[14]

Darcy himself became a source of contention within the district because of his opposition to Earl Browder's transformation of the Party into the Communist Political Association (CPA) in early 1944. Darcy argues that Browder had already sold out the Party's Southern organizing campaign in exchange for the administration's acceptance of his winning a congressional seat in New York. Whether this allegation is true or not, Darcy, along with William Z. Foster, dissented from Browder's move. Foster remained silent. Darcy, however, after being refused access to Party media, publicly criticized Browder and was expelled from the Party.[15]

Darcy was a dynamic and impressive leader, according to virtually all local Communists. He was a compelling and popular public speaker. Yet many, at least in retrospect, find him to have been arrogant and self-serving. Ideologically and strategically, Darcy was a Popular Front advocate. What he opposed and felt contempt for was Browder's distortion of the Popular Front through the elimination of a clear Party position and identity within all alliances. Darcy was also critical of Browder's overestimation of the long-range stability of American capitalism and of the possibilities of a protracted U.S.-Soviet postwar alliance.[16]

Many local Communists were confused and upset by the expulsion of Darcy and the rise and then fall of Browder. But the ones in the service were too remote from the local scene to make sense of Browder's fall. A few recall that the Duclos letter's publication and Browder's expulsion occurred during either their last days in the service or their first days of readjustment to civilian life. Sally Turpin remembers challenging a local leader about Browder's "errors": "How could you not have told us these things?" But she soon reminded herself that rank-and-filers could ask the same of her. Harry Freedman says, "We all had trouble with it, don't let anyone tell you different." A few remember always being afraid that criticism would be met by an ambitious leader's counterattack. One speaks of feeling "very close to Browder"—"the Euro-Communist of his day"—and argues that he was "right in what he was trying to do." Most, however, say that they simply went along, rationalizing their decision by remembering the touches of dissatisfaction they had felt at Browder's radical revisions.[17] For the most part they were elevated by the Party's postwar hopes and expectations, unwilling to be disturbed over what seemed to be a single sore spot, and immediately engaged in new political and labor struggles.

■ *the progressive party movement*
When the war ended, the Communist Party, locally and nationally, seemed to be ready to continue its uneven climb from the obscurity and schisms of the twenties to an even more expansive and influential Popular Front position.[18] Even with the

instability created by the purge of Browder and the beginnings of the Cold War, the Party seemed well situated. Peggy Dennis and others see the mid-forties as the apex of the Party's influence and growth. Joseph Starobin suggests that at least until early 1948, the Party was "not swimming against the tide," although there were obvious difficulties given the rising Cold War environment. The national membership, including youth in the YCL, may have reached 100,000, and the greater Philadelphia rolls, according to some sources, may have approached 4,000 in 1947.[19]

Truman seemed to have lost his New Deal mandate, alienating labor with his "get tough" policies, facing progressive and liberal charges of tolerating corruption and of general ineffectiveness, and upsetting many with his belligerent attitude toward the Soviet Union.[20] Churchill's "Iron Curtain" speech deeply divided the American liberal and radical community. Factions struggled over the legacy of Roosevelt and the New Deal, with Henry A. Wallace emerging to challenge Truman for leadership. Two versions of the Popular Front—the Progressive Citizens of America (PCA) and the new Americans for Democratic Action (ADA)—faced off against each other. The PCA version, a continuation and a broadening of the thirties Popular Front, tied New Deal goals to friendship with the Soviets and pushed for improved labor and civil rights legislation. As the historian Norman Markowitz suggests, they needed and lacked "a surrogate Hitler" as a focus for attack. Instead they directed a few blows at Franco and Peron and then turned their weaponry upon the anti-Communist coalition developing in Washington.[21]

ADA represented the liberal challenge. No longer envisioning a world divided between "democracy" and "fascism," they instead fashioned a new demonology, in which the "Free World democracies" challenged "totalitarianism," left and right, Fascist and Communist (or "Red Fascist," as some preferred). ADA liberals excluded Communists from participation in activities, calling for a recognition that Communists could not be part of any possible progressive movement by virtue of their allegiance to a foreign power and their contempt for democratic and libertarian processes. The ADA supported Truman's foreign policy, especially after the promulgation of the Marshall Plan.[22]

The critical moment in this postwar period was the decision to challenge Truman with a third-party movement, the Progressive Party, led by Henry A. Wallace and staffed, ultimately, by Communists and other radicals. Most of the subjects within my sample participated in the Progressive Party campaign, entering "Gideon's Army" with great hopes. Yet the movement was scattered to the winds, crushed by the Cold War atmosphere and Truman's ability to abscond with much of the Progressive Party's program and, consequently, most of its constituents.[23] From this point the Communist movement, nationally and locally, faced defeat, repression, erosion, and finally collapse. How did participants experience the Progressive debacle and the subsequent downhill slide?

Most Philadelphia Communists found the Progressive Party crusade exhilarating and invested great hopes in it: "We were gonna win," Angie Repice recalls. And even if they did not, the Progressives were involved in a long-term venture, the creation of an independent, labor-oriented party. Several veterans, however, remember noting signs of a coming defeat. Sally Turpin went to a Shibe Park rally for Wallace and noticed that most of those in attendance seemed to be from New York. She worried about the failure to bring out Philadelphia people and the need to bus in loyalists. Mark Greenly went from door to door in working-class Kensington and found that workers, while liking Wallace, would not tolerate a Dewey victory and therefore planned to vote for Truman. Those involved in fundraising quickly realized that old Popular Front sources had generally dried up. Most participants simply hoped for an impressive vote, understanding that expecting victory was unrealistic. Their stated commitment was to build a party of working people that would reject Henry Luce's vision of an American Century and a Pax Americana.[24]

Left-wing trade unionists found the Progressive experience very difficult. By supporting Wallace, many Communist-oriented labor leaders risked alienating their constituents. Some, like Mike Quill, broke with the Party on this issue. Others waffled. But as one local source put it: "Most [Communists] trade unionists didn't have the time to question" the Party's mandate. The left-wing unions were facing severe challenges from the emerging Reuther forces in any case, but several union veterans feel that the Wallace campaign sped up the process by which the Left-Center CIO coalition was destroyed and the Left purged from the labor movement.[25]

Many Philadelphia Communists express deep disappointment with the results of the 1948 election. Wallace and the Progressive Party did very poorly, well below even the most modest estimates.[26] A few participants continue to affirm the value of the campaign; one views it as "a profound contribution to independent political action." Even its staunchest supporters, however, admit that the Party erred in taking such a dominant role, though many others point out that given the narrow base of the Wallace movement, there was no one else to do the work. Harry Freedman charges that the Communists simply did not do their homework, failing to match the Democrats in providing money for election-day volunteers, getting out to vote, and doing all of the little chores that make for a successful electoral campaign on the local level. Even in Party strongholds in West and North Philadelphia, the Progressives showed disappointing results. Most participants feel that the movement was welcomed or at least tolerated in the predominantly Jewish neighborhoods where most Party members lived but faced harrassment in other areas.

The Progressive Party movement brought to the surface questions and problems with roots in earlier experiences. Several members felt uneasy about Party manipulation of the Progressive movement. One section organizer describes how the Party sent delegations of Communist-led community groups to persuade

Wallace that he had broad grass-roots support. Meyer Weiner tells of secret Party clubs for those working within the Progressive and other mass movements. He adds that there were regular one-to-one clandestine meetings between Party functionaries and Progressive Party leaders who were secret Communists. In some cases, Progressive leaders formally dropped from Communist Party rolls but maintained de facto ties.

The Wallace campaign was a significant but not decisive step in the collapse of the Communist Party as a force in American politics. Several participants now argue that it might have been wiser for the Party to push for a Wallace primary challenge, accepting defeat in the short run. A small party without deep roots in mass constituencies was unlikely to maintain itself, given the strategic and political needs of a bipartisan Cold War policy, not to speak of the needs of a Soviet-dominated Communist hierarchy more interested in embarrassing the United States than in nurturing an indigenous anticapitalist movement.

Remarkably, most Communists, though upset by the 1948 results, reimmersed themselves in political work, too engaged to mull over the obvious secular trends. Meyer Weiner was not demoralized by defeats, since he was "working with good people," with "heroic things done every day." He still feels that it was "a marvelous period to live through," one in which "very little . . . was routine." The elan and the perseverance of most subjects are impressive. The work at hand kept many going; there was little time to waste on getting discouraged. But as Stan Wax reflects, "the gaiety changed to real seriousness." Even more than in the period from 1939 to 1941, hard times were upon the faithful. Arenas for organizing began to shrink in neighborhoods and shops. The Party moved in two directions: outward, toward major peace campaigns like the Stockholm Peace Pledge and the militant defense of indicted Party leaders and minority people like the Trenton Six, the Martinsville Seven, and Willie McGee;[27] and inward, toward steeling the Party, purging it of its excess and its faint-hearted and doubtful, preparing for underground existence and the coming repression, expecting fascism, attacking Party revisionism, "Browderism," "Titoism," and white chauvinism. Just when the Party most needed allies and sympathizers, it entered a Third Period–like isolation.

■ the second red scare: mccarthyism

As Michael Harrington notes, 1948 was "the last year of the thirties."[28] Truman's first loyalty procedures of 1947 started a process that reached its highest and ugliest development in the person of Senator Joseph McCarthy. McCarthyism, or the second red scare,[29] resting on Cold War premises and seeking a rollback of progressive, particularly labor, accomplishments associated with the New Deal, focused its wrath on the American Communist Party.[30]

The official Party response was to assume that fascism was on the American agenda and take drastic measures, including the creation of an elaborate underground network, to prepare for it. Party members were activated to struggle against the threat of atomic war, presumably to be launched by the United States against the Soviets. Many Philadelphians accepted this analysis and expended enormous energy working to defeat militaristic policies through such massive propaganda efforts as the Stockholm Peace Pledge. Others involved in the same efforts felt that the Party was exaggerating the danger of a coming fascism by confusing the suppression of the Party with that of the working class. In all cases, members recognized the period as one "of intense struggle to maintain ourselves."[31]

Party membership dropped precipitously, in part because of the falling away of the timid, in part because many loyal members dropped their formal affiliations under the duress of the Taft-Hartley Act and other measures requiring loyalty oaths and anti-Communist statements, and in part because the Party deliberately trimmed its sails, fearful of government infiltrators and suspicious of the loyalties of marginal participants. National membership dropped from 54,174 in early 1950 to 24,796 in early 1953.[32]

Mario Russo, a cadre with considerable organizing experience, argues that the Party was also threatened by the unexpected affluence of the postwar period. Suburbanization, he believes, had a devastating impact on organizing efforts. By the early fifties, some of the older ethnic neighborhoods were breaking up as middle-class and even working-class people moved to places like Levittown, Cherry Hill, Abington, and the Far Northeast. The link between workplace and residence, a key element in reaching industrial workers, began to erode as workers commuted from their tract homes to distant plants in suburban industrial parks. The highway lobby, in its own way, undermined radical organizing efforts.[33] At the same time, some old Party members, beneficiaries of the new affluence, moved from city enclaves to suburban sprawl and simply dropped out. The Party was ill-prepared for this transformation of American and, in particular, working-class life. The traditional adversaries remained—anti-labor capitalists, conservative Republicans, Dixiecrats, reaction-aries of all stripes; for Communists, however, political events obscured the underlying trends that were transforming the everyday life of large numbers of Americans. These cultural trends were cutting off approaches that had achieved some success in the past: corporate capital would begin to fight unionization with more sophisticated tools, working-class suburbs would strain workplace bonds, highway construction and shopping malls would subvert neighborhood taverns and other centers of proletarian discourse. The Party's frame of reference denied the possibility of a rising standard of living, anticipated severe depression, and for a short but disastrous period predicted fascist dictatorship.

Surprisingly, a number of activists faced the early fifties with hope and enthusiasm. Like Jessica Mitford, many could "hardly imagine living in America in those days and *not* being a member."[34] The younger members, born in the late twenties, too young to have participated in the struggles of the thirties or even the war years, deeply involved in the Wallace campaign, sought to build a movement in the midst of massive repression. Moe and Sarah Levy were not the only young couple who went off as colonizers at this time. At least until the Korean War broke out they anticipated an economic crisis, if not a severe depression, and they assumed that workers would then be more attracted to militant activity.

Most members focused on peace efforts, gathering signatures for the Stockholm pledge, or engaged in support activities for the growing number of indicted Communist leaders and for local civil rights struggles.[35] Events in Korea, a hot war, made it virtually impossible to find a hospitable environment for peace agitation or for any activity labeled "Communist." Mike Caldwell recalls, "The atmosphere changed so fast." Both governmental prosecutions and public intolerance escalated.

Most of the cadres "just hung in there," holding on to a very tenuous "United Front idea," trying to maintain the Party, revive the Progressive Party movement, and rally all progressives against what Communists categorized as "red-baiting." Under severe attack, the hard core of the Party held. Most simply threw themselves into their political work. Many were defiant. Ike Samuels, called before McCarthy's subcommittee, asserted, "I have more patriotism in this little finger than you have in your whole body." He fondly recalls neighbors raising their pinkies at him to remind him of his daring act. Others, less in the limelight, faced harassment, FBI visits, surveillance, phone taps, loss of employment, and abuse of their children and their families. Many were scared and became exceedingly cautious; others "told the FBI to go screw." Al Schwartz tells of comrades bringing their left-wing libraries to him for safekeeping, but another activist insists, "We didn't give away our books."

Moe Levy emphasizes that the Party's organizational network, at least in remote areas, fell apart. He was subpoenaed by a congressional committee in the fifties. The Party offered him no guidelines; he had to take over all leadership efforts in his industrial section. He advised local workers also subpoenaed to tell the committee the truth about their activities in the hope of saving their jobs. In fact, those who ignored his advice and took the Fifth Amendment were fired; the others, finally supported by the national union because of Levy's efforts, got their jobs back. Levy threatened to publicly charge the union, a very conservative one in heavy industry, with being Communist if it did not support these workers. He himself was fired; his boss expressed friendship and regrets but said that it was too risky to keep him on.

Some Communists were shunned by old neighbors who had once been more sympathetic to left-wing causes and even by former Party members. Yet many found surprising support and protection from neighbors. One scarred couple moved to a new neighborhood, made new friends who "restored their faith in mankind," and proceeded to become neighborhood activists again.

Johnny Tisa found his union expelled from the CIO and the local under attack from an anti-Communist slate. They won a battle for representation in the early fifties but finally faltered under grand jury investigations and fears of prosecution. He had to merge his now smaller union with other besieged unions to survive.

Sammy Cohen spent this period in an outlying section of Philadelphia that included some old immigrant workers, "sectarian, proud, beautiful people" who wanted to face McCarthyism openly. They declared, "We're communist!" and were willing to register under the McCarran Act.[36] Fearing that some might be deported, he persuaded them to desist. He spent much of his time servicing the Party underground, aiding messengers who appeared and then disappeared at all hours and moments, creating harrowing scenes of late night rendezvous and mysterious phone calls.

Many remember the period of underground activities as painful, lonely, at times pathetic, and even ridiculous. In 1951, in anticipation of a coming fascism, the national leadership ordered many cadres to disappear; there was a "deep freeze" for those hiding in order to stay out of prison, a "deep, deep freeze" of trusted cadres ready to take over leadership if others were arrested, and an "O.B.U."—an "operative but unavailable" leadership—of disguised cadre, acting as the link between open and "frozen" categories.[37] Most now consider the underground period a mistake. Meyer Weiner recalls going on vacation to Cape Cod only to bump into a crew of supposedly underground district cadres. Several Philadelphians were sent underground with their families. They had to change their names and their children's, move to other towns, and try to survive. A few managed to share such ventures with other couples also in hiding. But most simply felt isolated and bewildered by this turn of events. Many of those sent underground had to leave their families. Cadre morale suffered, "scores of nervous and mental breakdowns occurred," and many began their first serious questioning of the viability of the Party.[38] One veteran cadre, after several years of seemingly meaningless hiding, simply went home to resume his private and political life. Many remember feelings of paranoia, the fear of detection, the intricate games used to keep in touch with loved ones. Several Philadelphians hid underground cadres in their homes for short or long stretches. All assumed that the FBI was well aware of their amateurish efforts.

At this point, with families separated and members fearful of prosecution and imprisonment, the Party began its own witch-hunt, turning in upon its membership. The organizational structure of the Party had already been weakened by the security-inspired limitation of membership in Party clubs to between three and five and the decision to have fewer meetings. Now it imposed on itself vigorous campaigns to eliminate white chauvinists, Freudians, and all kinds of revisionists.[39]

The second red scare had a fearful effect on the children of most Philadelphia Communists. Many speak poignantly of how their children suffered from emotional problems initiated, or at least exacerbated, by the traumas of the period. One child, formerly a charming extrovert, became fearful of playmates and was frequently found crying in class by the kindergarten teacher. Many local Communists recall how neighborhood youths ostracized and baited their children, taunting them about their parents being executed "just like the Rosenbergs." A few parents reflect that at the time they were so busy trying to survive financially and struggling to remain politically effective that they did not realize how much the political repression was affecting their children. Sensitive children, not wanting to add to their parents' burden, often hid their pain and fears and concealed their symptoms. Ruth Shapiro notes that one of her daughters only recently told her about the severe stomach cramps she experienced daily throughout her youth.

Old political comrades "huddled together," supporting one another as much as possible. They called on the Party's remaining subculture and social network to sustain their lives and those of their children. One woman emphasizes "the tight circle that we stayed close to before, during, and after" the McCarthy period. Some became closer to their own families. Many tried to remain in the ethnic pockets with Communist linings that contained at least some understanding and tolerant neighbors.

Party members relied on such institutions as the radical Jewish IWO schools and the progressive summer camps often directed by sympathetic Quakers to provide a supportive environment for their children. Several children speak enthusiastically about their experiences in these progressive institutions.[40] Mostly, however, the more informal social networks of Party members served to bolster morale, sustain a sense of meaning and purpose, and provide the kinds of everyday contact that sustain group identity.

Many Communists faced occupational crises. They were blacklisted from many shops and offices and were sometimes too well known to get conventional jobs. Mark Greenly found himself stuck in a business that "nauseated" him; he dreamed of becoming a commisar of insurance so that he could obliterate it in the name of the revolution. Twenty-six Philadelphia public school teachers were fired for "incompetence"—that is, for refusing to answer questions about their politics.[41] Such people had to find jobs in fields outside their training and work experience. Some relied on family, and others found assistance within the Party network. Certain institutions manned by Party sympathizers and civil libertarians became havens for victims of political repression. It was a source of resentment among black Communists that they did not have as much access to this network as the mostly Jewish white Communists. A few black members did eventually find havens in such institutions, and several blacks called on their own community resources and the network of church or college fraternity activities and associations.

The dominant civil liberties case in the area was the Smith Act prosecution of nine district Party leaders in 1953.[42] Many Philadelphia Communists, including some interviewed defendants, speak proudly of how the defense was handled. It merits attention as the first such case to be defended by prestigious non-Left attorneys along civil libertarian lines.[43]

One participant recalls the debates within Party leadership over defense strategy. One side argued for a Foley Square model. Named after the site of the federal court where the national Party leaders were tried, this was a defense of the Party and its principles and positions. The other side called for a more civil libertarian approach along First Ammendment lines. Several who argued for the latter approach felt that many within the Philadelphia progressive community would rally to a defense of free speech but not to a particular defense of the Party's line. The civil libertarian approach won with minor dissent. The district leaders then persuaded the president of the local bar association to help them gain counsel, arguing that it was disgraceful for the legal profession to evade defending unpopular causes. The wives of the Smith Act defendants played a particularly valuable role in securing legal representation for their husbands.[44]

The Party's national office, according to several sources, pounced on this modest strategy and sent a functionary down to Philadelphia to lay down the law, threatening all the district leaders with expulsion. The district officers held their ground and established a First Amendment defense. They were convicted but later exonerated on appeal in late 1957.[45]

Mike Caldwell, reflecting the sentiments of a substantial minority, feels that in this period the Party abandoned working-class organizing to concentrate on raising money from "bourgeois" sources to manage its defense efforts. It would certainly have been difficult for a smaller, weakened Party under attack from the government, in the courts and at every level of daily life to invest energy and resources in industrial organizing; and given the Party's constituency and the politically repressive environment, such an investment would probably not have paid off. Caldwell's feelings, however, reflect significant tensions within the Party that were kept within bounds while all were on the defensive but that would erupt by the mid-fifties.

Paradoxically, the strains of the McCarthy period sustained members, forcing them to suppress tensions, ambivalences, and questions that had begun to fester with the Party's decline in the late forties.[46] The reactionary assault diverted many loyalists from facing the increasingly apparent fact that the movement they had joined with the expectation of its ultimate triumph was in critical condition.

Depression-generation Communists were characteristically in their middle to late thirties or early forties when Dwight David Eisenhower took office. The responsibilities of adult life, long subordinated to the passions of commitment, could no longer be put off. As the remaining faithful hoped for the gradual softening of McCarthyism and prepared to rebuild their movement and their Party, they simultaneously worried about paying the bills, raising their children, finding a secure and hospitable neighborhood, and getting older.

■ *1956*

Although Smith Act prosecutions and appeals continued and congressional committees persisted in investigating Communists and progressives, the second red scare had begun to slow down by 1956. Philadelphia activists, while still tied up in court proceedings and the problems of everyday life, sought to revive their organization and extend their political efforts. Before any kind of breathing spell could occur, however, a series of crises initiated in the Soviet Union and Eastern Europe exploded. These traumatic eruptions would result, finally, in the decimation of the district Party structure and membership.

Joseph Stalin died in 1953, and all of the Communist world mourned the loss of "the best loved man on earth in our time."[47] Unashamedly emotional and extravagant eulogies poured from the Party press. The struggle for succession did not shake up district members until the famous Twentieth Party Congress in the Soviet Union, featuring Nikita Krushchev's speech on Stalin's crimes. The address was presented behind closed doors and then published, first in the Western press. Finally published by an aroused *Daily Worker*, it exploded myths and loyalties, shattered faiths, and produced soul searching among many Party members.[48]

At the national level, a struggle intensified over the future direction of the Party. The Old Guard, led by William Z. Foster, called for minor adjustments, striking some rhetorical blows against "the cult of personality," but holding firm for a pro-Soviet line. This orthodox faction, while admitting errors in economic forecasting and political analysis, reverted to a Popular Front domestic strategy. At first cautiously and then more aggressively, it struck out at all dissenters from Stalinist orthodoxy.[49]

The dissenters, often called Gatesites after John Gates, the reform-minded editor of the *Daily Worker,* called for "de-Stalinization." They had no united program: some wanted the Party liquidated; others saw democratizing and revitalizing the Party as the only hope. The reformers were deeply affected by the revelations of endemic Soviet injustices—the rigged trials of the late thirties and early fifties, the executions not just of adversaries and innocents, but of loyal Communists, and Soviet anti-

Semitism under Stalin, especially after the war. Those who remained committed to the Party offered what some would later call a model for Euro-Communism—independence from Soviet domination, a more democratized and open Party structure and process, and a recognition of the difficulties of socialist revolution in advanced capitalist democracies.[50]

In addition to these two factions, there was a determining group, usually called "moderates," associated with Party Secretary Eugene Dennis. This swing group, also disparate and sensitive to which way the wind was blowing, preferred at first to play it safe. They had been through many Party purges and battles and refused to commit themselves until absolutely necessary. Initially they tilted toward reform but in the final counting joined with the Fosterites in restoring orthodoxy by 1959.[51]

The Hungarian uprising in October played a critical role in deepening the rift within the Party and generating the alliance that would defeat the Gatesites. Communists had to come to grips with the fact that Soviet troops had entered an independent nation to crush a rebellion, whether defined as socialist, nationalist, or "clerical fascist." Even many of those who came to defend the intervention did so with deep reservations and lasting anguish. How, some asked, could it be alleged that fascism was still so strong ten years after the triumph of a "people's republic" in Hungary?[52]

In the Philadelphia area, as elsewhere, many members simply drew away from the Party, without fanfare or formal acts, feeling betrayed and disillusioned. Fred Garst now speaks of how Communism "requires the abdication of a certain portion of your ego." Al Rein, with growing children, struggling to hold a job, says he "simply drifted away from the movement," somewhat affected by the Khrushchev speech, but mostly just exhausted. One veteran who departed in 1956 says that he experienced "a general feeling of malaise," the result of "banal discussions, . . . too many decades of incestuous discussions." He welcomed the Khrushchev revelations as "a breath of fresh air" but did not see any point in struggling from within; instead, he joined those who left to pursue their private lives and to focus attention on long-neglected careers and families.

The plight of many Communists was quite severe. Many were either approaching or already in their forties. After doing Party and Party-related work for many years, they often lacked the credentials for professional jobs. Their children were in school, constantly needing new clothes; their spouses longed for respite, perhaps even nice vacations. Many had no job security, no pension plans. In the midst of such personal and family crises, Party members had to attend to crucial decisions concerning their political identities and loyalties.

One black activist resigned, feeling particularly bitter about the Jewish Communists who fled her neighborhood: "As the neighborhood began to change, their houses went up for sale." She angrily concluded that all of the talk of integration and racial harmony was "just rhetoric on their part" and declared, "The hell with these people and the false position they were taking."

Most Philadelphia Communists, however, struggled passionately with the mid-fifties Party crisis. Ruth Shapiro, who felt "relief from bondage" when the Stalinist myth exploded, recovered to enjoy the new freedom encouraged within the Party in mid-1956. But counterattacks from Fosterites made such freedom increasingly tenuous. One twenty-year veteran wanted the dissolution of the Party to be a discussion topic, feeling that all views had to be aired before any decision could be made. But a top district leader started a whispering campaign against him, charging him with emotional instability and anti-Communism. He thought, "I could have been Rajk or any of those guys that were purged and rehabilitated."[53] Another top cadre, a proponent of a more open and democratic Party who continued his membership even after orthodoxy had triumphed, felt deeply troubled over his own potential for the kind of political repression committed under Stalin. Many others admitted that they too might have executed innocent people if in power. It was a deeply humbling moment.

Some, particularly Jewish Communists, turned back to their roots. Otto Kramer says that the 1956 crisis "removed the rock of faith, the rock of support" that had sustained him and others for so long. He did not become anti-Communist or anti-Soviet, but he began to develop greater interest in his Jewish heritage. Ben Green, another second-generation Jew, recalls during the early fifties that "some of the truth was beginning to seep through" to him concerning Soviet anti-Semitism. He began to read the non-Party press to follow such charges and documentation. After the Twentieth Party Congress, he stopped attending meetings and refused to pay dues. He considered withdrawing from politics altogether, but instead began to work out a way to integrate his new anti-Stalinist socialism with sensitivity to Jewishness.

For many members, local tensions and disappointments were the chief sources of disillusionment. "It wasn't Hungary that was the key," or other international issues, although Sally Turpin admits being disturbed by the Soviet invasion; rather, she was annoyed at the policy of sending whites into the black ghettoes to agitate and sell *Workers*: "I was convinced that it wouldn't work," but "no one wanted to hear this, so I said to hell with this." Such tactical grievances were magnified by the increasing impotence of the Party and by the mid-fifties trauma.

By late 1956 and early 1957, district membership had dropped to no more than a thousand. The district leadership had to accept the elimination of the Pennsylvania edition of the *Worker* in early 1956, while their own pending appeals faced delays. Few recruits were entering the Party, and consequently the average age of members was steadily rising.[54]

There were minor bright notes in this period. In the summer of 1956, the American Legion and the Veterans of Foreign Wars tried to prevent the actress Gale Sondergaard from performing in a local production of "Anastasia." Despite pickets, the opening night was packed and the blacklisted Miss Sondergaard received "prolonged applause."[55] The political repression of the McCarthy era was starting to lift, though the thaw came too late to revive the Party.

District leaders for the most part aligned themselves with the reform-minded faction of the Party and, with few exceptions, left the organization at the end of the fifties as it became apparent that orthodoxy had triumphed. Virtually an entire generation of Party cadres decided that the American Communist Party was no longer an effective vehicle for social change. As Maurice Isserman recently noted, "A full three quarters of the American Communist Party membership, people who had stayed with the movement in the worst years of McCarthyism, quit in the year or so after the events of 1956."[56] This core group, supportive of the Khrushchev speech and critical of Soviet actions in Hungary, drew conclusions about the nature of democracy and the right of self-determination from these events. For example, they refused and still refuse to accept the argument that presenting unpleasant truths about socialist countries is playing into imperialist hands; they simply state that the truth is always revolutionary. And they refuse to accept the Soviet explanation of the Hungarian intervention; they are skeptical of Soviet claims about fascist predominance and unwilling to justify further Soviet domination over a resentful people.

A number of scholars suggest that the Party split in the mid-fifties between "hard-line" and reformers, Fosterites and Gate-sites, followed generational, class, and ethnic lines.[57] The orthodox faction, ever loyal to Soviet cues, is assumed to include the old immigrant, IWO-based, foreign-born, and often Yiddish-speaking Communists who refused to believe allegations about Soviet anti-Semitism. Such members had no place else to go and consequently were reluctant to abandon the protective if shrinking subculture and social network within which they were raised and nurtured.[58]

Old Party stalwarts also remained, according to this view, especially those who came into the movement before the construction of the Popular Front if they had not, indeed, joined as charter members. Foster, for example, predates the Party, having already established himself as a working-class organizer in the 1910s. They were "purer" Bolsheviks, trained in class struggle and always somewhat uncomfortable with the modified rhetoric and reformist practices of the Popular Front period. Several observers insist that this group of charter members plus the twenties recruits always maintained control of the Party, whatever the particular tactical phase.[59]

Finally, the hypothesis argues that the more working-class components of the Party remained loyal, whereas the more "petty-bourgeois," intellectual, and professional elements broke ranks. Such a view notes the pro-Fosterite role of the New York seamen in the mid-fifties struggles. One counterview accepts all of the above groups as part of the orthodox faction but includes such professionals as doctors, lawyers, and businessmen as the "most intransigent" Fosterites.[60]

On the other side of Party barricades this hypothesis places the second-generation, Jewish American, thirties Communists of the Popular Front period, now become anti-Stalinist and reform-minded. George Charney describes this Depression generation:

> As products of the 1930s, we had acquired an implicit faith in the Soviet Union as the "land of Socialism." Our illusions about Soviet democracy and justice were greater, and so was the shock of disillusionment. Furthermore, our people, more typically American, had an enduring though unarticulated pride in our democratic traditions.

Gabriel Almond argues that Bolshevik ideology was less strongly instilled in Popular Front–era members who were not part of the "insider" group and that such members were likely to be less active as well—that is, noncadre.[61] One still-orthodox Marxist-Leninist speaks harshly of "these Jewish Browderite hacks . . . mostly New Yorkers who remained tied to their parochial beginnings, all unsuccessful writers, none of whom had ever organized any workers in their lives, or participated in or led any struggles." A more temperate view is that the thirties recruits were more Americanized and therefore more aware of the development of American class consciousness. They were upwardly mobile and quite comfortable with a Popular Front ideology that seemed to resolve the contradiction of dual loyalties. They differed from the more Bolshevik older members in their populist responses to American democratic traditions, FDR, John L. Lewis, and the Spanish Republic.

My very limited Philadelphia sample lends some support to this hypothesis. For example, all of the twelve Philadelphia Communists falling into the category of the second-generation Jewish American members of the Popular Front era are self-defined anti-Stalinists who broke with the Party in the mid-fifties after failing to transform it.[62] They clearly left the Party for such ideological reasons as Soviet anti-Semitism, Stalinist repression, and, very often, Hungary. Despite the argument that finds them less ideological, and even less Marxist in their Popular Front assimilation to New Deal liberalism, most remain emphatically socialist more than twenty years after quitting the Communist Party.

The orthodox supporters of Foster, intransigent Stalinists, cut across generational, ethnic, sexual, and class lines with hardly any discernible pattern. The orthodox claim to be more working-class in background and identification, but such self-serving contentions must be viewed with appropriate skepticism.

Thirties Communists were less Bolshevik in the sense that they were part of a vital and growing movement that was clumsily trying to become indigenous—that is, Americanized—in both membership and constituency. Among cadres at least, the Popular Front ideology was both subordinated to and integrated into an economistic socialist strategy. James Weinstein argues that the Party, lacking a public vision of socialism, found its "private vision"—the Soviet model—shattered in 1956.[63]

What remained is what one might call a popular vision—an integrated if contradictory set of assumptions and values, a cluster of metaphors. Most Depression-generation veterans of the Communist Party maintain a populist hope that is rekindled by Pete Seeger folksongs about working people, movies like *Norma*

Rae and *Harlan County, U.S.A.*, and memories of sit-downs, unemployed marches, and anti-eviction actions. Such a populism, while deeply American, presupposes an internationalism that is periodically tested and strained by nationalistic behavior of Communist countries. Old Leftists are still moved by the concept of a unified world of working people, from Spain to El Salvador.

There is a tension in this popular vision between a populist-internationalist egalitarianism and a belief in socialism as planning, between its democratic vision and its assumptions about "objective conditions" and Scientific Socialism. Many Old Leftists, still uncomfortable with any dimensions of culture that belie their universalistic hopes—ethnicity, religion, sexuality, aggression, the psyche and emotional life—fall back on a belief in Progress, Science, and Reason (all in prenuclear, pre-Holocaust capitals). The popular vision is muted for most Old Leftists and occasionally comes close to flickering out, but it holds; tempered by sobering experiences, revised by new insights, still the socialist dream holds.

eight

coping

It is now more than two decades since most Philadelphia Communist activists abandoned the Party. Their experiences, before and since that denouncement, offer radicals soberly regarding the last years of the twentieth century a set of guidelines, hopes, and warnings. The history of how they have coped with the stubborn ideological terrain of American society stands as a crucial legacy for those seeking to chart a socialist future. What they accomplished, how they faltered and failed, are strands in an all too thin history of American radicalism. Most of all, I wish to emphasize how so many of these children of the Depression managed to maintain their socialist values and practices over a lifetime. In a culture ravaged by a cult of the celebrity (whom Daniel Boorstein once characterized as "a person who is known for his well-knownness"), it is essential to find ways through the ephemeral.[1] The Old Leftists I interviewed were not "superstars", they will never appear in *People Magazine,* and they have not recycled their consciousness with psychobabbled liberation, evangelical faith, or Wall Street hype. They are quite ordinary people who entered and then remained within a small American left. Knowing that the road remains long, present-day radicals need to reflect on how Old Leftists coped and sometimes flourished.

What becomes of former Communists who have spent the better part of their lives organizing, proselytizing, attending meetings, and living within a special and somewhat insular social network? First of all, they had to find ways of managing financially. Many faced a blacklisting job market and had to accept what they hoped would be only transitional jobs. A few college-educated ex-Communists had to work at low-paying service jobs, driving delivery trucks or working as clerks in retail stores. Some Philadelphia Communists returned to school in their forties to start new careers. Several found employment through the social network of Party veterans and sympathizers, with which they were still in contact although no longer members and which worked through institutions, schools, and businesses that had become occupational havens.

Many Old Leftists say that they "took off the shackles from their personal lives." Although still harried by economic insecurity, long working hours, and in some cases double duty as workers and students, weary veterans of Party battles gave themselves as much time as possible for relaxation and leisure. They read Trotsky, Orwell, Djilas, Freud, material long forbidden by Party mores and went to the theater, and the ballpark. Parents, particularly fathers, who felt remorseful about neglecting their children could now try to make up for lost time. As Chapter Five indicates, some marriages fell apart without the bond of Party identification; couples discovered that they had very little else in common. Not everything was retrievable. But, in general, life became significantly more relaxed.

There is a certain mythology about the ability of former Communists to become extremely wealthy capitalists of a particularly ruthless and unscrupulous sort. A monograph on "Bolshevik businessmen" may be possible on a national scale, but an examination of social class and occupation within the Philadelphia sample does not indicate that this pattern was the norm. A few Philadelphia ex-Communists interviewed have become wealthy. Such success is viewed skeptically by several of those interviewed; I heard some allegations of unethical business practices and ruthless behavior. Others respond that such charges are mere envy and rooted in personal animosities. More significant, however, is the small number of such cases and claims. Former Communists often achieved affluence, but few achieved great wealth.[2]

Some observers make the related charge that rising levels of affluence led most old Communists to dilute their political values and make a comfortable settlement with mainstream America. The evidence presented here suggests otherwise; in fact, there does not seem to be any correlation between the social class and the political values and behavior of Old Leftists.

☐ *johnny tisa*

Johnny Tisa's experience, while not typical, stands as a measure of the efforts of many. He found himself in the mid-fifties stranded without a union base, with nothing in the bank, no prospects, and a growing family to feed. Tisa was forty years old, a high school graduate. He went to the Italian market in Camden to find out what items were marketable and discovered that pet food offered some possibilities. Borrowing a hundred dollars from a friend, Tisa purchased pet food from a North Jersey wholesaler, sold it, and reinvested the profits in more pet food. He and his family worked long hours to build the business and finally became established as successful retail merchants.

Tisa, a hearty and animated man, had little time for political involvement during this trying but rewarding period. There were occasional activities, such as attending rallies or signing petitions, but for the most part his business required a seven-day-a-week effort. In the sixties, however, the anti–Vietnam War movement reactivated him: "I went into that wholeheartedly." He even rejoined the Party, calling it "still the vehicle for revolutionary change." "I could make criticism but what other organization is trying to rebuild itself in basic industry?" Unlike several other remaining Party loyalists, Tisa speaks cordially about those who disagree with his reaffiliation. He remains optimistic. "The balance of forces is toward socialism and getting better every year." He is active with the Veterans of the Abraham Lincoln Brigade and has recently completed a book of Spanish Civil War posters with graphics by his son. He is presently working on his Spanish Civil War diary.

Tisa does not communicate dogmatism; in fact, he is not particularly comfortable with ideology and theory. He is a working-class radical, with strong loyalties, pride in his life, and an ecumenical approach. This direct, unpretentious and thoroughly likable man lives in a simple South Jersey home; during the interview, he offered a glass of water. I accepted.

□ abe shapiro

Abe Shapiro is professorial and yet without pretense. When he gets excited, his voice rises and booms; when conversation evokes humor, his laughter shakes the room. Beneath Shapiro's intellectual vitality is a subtle stoicism that surfaces when he describes the years during which he was blacklisted from teaching. He was fired from the Philadelphia school district in November 1953, following the House Un-American Activities Committee investigations that allowed the superintendent to rationalize his dismissal of twenty-six teachers. "I lost my job Friday and returned to work for the company on Monday," he says. "The company" was his father's small retail business. He worked there from 1953 to 1968. "it was simply a job, no more," Shapiro recalls, giving a hint of the frustration such work must have engendered.

Abe Shapiro never expected to regain his teaching job. He simply pursued his own studies, rigorously kept up with the literature in fields of interest, and after ideologically breaking with the Party in the mid-fifties, became involved with a local peace organization. A committed democratic socialist and Marxist, Shapiro believes that ongoing political effort is less a choice than a necessity.

He maintains friendships with a score of Old Left comrades despite many disagreements over key issues like the Soviet Union and Israel. "This once very close group is no longer ideological," he says. "It's kept together by friendship. People are active, but by their own choice; the common utopia they had when they were young no longer exists; now they have the bond of friendship." Shapiro concludes, "When you are young, everything is politics," implying that now his political generation engages in "idle chatter" and reads less. Shapiro struggles against such currents, still intent upon making sense of a world characterized by a "winning of reason," still believing that the point of "chatter" is to find ways of converting thought into effective action. He has remained active in the peace movement, was involved in civil rights support work, and is constantly bringing people of all ages together to grapple with contemporary social issues.

In the late sixties he returned to his teaching position in the Philadelphia public school system. Despite frustrations, he struggles to democratize his often obtuse union and to teach critical thinking to his wary students. Abe Shapiro takes frustration for granted as part of a radical's burden and seems to derive satisfaction from puncturing left-wing shibboleths, particularly those that deny the kind of patience his life exemplifies. Sometimes he pontificates; mostly he strives to learn. Abe Shapiro, after more than forty years, remains a socialist teacher.

Again and again, one is struck by the refusal to allow any feelings of pessimism or self-doubt to interfere with Old Leftists' drives to make lives for themselves. These were and are achievement-oriented people, only comfortable when putting in long hours at work or its equivalent—politics or hobbies. One finds few complaints about boredom or paralysis of the will, few tortured, ambivalent souls, few incapacitated dreamers. Meyer Weiner, speaking for many others, concludes, "I have no bitterness in me; my life has been the best possible for me."[3]

Many speak proudly of the training they received as Communists, a training in self-discipline, organizational and administrative skills, social and public relations, precise record keeping, patience, and hard work. Others add that most Communists already had personalities and social backgrounds that made them likely to succeed in the business and professional world and that Party involvement simply delayed material achievements. Indeed, one can argue that these Depression-era activists were simply catching up with their non-Communist generational peers. In addition, the special training and experience of Party members seem to have bolstered and fashioned native qualities. As Edith Samuels says, "You became a disciplined person, responsible for your idealism."[4]

Such disciplined veterans of the Communist movement have indeed been centrally involved in virtually every significant progressive organizing effort in the Philadelphia area. Depression-generation Old Leftists have worked within all of the peace groups—Women's Strike for Peace, the Women's International League for Peace and Freedom, Committee for a SANE Nuclear Policy, Businessmen for Peace (an anti-Vietnam War organization), and Resist (a support group for Vietnam draft resisters). They have also been active in early civil rights groups like the Friends of SNCC (Student Non-Violent Co-ordinating Committee), the Congress of Racial Equality, the National Association for the Advancement of Colored People, and the Southern Christian Leadership Conference, although for the most part their efforts in this area have focused on extending racial harmony and residential and school integration within their neighborhoods. Many have worked within the reform wing of the Democratic Party, sometimes holding minor local offices and responsibilities, in a few instances becoming influential at city and state levels. In

Old Leftists' loyalty to early ideals and values is impressive. Within my sample, seven respondents are best described as orthodox Stalinists, still loyal to a Soviet vision of socialism and critical of all deviations as "revisionist" or "Maoist." The largest proportion are comfortable describing themselves as Marxists and democratic socialists, specifically denying that they are either Stalinists or social democrats. This group is attracted to the explorations going on under the label of Euro-Communism and, in some cases, to the growth of a left-wing in the socialist world, especially the tendency associated in the United States with Michael Harrington. Several are either active in or sympathetic to Harrington's Democratic Socialist Organizing Committee, though others remain wary of its connections with Western European Social Democrats. Several figures within this rather heterogeneous group are much more suspicious of all parliamentary maneuverings, including those of the Euro-Communists, and remain left-wing, anti-Stalinist independents. All of these "plain" Marxists opposed the Soviet intervention in Czechoslovakia and invested some hope in "socialism with a human face." Two respondents affirm social democracy, hoping for a Swedish-type evolutionary model for the United States, while one subject leans toward a humanitarian pacifism and a decentralized communalism.

Few have replaced the Soviet "god" with any other. They are generally discouraged by the nationalistic behavior of socialist countries; some focus criticism on the Soviet Union, a few on China, but most simply feel that they tremendously underestimated the force of nationalism and now have little sense of how to limit its destructiveness. Some found encouragement in the Cuban Revolution; many more were moved by the struggle of the Vietnamese against American military power. The most characteristic stance is that all foreign lessons must be carefully applied within the specific and distinctive experiences of the United States.

Generationally, Old Leftists stand between their 1905er parents, immigrant Jewish and Southern European Catholic, and their children, fully Americanized and raised in the fifties or sixties.

Thus, they stand between a world of *shtetl*, ghetto, and peasant village and one of suburb, rock and roll, and mass consumption.[7] Interestingly, the majority of them identify more with their parents than with their children. Indeed, many communicate anxiety and ambivalence about their children, somehow wishing that their preferences were more balanced. The Old Leftists share with their parents, including the older Party generation, a belief in the intrinsic value and necessity of human labor. On the other hand, they are not "Old World" as their parents often were; they identified with everyday American cultural life—movies, radio, and spectator sports. Most Depression-era Communists grew up with Jack Benny, Joe DiMaggio, and Rita Hayworth, wasting time, as their parents saw it, playing in the streets and dreaming Hollywood dreams, albeit from a class perspective.

They were heartened by the revival of political activism in the sixties but disturbed and sometimes angered by the decade's flamboyant bohemianism. "My generation was molded by the Depression," Milt Goldberg concludes; Laura Blum adds, "We're the product of a depression psychology." They are therefore conscious of the value of money, even the ones who are quite affluent, and bewildered by the apparent irresponsibility toward money they see in their children. Milt Goldberg, for example, winces when his adult son buys his lunch; he himself still makes his own and brings it to work. While most Old Leftists enjoy travel and certainly are not miserly, they remain savers rather than spenders.

Many have mixed feelings about the much proclaimed changes in values and sensibility associated with the sixties and seventies. They tend to complain, "Our children are products of a hedonistic generation," less willing to struggle to preserve marriages and families, more interested in self-fulfillment, less politically interested or active. They are certainly at odds with the changes in sexual attitude of recent times. Some recall severely repressive sexual upbringings; one woman says that her husband never kissed her until he proposed. Thirties Communists typically think of sex as a natural and pleasurable activity and remember the loosening of already eroding Victorian standards in the 1920s and 1930s. They are tolerant of premarital sex, critical of most forms of censorship relating to sexuality, and decidedly not prudish. They are, however, amazed at what they perceive as the contemporary mania about sex, recalling that their generation never made it such a center of either conversation or thought. One woman admits, "Communists were not that far ahead of the rest of the community" on such matters. Tessie Kramer offers the shrewdest observation, arguing that there was little or no difference between her generation and that of the 1960s where behavior is concerned. But her generation was circumspect, whereas "the sixties scorned to be discreet."

Old Leftists are very ambivalent about the women's movement. They readily agree with its egalitarian goals and express regret that it was not on their own political agenda. A few women, in fact, speak very forcefully about the limitations Party sexism imposed on their careers. Yet there is a strong undercurrent of resentment and mistrust among many old Communists, men and women, concerning what they view as the hedonism and selfishness of the contemporary women's movement. A few veteran radicals— again, both men and women—refer to some contemporary feminists as "man-haters." When discussing feminism they typically begin with affirmations of the constitutional and economic goals of feminists but soon focus on those aspects, particularly lesbianism and assertions of uninhibited sexuality, that they feel undermine marriage and the family. On the other hand, it is no mere sop when Old Leftists affirm a movement that values women as fully competent participants in society and seeks to generate social and cooperative systems of home maintenance and child care. And perhaps it is no coincidence, as Sara Evans suggests, that "red-diaper" feminists of the sixties, taught by their mothers about the nature of various kinds of oppression, spearheaded the attack on New Left sexism.[8]

Those interviewed do not appear to be particularly introspective or insightful concerning the subtleties of human behavior. The men especially, tend to be highly rationalistic, goal-oriented, and straightforward. Several speak of their insensitivity to the emotional life of their children or spouses during their Party period. This is a generation taught by the Party to mistrust depth psychology as subjectivist and to treat Freud and psychoanalysis as a "bourgeois" phenomenon. Lenin was scarcely a guide to the mysteries of feeling, fantasy, ambition, fear, or any of the other affective components of life.[9]

Old Leftists worry about their own children, whom they describe as "progressive" but not activist, sympathetic to their political pasts but not carriers of the Marxist banner. Many of their children protested against the war, opposed the draft, and fought for civil rights and women's rights, and some still remain active into the early eighties, often as environmentalists, feminists, and cultural radicals. But very few have become full-time, active radicals; as one parent notes almost apologetically, "Our children are very politically aware, but not joiners." Many experienced serious conflict and pain when their children became involved in the more self-destructive and indulgent aspects of the "counter-culture." As one woman states, exaggerating for dramatic effect, "There isn't a Communist family that hasn't been caught up in some of this 'hippie' stuff."

Yet for the most part the children of the thirties radicals have adopted what the psychologist Kenneth Keniston calls the "core values" of their parents: liberal and egalitarian values, toleration, support for minority rights, opposition to superpatriotism, suspicion of corporations.[10] Raised by parents who wanted them to have the very best, they are now upwardly mobile professionals, artists, professors, and human service workers.

Some parents anxiously conclude about their children's politics, "At least they're not on the other side." Others feel greater confidence and pride in their children's activism. Sammy Cohen says of his school-age children, "Of course, they will be radicals," and describes their present political ventures. Laura Blum proudly proclaims that "our kids knew what we were doing," and then describes how her daughter's friends recently told her that her home was always more interesting than those of other friends because it lacked a religious atmosphere, encouraged open discussions on virtually any topic, always had interesting guests, and cultivated excitement about cultural affairs.

The issue of ethnicity continues to trouble the Old Left. For example, Philadelphia Communists and other progressives established a Jewish club, the Sholom Aleichem Club, in the 1950s when the IWO's Jewish People's Fraternal Order collapsed under governmental persecution.[11] After half a decade the organization included many of the Jewish Communists who had left the Party in the mid-fifties plus others on the edge of the movement. As Harry Freedman puts it, the club "provided a useful way for many of us who were the backbone of that organization to continue to be active around the major issues of our times." It had a committee that served as a virtual left-wing enclave, supporting civil rights groups and seeking to minimize the tensions and misunderstandings that began to appear as blacks moved toward more militant positions and Jews became more comfortable and politically moderate.

The club, consisting of perhaps 150 to 200 families, faced rising tension over Jewishness, especially as it related to Israel. In the mid-sixties conflict erupted over the club's decision to criticize Soviet treatment of Jews. Some orthodox pro-Soviet club members resigned; others disagreed but stayed. Meanwhile, the club continued to change, becoming less Marxist and more Zionist. During the 1967 Middle East war, "we got dogmatic, for one week," as Ben Green, a club leader, puts it. They allowed no discussion on the merits of supporting Israel, but simply raised funds to show their full support. Nevertheless, several members insist that the club is not Zionist and engages in "critical support" of Israel.

The continuing Old Left subculture also generated a modest summer club that has always been mostly Jewish and has become increasingly apolitical over the years. Edith Samuels, using a form of affirmative action that antagonized many members, finally brought black members into the club. While none of those interviewed have experienced such a hardening of the ideological and moral arteries, apparently many other former Communists and fellow-travelers, and their relatives and children, have adopted the ethnocentric and parochial values and interests of the affluent American bourgeoisie.

The most explosive and consequently most avoided issue is the state of Israel. It is the point of departure for the present passions of many Jewish ex-Communists. A solidarity with the Soviet position on Palestinian rights exists among the remaining orthodox Stalinists. Among the democratic socialists one finds a belief that Palestinian rights must be recognized by a more generous Israel and that the Palestinian Liberation Organization must finally accept the right of Israel to exist.[12]

Despite the virtual demise of the Communist Party in the late fifties, a social network still exists of people who shared in its political life and camaraderie. That social network has had a significant effect on the political and even cultural life of Philadelphia—especially the area's peace groups and many neighborhood efforts challenging "politics as usual." The Communist Party contributed to the training of possibly tens of thousands of Philadelphians in the skills of organizing; leaving the Party did not necessarily deprive them of those skills. Individuals, usually in touch with other individuals, simply did and continue to do what they always have done—organize.

The intensity of political life since the break with the Party is lower for most. Parents become grandparents, and physical activity is limited by age or illness (although one feels compelled to note the amazing courage and energy of one physically disabled Old Leftist who does more political work than a boatload of Marin County joggers). A few veterans of older political wars chastise their peers for shifting toward what Henry Blum cynically calls "tennis materialism," the good life. Old Leftists are always hard on themselves.

The vitality of the Old Left local social network is impressive. Many speak of friendships that have lasted over forty years, and several argue that Philadelphia's Old Left network is remarkably close, intimate, and stable. It is unlikely that one can be involved in local progressive political activities without at some point discovering a role being played by someone or some group with roots in the Communist Party experience.

Vivian Gornick argues that there was a passion within the Old Left, the Communist movement of the thirties, that held ground until the crisis of 1956. Most Philadelphia Old Leftists, many of whom have read Gornick's book, affirm that intensity and sense of community. But many tightly organized groups have generated passion and community, including some of dubious merit, like religious cults. What makes the Communist movement unique is that its passion created a community, a subculture, and strong social networks committed to particular changes within the United States and to an often vague but remarkably steady vision of socialism. It is not coincidental that so many Old Leftists have continued to live by their political beliefs, engaging in progressive and radical activities and deriving nourishment and comradeship from the social networks they built many decades ago.

The Old Left political experience offers no conventionally defined "lessons" for contemporary radicals. Would that life could be so simple and straightforward! Nevertheless, an understanding of the Communist Party's thirties generation enriches one's identity as a part of the ongoing effort to build a socialist movement in a nation still clinging to a mythology of a *middle-*classless society.

Certainly, we need to pay attention to the subculture and the social networks we build. The context within which radicals operate plays a critical role in how they deal with the inevitable frustrations and failures. The New Left talked a great deal about community and solidarity but often subverted such goals with its penchant for the protean life. The various citizens' movements of the seventies indicate how important neighborliness and a sense of rootedness are, particularly in an era when television, electronic space games, home computers, and humongous portable radios seem to box people into isolation and antisocial patterns.[13]

Radical subcultures have too often been exclusive, a protected terrain for battered radicals or ideologically arrogant ones. The Communist Party's subculture suffered from such insularity. More recently, university-based enclaves like Berkeley, Madison, and Cambridge have demonstrated a tendency to organize themselves in a way that restricts their ability to connect with the lives of ordinary people.

Political movements have to be in but not of the world. Edith Samuels talks of the inherent tension between "cadre needs" and "family needs." Workaholic Communist men often match corporate executives in their neglect of personal life and family. For some radical leaders, such single-mindedness may be essential. But for most participants in social change movements, a balance between work, politics, and personal life is highly recommended.

The life cycle of organizers deserves analysis so that a more realistic view of age-specific needs and tolerances can be developed. Certainly young people without children, unmarried or married, are capable of a level of political work beyond the capacity of most parents. Youth carries with it a level of enthusiasm and energy that is special and unique. Many Communists recall monumental schedules from their student and YCL days. The dawn of political awakening brings with it expectations that are incredibly energizing. Ben Green heard about the San Francisco general strike of 1934 while on his honeymoon. He thought, "The revolution is at hand." Others, although less euphoric, recall being lifted by events and barely fazed by failures. They were willing to work interminable hours with no thought to remuneration. They did not consider professional credentials or careers; they assumed the future would be bright and were too much involved in the dramatic present to worry about their next jobs.

An organizing strategy must value and encourage such youthful energy but must also recognize its inevitable limits. Organizers with family responsibilities will only remain totally mobile and completely given to their work at tremendous personal cost. Indeed, one can argue that the experience of responsibility and residential stability gives an older organizer better insight into and empathy with other Americans, who are usually too busy with work, laundry, dishes, household repairs, and family concerns to attend meetings and engage in political activity.

The best feature of the old Communist Party remains the bonds created by shared political work, robust discourse, and ongoing friendship. As Joseph Starobin observes, "Not intended to be a family but a quasi-military elite, forged for stern historical tasks, it was in fact a family to many."[14] As a family, it included marriages, child rearing, and all of the other institutions and arrangements involved in generational continuity. The formal Party definitions of political activism give the ways in which Communists arranged their domestic lives a special significance. In deciding on a political career of a particularly stringent type, Communists, male and female, constructed a social and domestic life in which "the personal" often contradicted "the political."[15]

Contemporary tasks are both clearer and more difficult. Radicals need to establish egalitarian, nonpatriarchal relations within all their primary groups, marital and communal, heterosexual and homosexual, to allow men and women to engage the world according to their abilities and interests without sacrificing their responsibilities to others, particularly the next generation. We are in a difficult time in which the "cultural contradictions of capitalism" are unfolding in ways that confuse and distort our perceptions.[16] The old bourgeois, patriarchal ways are crumbling, but the Left cannot afford to stand as the countercultural, bohemian flip-side of modern hedonism. The current surge of the Moral Majority is a rearguard action that will soon receive its comeuppance; we are not about to return to that fundamentalist world, despite some very real short-term threats. Most of America is more enamored with the decadence of Atlantic City casinos, T.V. soap operas, and designer jeans. The Old Left, at its best, was neither bohemian nor Victorian in its social life. The people I interviewed value the sense of responsibility they found and nurtured in the Party, in their social circles, and in their own families. We do not have to imitate them; rather, we should place such traditional values and behavior in settings that no longer victimize women, old people, and children.

At the same time, we need to understand why so many Americans have turned toward the demagogic cultural solutions of the Moral Majority, Phyllis Schlafly, and Jesse Helms. They legitimately fear crime and lawlessness, worry about what sexuality means without some connection with procreation, are concerned with the tension between self-fulfillment and child rearing. In struggling for the right of women to control their bodies, affirming the civil liberties of gays, and remaining open to alternative ways of organizing personal relationships, the Left has to take more seriously the fears, anxieties, and concerns of working-class Americans.

Most American radicals have preferred a more ecstatic perspective, with roots in Protestant millennial visions of a blessed community and Popular Front—style evocations of the abstract "people," who, like the Joads, simply carry on. More recently the rise of the therapeutic vision has further removed many radicals from a clear assessment of human behavior. The plethora of therapeutic fads associated with the human potential movement are the bourgeois counterpart to utopian visions of a new socialist man. Jerry Rubin's journey from the Yippies to Esalen to Wall Street is an emblem of the way in which the status quo of oppression can coexist with the pursuit of perfection.

Too many of my Sixties comrades sought authenticity in their personal lives, their friendships, and their marriages only to find themselves facing the return of repressed guilt and rage.

Countercultural libertarians find themselves on the same wave length as many Communists when their utopian experiments collapse. When expectations are unrealistic, when Stakhanovites do not emerge to enthusiastically increase output, when Red Guard units seek petty vengeances, when Cuban workers resist moral incentives, when mates experience jealousy despite their proclamation of open marriage, when union leaders resign themselves to the poor prospects for worker democracy, one discovers a common thread of illusory hopes and subsequent reprisals. As antirevolutionary thinkers have correctly stressed, when utopian dreams go awry, justifications for repression emerge.[17]

My not so hidden agenda is to extend my analysis of the Old Left subculture to the contemporary problem of maintaining a radical praxis in a nonradical environment. Counter-cultural enclaves and "Liberated zones" only work for the privileged, and even then they may not work as anticipated. Radicals must be more sober about human behavior without losing their commitment to a more humane social order. Our Federalist founding fathers provided us with a model (albeit a bourgeois and now dated one) that tried to put human frailty, self-interest, and aggression to work in the interest of the community. Aggression and destructiveness in no way determine a social order; one could suggest that the Hobbesian view of human nature virtually demands a socialist society to temper selfishness and limit malevolence. Indeed, if human beings are selfish and power-seeking, how can one accept the kind of institutional power presently in the hands of corporate leaders? While it is undoubtedly true that absolute power corrupts absolutely, it is not true that power itself is corrupting. The concentration of power is most harmful to a democracy; it corrupts the powerful and infantilizes the powerless. To seek the absence of any power, an underlying wish of countercultural and therapeutic communities, merely concedes it to those less enamored with utopian dreams. The gloomiest view of human nature suggests the need for controls of the consequences of human selfishness, particularly in an era when ecological disaster has become a legitimate fear. It, of course, follows from this argument that the Soviet model of Party dictatorship with its rejection of a pluralistic system of checks and balances is to be found equally wanting.

The rejection of radicalism by working Americans stems in part from a suspicion of radical visions. Their experience teaches them that there are consequences to all choices and that reality is fundamentally tragic. They did not accept the old Communist Party's "private vision" of a Soviet workers' paradise, or any of the more recent Third World substitutes. American workers, like their Polish counterparts, understand that if socialism is merely Soviet reality writ large, there is no point in being a socialist. Leftists, Old and New, have too long had a propensity to romanticize struggling revolutionizing societies—the Soviet Union, China, Cuba, Vietnam, even Cambodia.[18]

At least Old Left Communists understood that they had to communicate with working Americans. They did not always succeed, for some of the reasons noted above, but their activism was grounded in the knowledge that no socialist movement could advance without persuading working people of its merit. James Weinstein correctly argues that the Party members of the Popular Front period went too far in their conformist drive to be thoroughly American and authentically of the people.[19] But at least they understood which constituencies had to be addressed.

More recent radicals, caught up in the abstractions of the counterculture and their libertarian and utopian goals, need to be more sensitive to the desire of working people to maintain as much stability, order, and meaning in their lives as possible. The consequences of the radical refusal to come to grips with the "old-fashioned" beliefs of possible constituents are brutally articulated by Christopher Lasch.

> Having written off demands for law and order as the expression
> of the proto-fascist mentality of the American working class,

intellectuals wonder why working-class discontent often takes the form of anti-intellectualism, opposition to McGovernite "new politics," or of a "profound conservatism." When the alternatives held up to "middle America" are a totally permissive paradise, a socialist utopia modeled on Cuba or the USSR, or a "language located beyond the rhetoric of the "real," it is not surprising that ordinary working people in this country refuse to become revolutionary.

. . . The Left has turned its back on its proper constituency—the people who cling to family life, religion, the work ethic, and other ostensibly outmoded values and institutions as the only source of stability in an otherwise precarious existence. The Left has chosen the wrong side in the cultural warfare between "middle America" and the educated or half-educated classes, which have absorbed avant garde ideas only to put them at the service of consumer capitalism.[20]

The Old Left, rooted in the labor struggles of the thirties, rarely dealt with such problems. In fact, two of their central limitations were at the other extreme—obliviousness to matters of the psyche and the toleration of cultural forms—for example, patriarchy—that their formal ideology rejected.

All adherents to the Left need to learn from the American Communist Party experience. We need to celebrate their victories in establishing mass industrial unions, furthering humane social welfare practices, contributing to a better standard of living for working and poor people, fighting for racial justice, standing up early and leading the fight against barbarism, and, finally, being part of the radical tradition that has had some success in demonstrating that democracy and capitalism are incompatible.

That Philadelphia Communists, like others, have had shameful moments is also true. Eric Bentley is probably exaggerating when he argues that Communists "have the worst record of perhaps any radical group that ever existed for intrigue, unscrupulousness, and inhumanity,"[21] but there is enough truth in his words to temper any impulse to glorify the Old Left. And yet even Bentley admits that "very many Stalinists continued to be men."[22]

I have met and interviewed many of these men and women and hope that some of their personalities, dreams, struggles, successes and failures, errors and hurts have come alive in these pages. These are good, decent, and eminently fallible people. The "true believer" model, while appropriate to a small percentage of Communists, is too abstract and ideologically slanted. Too often critics treat the Communist Party, U.S.A., according to its own arrogant standards of specialness—as "the Party"—subjecting it to standards of consistency and ethics rarely if ever met by any other political agency. Ultimately it was a party and a movement that energized hundreds of thousands of men and women to struggle for a more equitable social order.

That they did not succeed in fulfilling all of their hopes is less noteworthy than the fact that most of them still have them. Such hopes may be tempered by certain realities, but perhaps all would find satisfaction with the modest anticipation that under socialism, "man ceases to suffer as an animal and suffers as human. He, therewith, moves from the plane of the pitiful to the plane of the tragic."[23]

notes

■ *chapter 1*

1. Kirkpatrick Sale, *SDS* (New York: Random House, 1973), pp. 60–68. Trotskyists (or Trotskyites, Trots) were followers of the Soviet revolutionary Leon Trotsky, who was purged and finally murdered by Stalin's agents. Shactmanites were followers of Max Shactman; who led a break from Trotskyists in 1940.

2. C. Wright Mills, "The Politics of Responsibility," in *The New Left Reader*, ed. Carl Oglesby (New York: Grove Press, 1969), pp. 23–31; William Appleman Williams, *The Contours of American History* (Cleveland: World Publishers, 1961); James Weinstein, *Ambiguous Legacy: The Left in American Politics* (New York: New Viewpoints, 1975), esp. ch. 3, 5, 6.

3. Erich Fromm, ed., *Marx's Concept of Man* (New York: Frederick Ungar, 1969).

4. Herbert Marcuse, *One-Dimensional Man* (Boston: Beacon Press, 1964).

5. Ibid., pp. 79–83, 254–57.

6. See especially Wilhelm Reich, *The Sexual Revolution* (New York: Noonday Press, 1962), part 2.

7. Karl Marx, *Economic and Philosophic Manuscripts,* selection in *Socialist Thought: A Documentary History,* eds. Alfred Fried and Ronald Sanders (Garden City, N.Y.: Doubleday, Anchor Books, 1964), p. 290

8. See, for example, Gabriel Almond, *The Appeals of Communism* (Princeton: Princeton University Press, 1954); Nathan Glazer, *The Social Basis of American Communism* (New York: Harcourt, Brace & World, 1961); Morris Ernst and David Loth, *Report on the American Communist* (New York: Praeger, 1952); Frank Meyer, *The Moulding of Communists* (New York: Harcourt, Brace, 1961). The best-known and most influential of such studies is Eric Hoffer, *The True Believer* (New York: New American Library, Mentor Books, 1962).

9. On deviance, see Howard S. Becker, *Outsiders: Studies in the Sociology of Deviance* (New York: Free Press, 1963).

10. See Richard Flacks, *Youth and Social Change* (Chicago: Markham, 1971), for an excellent account of who became a radical in the sixties.

11. Louis Hartz, *The Liberal Tradition in America* (New York: Harcourt, Brace and World, 1955).

12. For the clearest and most self-righteous expression of this viewpoint, see Arthur Schlesinger, Jr., *The Vital Center* (Boston: Little, Brown, 1948).

13. See Richard Hofstadter, *The Paranoid Style in American Politics* (New York: Alfred A. Knopf, 1965).

14. Peter Clecak, *Radical Paradoxes* (New York: Harper & Row, 1973).

15. See note 8; also Irving Howe and Louis Coser, *The American Communist Party* (New York: Frederick A. Praeger, Praeger Paperbacks, 1962); David A. Shannon, *The Decline of American Communism* (New York: Harcourt, Brace, 1959); Daniel Bell, *Marxian Socialism in the United States* (Princeton: Princeton University Press, 1967); Theodore Draper, *The Roots of American Communism* (New York: Viking Press, 1966), and *American Communism and Soviet Russia* (New York: Viking Press, 1960).

16. See Maurice Isserman's thoughtful essay, "The 1956 Generation: An Alternative Approach to the History of American Communism," *Radical America* (March–April 1980), pp. 43–57, for a useful framework.

Isserman argues that too many scholars, hostile and empathetic, "treat the people who joined the CP in the 1930s as the passive agents of a politics imposed on them from above and without." He contends that in many ways such thirties Communists "shaped the Party to fit their own needs and expectations," pp. 43–4.

17. Tamara Hareven, "The Search for Generational Memory: Tribal Rites in Industrial Society," *Daedalus* (Fall 1978), p. 141.

18. Ibid., pp. 142, 143.

19. William W. Moss, *Oral History Program Manual* (New York: Praeger, 1976). To protect anonymity, interview material has not been included within footnote references, except in reference to Sam Darcy, whose national experiences have already brought him a degree of recognition.

20. Almond, *Appeals,* pp. xii, 401. Almond, with scanty evidence, found a high proportion of American Communist subjects viewing the Party "as a means of solving the personal problems of rebelliousness, isolation and the need for certainty and security" (p. 172). On the basis of the case studies he evaluated, he concluded that "many of the families described involved weak fathers and dominating mothers" (p. 288).

21. Vivian Gornick, *The Romance of American Communism* (New York: Basic Books, 1977), pp. xi–xii.

22. Arthur Liebman, *Jews and the Left* (New York: John Wiley & Sons, 1979), p. xi.

23. Glazer, *Social Basis,* p. 127.

24. Annie Kriegel, "Generational Difference: The History of an Idea," *Daedalus* (Fall 1978), p. 29.

25. Isserman, "The 1956 Generation," argues that it is "useful to think of the history of the CP from about 1930 through 1956 as a whole, and as the history of a single generation" (p. 46).

26. André Gorz, *Strategy for Labor* (Boston: Beacon Press, 1968).

27. Stanley Moore, "Utopian Themes in Marx and Mao," *Dissent* (March–April 1970) and *Monthly Review* 21 (June 1969). As Peter Clecak notes, Moore's piece is the only article ever to appear in both journals, *Radical Paradoxes,* pp. 305–306.

28 Ibid., p. 171, 175.

29. V. I. Lenin, "Two Tactics of Social-Democracy in the Democratic Revolution," in *Selected Works,* vol. 1 (New York: International Publishers, 1967), p. 542.

30. See Lenin, *Selected Works,* vol. 3, p. 362.

■ *chapter 2*

1. See Lewis Feuer, *The Conflict of Generations* (New York: Basic Books, 1969), for a shrewd but reductionist Freudian approach; see also note 8, Chapter 1.

2. Annie Kriegel, "Generational Difference: The History of an Idea," *Daedalus* (Fall 1978), p. 32.

3. Morton Keller, "Reflections on Politics and Generations in America, *Daedalus* (Fall 1978), p. 127; See also Norman B. Ryder, "The Cohort as a Concept in the Study of Social Change," *American Sociological Review* (1965), Kriegel, "Generational Difference," p. 29. The entire Fall 1978 issue of *Daedalus* is devoted to the concept of generations and contains some valuable and provocative material.

4. Kriegel, "Generational Difference," p. 32.

5. For the most thorough study of the effects of the Depression on an entire generation, see Glen H. Elder, Jr., *Children of the Great Depression: Social Change in Life Experience* (Chicago: University of Chicago Press, 1974).

6. For the most comprehensive accounts of early Party history, see Theodore Draper, *The Roots of American Communism* (New York: Viking Press, 1966) and *American Communism and Soviet Russia* (New York: Viking Press, 1960); Irving Howe and Lewis Coser, *The American Communist Party* (New York: Frederick A. Praeger, Praeger Paperbacks, 1962), pp. 1–174; James Weinstein, *Ambiguous Legacy: The Left in American Politics* (New York: New Viewpoints, 1975), pp. 26–43; Daniel Bell, *Marxian Socialism in the United States* (Princeton: Princeton University Press, 1967), pp. 122–33.

7. Draper's *Roots of American Communism* and *American Communism and Soviet Russia* provide the most detailed account of this process. Lovestonites were followers of Jay Lovestone, an American Communist Party leader purged in the late twenties as a "right deviationist."

8. Nathan Glazer, *The Social Basis of American Communism* (New York: Harcourt, Brace and World, 1961), pp. 42–52.

9. All selections from the "Little Lenin Library" of International Publishers, New York.

10. Howe and Coser, *American Communist Party*, pp. 175–272; Weinstein, *Ambiguous Legacy*, pp. 43–56.

11. Ibid.

12. Glazer, *Social Basis,* p. 92; Bell, *Marxian Socialism,* p. 141.

13. Weinstein, *Ambiguous Legacy,* pp. 63–64; Sam Darcy, a district organizer and national leader, stressed such local pre-Popular Front maneuvers (interview with Samuel Adams Darcy, 7 October 1978). Georgi Dimitrov, a Bulgarian, was a Comintern official best known for his role in the development of the Popular Front strategy.

14. Howe and Coser, *American Communist Party,* pp. 319–24; Bell, *Marxian Socialism,* pp. 143–44.

15. For example, Alexander Bittleman, "The New Deal and the Old Deal," *The Communist* (January 1934), called Roosevelt "a servant of Morgan and Co." (p. 89) and defined the New Deal as fascist (p. 81). Yet by mid-1939 James W. Ford wanted to "Bring the New Deal to Puerto Rico," *The Communist* (July 1939), pp. 634–40.

16. Howe and Coser, *American Communist Party,* pp. 319–86; Weinstein, *Ambiguous Legacy,* pp. 56–86.

17. The 1905ers' generation combined with native-born radicals already politically active prior to the Bolshevik Revolution (Foster, Browder) to form the pioneer Party group. The twenties generation are those who joined the Party between its formation and the Depression. This group played a major role in directing Party efforts, particularly in industrial organizing drives, during the Depression years. Note the birth dates of the following pre-1917 radicals: Anita Whitney (1867), Foster (1881), Charles Ruthenberg (1882), Max Bedacht (1885), Alexander Bittleman (1890), Browder (1891), Benjamin Gitlow (1891), William Patterson (1891). Twenties-generation Communists included Harry Haywood (1898), Jay Lovestone (1898), Hosea Hudson (1898), George Padmore (1902), John Williamson (1903), Benjamin Davis (1903), and Gene Dennis (1905). Thirties-generation Communists included Al Richmond (1913) and John Gates (1913). Annie Kriegel, *French Communists: Profile of a People* (Chicago: University of Chicago Press, 1972), presents a three-generation model for the French Communist Party, identifying 1924–1934, Popular Front, and Resistance generations (pp. 103–5). Two recent works on members of the twenties generation are: Kenneth Kann, *Joe Rapoport, The Life of a Jewish Radical* (Philadelphia: Temple University Press, 1981), and Vera Buch Weisbord, *A Radical Life* (Bloomington: Indiana University Press, 1977).

18. On Popular Front imagery, see Richard H. Pells, *Radical Visions and American Dreams* (New York: Harper & Row, Harper Torchbooks,

1974), pp. 292–329. The Liberty League was an corporate-financed anti–New Deal lobby group. Father Charles Coughlin was a Detroit-based Catholic priest whose nationwide radio broadcasts agitated against Jewish "conspiracists," Communists, and New Dealers. Huey Long, the Louisiana "Kingfish," was considered a serious challenger to Roosevelt until his assassination in 1935. All three were considered harbingers of a rising indigenous fascism by many liberals and radicals. The Soviet push toward economic growth was organized initially with a Five Year Plan, which began such heavily publicized projects as the construction of hydroelectric plants and the Moscow subway. Stakhanov was a Soviet coal miner whose alleged productivity under piecework incentives was presented as a model to other Soviet workers under Stalin in the mid-thirties. Mussolini's Italy attacked Ethiopia in 1935. On New Deal politics, see William E. Leuchtenberg, *Franklin D. Roosevelt and the New Deal* (New York: Harper & Row, 1963), passim. On Soviet economic growth, see J. P. Nettl, *The Soviet Achievement* (New York: Harcourt, Brace & World, 1967), pp. 115–50.

19. Dolores Ibarruri, "La Pasionaria," was most associated with the slogan of the defense of Madrid, *"no pasarán."*

20. For an evaluation of the importance of the Spanish Civil War to American radicals, see John Gates, *The Story of an American Communist* (New York: Thomas Nelson & Sons, 1958), pp. 42–67, and Robert A. Rosenstone, *Crusade of the Left: The Lincoln Battalion in the Spanish Civil War* (New York: Pegasus Press, 1969).

21. The revival of folk music in the period of the Popular Front was part of a populist reassertion of American values and traditions, often sentimental and nostalgic and at times even cynical. Communists and progressives were likely to have been moved by Steinbeck's *Grapes of Wrath* (if not the novel, then the film) and Odets's *Waiting for Lefty, Awake and Sing,* and *Golden Boy.* Many subjects also noted that they were influenced by Beard, especially his *An Economic Interpretation of the Constitution,* and Parrington, the cultural historian whose three-volume work *Main Currents in American Thought* established progressive and conservative strains in our culture. The Popular Front acceptance of mainstream, even conservative, traditions is best evaluated in Pells, *Radical Visions,* pp. 292–329. See also Joe Klein, *Woody Guthrie: A Life* (New York: Alfred A. Knopf, 1980), pp. 145–48 for the Popular Front milieu and, overall, for a sensitive portrait of the Popular Front's foremost culture hero.

22. Pells, *Radical Visions,* p. 298.

23. Ibid., pp. 292–329; Weinstein, *Ambiguous Legacy,* pp. 56–86.

24. *Daily Worker,* 1 May 1938, 4 July 1938. On the worship of John L. Lewis, see Len DeCaux, *Labor Radical* (Boston: Beacon Press, 1970), pp. 222–47. For the embarrassing and puerile side of Popular Front Americana, which was well represented, see Granville Hicks, *I Like America* (New York: A New Modern Age Book, 1938). See also Maurice Isserman, "The 1956 Generation: An Alternative Approach to the History of American Communism," *Radical America* (March–April 1980), pp. 46, 48.

25. Arthur Liebman, *Jews and the Left* (New York: John Wiley & Sons, 1979), pp. 285, 135–325.

26. Headquarters later moved to 19th and Market, and later still, in the late thirties, to 250 S. Broad Street; both are downtown addresses.

27. Glazer, *Social Basis,* p. 6. See also Gabriel Almond, The *Appeals of Communism* (Princeton: Princeton University Press, 1954), p. 221. In Almond's sample 34 percent were from "Left" backgrounds, 16 percent from liberal, "Moderately Left," 3 percent from monarchist or fascist, 16 percent from conservative, and 15 percent from apolitical ones. The Workmen's Circle, or Arbeiter Ring, founded in 1892, was a Jewish fraternal order with close ties to the Socialist Party and the Jewish trade-union movement. "The International Workers Order," founded in 1930, was a multiethnic fraternal order closely associated with the Communist Party. The Bund, founded in Vilna in 1897, was a Jewish socialist working-class party in Eastern Europe. The Farband, the Jewish National Workers' Alliance, founded in 1912, was the fraternal order of the Labor Zionists. For detailed accounts of all the above, see Liebman, *Jews and the Left,* pp. 284–325.

28. In Gabriel Almond's sample, thirty-four were middle-class and thirty working-class (*Appeals,* p. 401).

29. Peter Muller, Kenneth C. Meyer, and Roman A. Cybriwsky, *Philadelphia: A Study of Conflicts and Social Cleavages* (Cambridge: Harvard University Press, 1976), pp. 18–22.

30. 17 August 1948, p. 1.

31. Peggy Dennis, *The Autobiography of an American Communist* (Berkeley: Creative Arts Book Company, 1977), p. 26.

32. Vivian Gornick, *The Romance of American Communism* (New York: Basic Books, 1977), pp. 4–9, 53–59. The Coops were the Co-operative Houses in the Bronx built in the twenties by the United Workers

Co-operative Association, a Communist, mostly Jewish organization of garment workers.

33. Of the seventeen from identifiable Philadelphia high schools, six attended the academically elite Central High School, while the remainder studied at the disproportionately academic and Jewish Overbrook, West Philadelphia, Southern, Olney, Gratz, and Northeast high schools. The majority of those who advanced to college attended local schools, either the prestigious University of Pennsylvania or the more plebian Temple University. In addition, two completed specialized technical programs. At the graduate level, four completed professional school and three earned doctorates in academic programs. Sex seems to have had little or no significance as a variable in educational accomplishments. Of the ten women, two were high school drop-outs, four completed high school, and four graduated from college. All four female college graduates continued their training at the graduate level, but it is significant that they chose such sex-defined fields as elementary education, social work, and nursing. The men did their graduate work in law, medicine, dentistry, and public administration, as well as in the human service area. Among the Jews of the sample, thirteen (of twenty-three) were college graduates. All of the holders of advanced degrees were Jewish. Indeed, of the ten Jews who halted their education after high school graduation, five are women. Within the very small black sample, three of four completed college.

34. Glazer, *Social Basis*, p. 6; Almond, *Appeals*, pp. 172, 243, 288.

35. For an impressionistic picture of the thirties, see Studs Terkel, *Hard Times* (New York: Avon Books, 1971). For a fine cultural analysis, see Pells, *Radical Visions*.

36. Almond notes that only 27 percent of his sample had read the Marxist classics before joining the Party (*Appeals*, p. 100).

37. Liebman, *Jews and the Left*, p. 373; see also Richard Flacks, *Youth and Social Change* (Chicago: Markham, 1971), for a sense of the characteristics of sixties radicals.

38. Robert D. Hess and Judith V. Torney, "Patterns of Growth in the Emergence of Political Attitudes," in *The Seeds of Politics*, ed. Anthony M. Orun (Englewood Cliffs, N.J.: Prentice-Hall, 1972), p. 47, designate four steps toward radical political socialization: awareness, conceptualization, subculture involvement, and active participation.

39. Richard Wright, "Memoir," in *The God That Failed*, ed. Richard Crossman (New York: Bantam Books, 1965), p. 106. Wright also

emphasizes that the Soviet Union's apparent benevolence toward its own backward peoples and its theoretical positions on nationality and colonialism greatly impressed him (p. 117).

40. Gates, *Story*, p. 17; David A. Shannon, *The Socialist Party of America* (Chicago: Quadrangle Books, 1967), passim; Bell, *Marxian Socialism*, passim. See also Hal Draper, "The Student Movement of the Thirties: A Political History," in Orun, *The Seeds of Politics*, pp. 24–40.

41. Harvey E. Klehr, *Communist Cadre* (Stanford: Hoover Institution Press, 1978), p. 83; Glazer, *Social Basis,* p. 117.

■ *chapter 3*

1. Frank Meyer, *The Moulding of Communists* (New York: Harcourt, Brace, 1961); Philip Selznick, *The Organizational Weapon: A Study of Bolshevik Strategy and Tactics* (New York: McGraw-Hill, 1952); Morris Ernst and David Loth, *Report on the American Communist* (New York: Praeger, 1952).

2. See Annie Kriegel, *The French Communists: Profile of a People* (Chicago: University of Chicago Press, 1972); Donald L. M. Blackmer and Sidney Tarrow, eds., *Communism in Italy and France* (Princeton: Princeton University Press, 1975); Harvey E. Klehr, *Communist Cadre* (Stanford: Hoover Institution Press, 1978); James Weinstein, *Ambiguous Legacy: The Left in American Politics* (New York: New Viewpoints, 1975); David A. Shannon, *The Decline of American Communism* (New York: Harcourt, Brace, 1959); Joseph R. Starobin, *American Communism in Crisis, 1943–1957* (Berkeley: University of California Press, 1972).

3. See, in particular, Kriegel, *French Communists*. See also Gabriel Almond, *The Appeals of Communism* (Princeton: Princeton University Press, 1954); Nathan Glazer, *The Social Basis of American Communism* (New York: Harcourt, Brace and World, 1961).

4. Mark Naison, "The Communist Party in Harlem, 1928–1936" (Ph.D. diss., Columbia University, 1976), "Marxism and Black Radicalism in America," *Radical America* (May–June 1971), "The Communist Party in Harlem: A Case Study in the Reinterpretation of American Communism," *Radical History Review* (Fall 1976), "Harlem Communists and the Politics of Black Protest," *Marxist Perspectives* (Fall 1978); James Prickett, "Communists and the Communist Issue in the American Labor Movement, 1920–1950" (Ph.D. diss. U.C.L.A.,

1975); Roger Keeran, "'Everything For Victory': Communist Influence in the Auto Industry during World War II," *Science & Society* (Spring 1979).

5. Klehr, *Cadre*, p. 3.

6. Mark Naison, "Historical Notes on Blacks and American Communism: The Harlem Experience," *Science & Society* (Fall 1978), pp. 330, 328; Naison charges that "too often scholars have used 'Stalinism' and 'Comintern domination' as *dei ex machina* to explain everything the Party did, abdicating their responsibility to make detailed empirical investigations of Party activity," p. 328.

7. Vivian Gornick, *The Romance of American Communism* (New York: Basic Books, 1977), p. 23.

8. See Anthony Downs, *Inside Bureaucracy* (Boston: Little, Brown, 1967), pp. 24–31 on the nature of bureaucracy and pp. 61–65 on informal structures.

9. One district leader told me that the Party headquarters was not willing to cooperate with this study because of what it considers to be recent scholarly distortions of Party history. For this study I read the *Daily Worker* from 1929 until 1957, focusing on the information about District Three, including the Pennsylvania supplement *Pennsylvania Worker* from 1947 to 1956. A number of sources have also made available assorted copies of Party and district newspapers, pamphlets, and mimeographs. Finally, heavy reliance has been placed on the invaluable information provided by knowledgeable and cooperative subjects.

10. On national structures, see Gornick, *Romance*, p. 120; Glazer, *Social Basis*, p. 50; Shannon, *Decline*, pp. 70–74. See also *Daily Worker*, 8 November 1929, 7 July 1946, and 7 May 1944, which listed the following twenty-three districts: New York, New England, Eastern Pennsylvania, Connecticut, Ohio, New Jersey, Michigan, Western Pennsylvania–West Virginia, Wisconsin, Northwest, California, Montana, Virginia-Carolinas, Minnesota, Iowa-Nebraska, Maryland, Louisiana, Oklahoma, Colorado, Missouri, Vermont, Texas, and Florida. On New York's predominance, see Starobin, *American Communism in Crisis*, p. 23.

11. The *Daily Worker* of 12 November 1934, for example, tells of a drive for 60,000 new subscriptions. New York was given responsibility for 30,000 and Philadelphia for 3,500 (6 percent), the third-highest quota among districts. See also 14 August 1943, 3 October 1946, and 9 November 1947 for drives indicating New York's primacy and Phila-

delphia's second or third ranking, with quotas ranging from 5 to 7 percent. In Vera Buch Weisbord's memoir, *A Radical Life* (Bloomington: Indiana University Press, 1977), she reflects the characteristic Party attitude toward Philadelphia: "Just when we were getting used to Philadelphia . . . a real assignment came: district organizer in Detroit" (p. 146). Shades of W. C. Fields!

12. On Philadelphia's class and ethnic distribution, see Allen F. Davis and Mark H. Haller, eds., *The Peoples of Philadelphia* (Philadelphia: Temple University Press, 1973), especially the articles by Dennis J. Clark, "The Philadelphia Irish: Persistent Peril"; John F. Sutherland, "Housing the Poor in the City of Homes: Philadelphia at the Turn of the Century"; Caroline Golab, "The Immigrant and the City: Poles, Italians, and Jews in Philadelphia, 1870–1920"; Maxwell Whiteman, "Philadelphia's Jewish Neighborhoods"; and Richard A. Varbero, "Philadelphia's South Italians in the 1920s." See also Sam Bass Warner, Jr., *The Private City: Philadelphia in Three Periods of Its Growth* (Philadelphia: University of Pennsylvania Press, 1968), pp. 161–223.

13. Gornick, *Romance*, p. 120.

14. Gornick speaks of the clubs as "the most important unit" (ibid., p. 70). She describes a New York City section consisting of twenty-eight open and two secret branches meeting every other week, public and private meetings alternating. She adds that this section contained between forty and fifty youth clubs for neighborhood children. Each year the branch sent one activist to attend the section organizers' special classes. This was a means by which the Party discovered and trained new cadres. For branch and club membership figures, see pp. 120–22. Gornick informs us that one Lower East Side area with a population of 250,000 had a section with 3,000 members. See also Jessica Mitford, *A Fine Old Conflict* (New York: Alfred A. Knopf, 1977), pp. 67–69, on branch and club life.

15. On Communist Party membership over time, see Daniel Bell, *Marxian Socialism in the United States* (Princeton: Princeton University Press, 1967), p. 141; Glazer, *Social Basis,* pp. 90, 92–93; Shannon, *Decline,* pp. 3, 364; Starobin, *American Communism in Crisis,* p. 114; Michael R. Belknap, *Cold War Justice: The Smith Act, the Communist Party, and American Civil Liberties* (Westport, Conn.: Greenwood Press, 1977), pp. 90, 202; Peggy Dennis, *The Autobiography of an American Communist* (Berkeley: Creative Arts Book Company, 1977), p. 159;

Theodore Draper, *The Roots of American Communism* (New York: Viking Press, 1966), p. 391; Jon Weiner, "The Communist Party: An Interview with Dorothy Healey," *Radical America* (May–June 1977), p. 26.

16. Glazer claims that in early 1929 the Philadelphia district had 481 members, of whom only 50 were native-born (*Social Basis*, p. 60).

17. Federal Bureau of Investigation File 61-6593 Sub A Section #2 (18 June 1943–16 February 1945), copy courtesy of Samuel Adams Darcy. The file lists district membership as of 22 January 1944 as 2,489, with 1,818 in Philadelphia proper.

18. On the Darcy affair, see Starobin, *American Communism in Crisis*, p. 65, 78; *Daily Worker*, 5 June 1944; FBI. File 61-6593, pp. 24, 25, 30. I have also greatly profited from conversations with Mr. Darcy on 7 October 1978 and 4 January 1979, and from conversations with other former district leaders.

19. Darcy claims that Jewish membership declined to approximately 50 percent by 1944, but no other source confirms such an estimate.

20. Glazer, *Social Basis*, pp. 41, 80; Draper, *Roots*, p. 392; Arthur Liebman, *Jews and the Left* (New York: John Wiley & Sons, 1979), p. 305.

21. In 1943, for example, the Party set up an Independent Voters Party with Jules Abercauph as mayoral candidate, after the Democrats had selected William C. Bullitt over Communist objections. The local Party attacked Bullitt vociferously as an "anti-Semite," a "racist," and a "fascist." For information on the election, won by Republican Barney Samuel by a wide margin, see "Bullitt Exposed," *Worker* reprint, n.d., and Samuel Adams Darcy, "The Last Crusade," pp. 558–65, an unpublished memoir generously made available to me by Mr. Darcy. Abercauph received only 4,330 votes, less than one percent (Philadelphia *Bulletin Almanac* [Philadelphia: Philadelphia Bulletin, 1944], p. 492).

22. Darcy speaks of luncheons with John B. Kelly and other Democratic Party leaders (interview, 7 October 1978).

23. Starobin, *American Communism in Crisis*, p. 36, observes, "In Philadelphia, the Communists connected themselves through local reform movements based on the city-wide CIO Councils . . . in such a way as to exert powerful leverage on the Democrats."

24. The more insightful efforts include Klehr, *Cadre*; Starobin, *American Communism in Crisis*; Naison, "The Communist Party in Harlem," *Radical History Review*; Glazer, *Social Basis*; Almond,

Appeals. Demonological approaches include Meyer, *Moulding;* Ernst and Loth, *Report;* and, perhaps the most influential, Eric Hoffer, *The True Believer* (New York: New American Library, Mentor Books, 1962). In a class by itself is Gornick, *Romance.*

25. For example, the *Daily Worker,* 19 April 1939.

26. For solid analysis of informal organization, see Charles Perrow, *Complex Organization* (Glenview, Ill.: Scott, Foresman, 1972), pp. 97–144. See also F. J. Roethisberger and William J. Dickson, *Management and the Worker* (Cambridge: Harvard University Press, 1947), passim. Almond, *Appeals,* after stressing formal indoctrination, nevertheless concedes, "It is indeed probable that for most individuals publications constitute only a secondary source of information about the party, while direct, first hand experience of those aspects of the party with which individuals come in contact constitutes their primary source of information. In this respect, the Communist movement may differ only in degree from most other associations in which publications and formal doctrine are far less important than communication in intimate groups and information from trusted associates" (p. 99).

27. Elizabeth Bott, *Family and Social Network* (London: Tavistock, 1957), states, "Conceptually, the network stands between the family and the total social environment" (p. 98). "In network formation . . . only some, not all, of the component individuals have social relationships with one another" (p. 58). It may be useful to view the social network of friends, relatives, and acquaintances as a subset of a subculture. For a comprehensive presentation of the radical Jewish subculture, both in Eastern Europe and in the United States in the early twentieth century, see Liebman, *Jews and the Left,* passim.

28. On social democratic politics, see James Joll, *The Second International, 1889–1914* (New York: Harper & Row, Colophon Books, 1966), and Peter Gay, *The Dilemma of Democratic Socialism* (New York: Collier Books, 1962). On the French and Italian Communist experience, see Kriegel, *French Communists,* and Blackmer and Tarrow, *Communism in Italy and France.* Almond, *Appeals,* p. 369, sees the American Communist Party (as well as the British) as an "aberration," in contrast to the French and Italian parties, which have taken on "the proportions of a subculture."

29. *Daily Worker,* 19 April 1939, 29 April 1939, 30 April 1939, 2 May 1939.

30. Gornick, *Romance,* p. 59.

31. Richard Sennett, *The Fall of Public Man* (New York: Alfred A. Knopf, 1977), esp. pp. 89–106, 294–340. Sennett is sensitive to the "confusion that has arisen between public and intimate life; people are working out in terms of personal feelings public matters which properly can be dealt with only through codes of impersonal meaning" (p. 248).

32. Gornick, *Romance,* p. 248, argues that this is what is most striking in the Communist: the gift for political emotion highly developed, the gift for individual empathy neglected, atrophied."

33. Ellen Kay Trimberger, "Women in the Old and New Left: The Evolution of a Politics of Personal Life," *Feminist Studies* (Fall 1979), pp. 436–439, stresses the privatization of emotions in the Old Left; Peggy Dennis, "Response," *Feminist Studies* (Fall 1979), p. 456, rebuts by emphasizing the Party interference in personal matters. I do not find these two views incompatable; Party members did privatize emotions, and yet the Party considered it appropriate to invade any domain in its own interest.

34. See Philip Rieff, *The Triumph of the Therapeutic* (New York: Harper & Row, 1968).

35. George Charney, *A Long Journey* (Chicago: Quadrangle Books, 1968), p. 29.

36. Mitford, *Fine Old Conflict,* p. 236.

37. Peggy Dennis, in her *Autobiography,* gives evidence that such friendships were much less common at the upper echelons of leadership. She excoriates the national leaders who "gave nothing of themselves" when her husband was in prison or, later, when he was dying. On the other hand, she praises neighborhood comrades for their genuine friendship and loyalty (p. 193). Annie Kriegel, *French Communists,* p. 221, finds little friendship but much "camaraderie" among French Communists.

38. Almond, *Appeals,* p. 160, presents a table on the social network distribution within his sample. It indicates that 14 percent maintained social relations entirely. Another 23 percent did so almost entirely within Party circles. Eight percent spoke of having social relations outside the party but with people "instrumental to the party." Among those who maintained relations totally outside of Party influence, Almond notes 22 percent who retained a "few friends," 19 percent who retained "many friends," and 9 percent who continued relations with most non-party friends.

39. In comparison, the Wisconsin district of the late thirties had 600

members, including 100 union officials and nearly 300 active in the CIO and AFL (Dennis, *Autobiography,* pp. 93–96); see also Steve Murdock, "California Communists: Their Years in Power," *Science & Society* (Winter 1970), who describes a Party district of close to 9,000 members in the late 1930s and as late as 1949 (p. 482).

40. Gornick, *Romance,* p. 22.

41. Starobin, *American Communism in Crisis,* p. 235.

42. Gornick, *Romance,* pp. 115–16.

■ *chapter 4*

1. For useful insights about ethnicity, see Milton M. Gordon, *Assimilation in American Life* (New York: Oxford University Press, 1964), and Nathan Glazer and Daniel P. Moynihan, eds., *Ethnicity: Theory and Practice* (Cambridge: Harvard University Press, 1975). In the latter volume, of particular value is Orlando Patterson, "Context and Choice in Ethnic Allegiance: A Theoretical Framework and Caribbean Case Study," pp. 305–49.

Max Weber defines an ethnic group as follows: "Those human groups that entertain a subjective belief in their common descent—because of similarities of physical type or of customs or both, or because of memories of colonization and migration—in such a way that this belief is important for the continuation of non-kinship, communal relationships" ("Ethnic Groups," in *Theories of Society,* ed. Talcott Parsons [New York: Macmillan, 1961], p. 306). For an attempt to relate ethnicity to class, see Gordon, *Assimilation in American Life,* pp. 51–54.

2. Harvey Klehr, *Communist Cadre,* finds this model, (Stanford: Hoover Institution Press, 1978), as well as sexual differentiation, useful in analyzing Party leadership, see ch. 1–3.

3. Vivian Gornick, *The Romance of American Communism* (New York: Basic Books, 1977), p. 25.

4. Arthur Liebman, *Jews and the Left* (New York: John Wiley & Sons, 1979), pp. 55–69, 347–54, 311–15, 492–526, 458–64. As Nathan Glazer noted several decades ago in *The Social Basis of American Communism* (New York: Harcourt, Brace and World, 1961), pp. 130–31, "no detailed understanding of the impact of Communism on American life is possible without an analysis of the relationship between American Jews and the American Communist Party."

5. Joseph R. Starobin, *American Communism in Crisis, 1943–1957*

(Berkeley: University of California Press, 1972), p. 23; Glazer, *Social Basis,* pp. 99–100; Theodore Draper, *The Roots of American Communism* (New York: Viking, 1966), p. 392.

6. Glazer, *Social Basis,* p. 49. In 1925 there were between 3,000 and 4,000 Jews in a Party with approximately 13,000 members. See Paul Buhle, "Jews and American Communism: The Cultural Question," *Radical History Review* (Spring 1980), p. 32.

7. Paul Buhle takes a more benevolent view of the Popular Front in "Jews and American Communism": "Was not the adherence to the Popular Front of Paul Robeson, Huddie Ledbetter, Woodie Guthrie, or young Pete Seeger the nearest equivalent to the Yiddishist literary, theatrical, and choral personalities around the *Freiheit* a decade earlier?" (p. 24). Overall, Buhle skillfully explores the Party's general "disrespect for cultural work" (p. 28) and yet tempers his criticism with consideration of the multiethnic environment the Party operated in. I found few second-generation Jewish Communists, however, who would fully agree that "Communism would provide . . . a vision to unify the Jewish past, the American proletarian present, and the golden future" (p. 17). See also Maurice Isserman, "The 1956 Generation: An Alternative Approach to the History of American Communism," *Radical America* (March–April 1980, pp. 46, 48.

8. They were not so comfortable with Irving Berlin's "God Bless America." See Joe Klein, *Woodie Guthrie: A Life* (New York: Alfred A. Knopf, 1980), pp. 140–41, for Guthrie's "This Land Is Your Land" as a counter to Berlin.

9. Gornick presents her interviewees as "every kind of American"; yet close to 65 percent of her sample is Jewish. For the most comprehensive accounts of Jewish–American Communists, see Liebman, *Jews and the Left,* passim, and Klehr, *Cadre,* ch. 2.

10. For example, John Gates never discusses his own Jewish background or expresses any identification with Jewishness in his memoirs, *The Story of an American Communist* (New York: Thomas Nelson & Sons, 1958).

11. On the three-generational pattern, see Sidney Goldstein and Calvin Goldscheider, *Jewish American: Three Generations in a Jewish Community* (Englewood Cliffs, N.J.: Prentice-Hall, 1968), and Gordon, *Assimilation in American Life.*

12. On Party programs and attitudes concerning Jews, Judaism, and

Zionism, see Melech Epstein, *The Jews and Communist* (New York: Trade Union Sponsoring Committee, 1959); Klehr, *Cadre,* pp. 37–52; Liebman, *Jews and the Left,* passim; Glazer, *Social Basis,* pp. 151–58.

13. For vivid examples of the kind of Jewish identification revived by the Popular Front's celebration of ethnicity, see the letters of Julius and Ethel Rosenberg in Robert and Michael Meeropol, *We Are Your Sons* (Boston: Little, Brown, 1975), especially pp. 33, 70, 197, 225.

14. Harry C. Boyte, *The Backyard Revolution: Understanding the New Citizen Movement* (Philadelphia: Temple University Press, 1980), p. 25.

15. On the Socialist Party, see Liebman, *Jews and the Left,* pp. 135–356. On the Communist Party, see Draper, *Roots,* p. 392. The largest federation was the Finnish, which accounted for 45 percent of the total. Other important federations, beside the Jewish, were the South Slav, Russian, Lithuanian, Ukrainian, and Hungarian. See also Glazer, *Social Basis,* p. 80.

16. On the 1905ers' hostility to Judaism, see Liebman, *Jews and the Left,* pp. 502–4. Yom Kippur is the most sacred of Jewish religious holidays, a day of atonement for the sins of the past year.

17. Mark Naison, "The Communist Party in Harlem in the Early Depression Years: A Case Study in the Reinterpretation of American Communism," *Radical History Review* (Fall 1978), downplays ethnicity, concluding that the Party, "composed almost exclusively of first and second generation immigrants," made great strides in fighting for black-white unity and racial equality (p. 88).

18. George Charney, *A Long Journey* (Chicago: Quadrangle Books, 1968), pp. 103–4. Charney, born in 1905, was a second-generation Jewish-American Communist.

19. Ibid., p. 105.

20. Gates, *Story,* p. 26.

21. On name changing, see Klehr, *Cadre,* p. 41, and Glazer, *Social Basis,* p. 211. See also Albert Memmi, *The Liberation of the Jews* (New York: Viking Press, Viking Compass Books, 1973), for many insights on name changing, pp. 31–42, self-hatred, pp. 107–24, and "The Jew and the Revolution," pp. 227–45.

22. On leadership, see Liebman, *Jews and the Left,* p. 527. Klehr, *Cadre,* pp. 39–40, finds that the proportion of Jews in national leadership declined over time. He adds that whereas foreign-born Jews were disproportionately in leadership, getting to the top early and being more

Americanized than other immigrant cadres, native-born, Depression-era Jews advanced quite slowly. By the thirties, the Party was trying to make room for blacks and working-class Gentiles. See also Gabriel Almond, *The Appeals of Communism* (Princeton: Princeton University Press, 1954), p. 140.

23. Harold Cruse, *The Crisis of the Negro Intellectual* (New York: William Morrow & Company, 1969), pp. 147–70, 497, and "My Jewish Problem and Theirs," in *Black Anti-Semitism and Jewish Racism*, ed. Nat Hentoff (New York: Richard W. Baron, 1969), pp. 143–90. Cruse tends to weaken his provocative hypothesis with vitriol.

24. Cruse, *Crisis*, p. 163.

25. Morris U. Schappes, "The Jewish Question and the Left: Old and New" (New York: Jewish Currents Reprint, 1970), pp. 13–14. Schappes charges that the Party finally recognized black national identity but never that of the Jews.

26. Charney, *Long Journey*, p. 102, notes that there was "ill-concealed resentment" of such affairs and adds that affairs between black women and white men "rarely occurred." Sara Evans, *Personal Politics: The Roots of Women's Liberation in the Civil Rights Movement and the New Left* (New York: Alfred A. Knopf, 1979), pp. 78–82, discusses the interracial sexual dynamics of the 1960s movement.

27. See Calvin C. Hernton, *Sex and Racism in America* (Garden City, N.Y.: Doubleday, 1965), for an insightful analysis of the impact of racism on blacks and whites, men and women.

28. On the reformist recruitment of blacks in Harlem, see Charney, *Long Journey*, p. 105. On high turnover among blacks, see ibid., p. 116; Glazer, *Social Basis*, p. 123; Wilson Record, *The Negro and the Communist Party* (Chapel Hill: University of North Carolina Press, 1951), pp. 117–18; Henry Williams, *Black Response to the American Left, 1917–1929* (Princeton: Trustees of Princeton University, 1973), pp. 26–27; Bert Cochran, *Labor and Communism* (Princeton: Princeton University Press, 1977), p. 228.

29. Record, *Negro and the Communist Party*, pp. 65, 136; Richard Wright, "Memoir," in *The God That Failed*, ed. Richard Crossman (New York: Bantam Books, 1965), pp. 106, 117.

30. Naison, "The Communist Party in Harlem," *Radical History Review*, pp. 68–69. Glazer, *Social Basis*, p. 180, idealizing somewhat, claims that "the party was the only institution in American life in which

Negroes commonly worked with whites on a level of equality, which was truly colorblind, which was really indifferent to issues of race."

31. Perhaps the tendency of black national Party leaders to be better educated than their white counterparts is the result of such discrimination in the job market. See Klehr, *Cadre*, p. 60.

32. Charney, *Long Journey*, p. 84.

33. Morris U. Schappes spoke in an interview in New York City, on 10 April 1979, of Party campaigns to discourage Jewish Communists from vacationing at Miami Beach because of its racially segregated facilities.

34. Liebman notes Jewish patronizing of Gentiles, "a mixture of hostility and superiority," in *Jews and the Left*, p. 534.

35. Liebman, *Jews and the Left*, p. 553. See also Irving Howe, *The World of Our Fathers* (New York: Harcourt Brace Jovanovich, 1976), passim.

36. Glazer, *Social Basis*, p. 123.

37. Gornick, *Romance*, p. 170. Glazer, *Social Basis*, p. 179, charges that these campaigns "hit the Jewish membership particularly strongly" and induced a "loss of Jewish fellow-travellers." Record, *Negro and the Communist Party*, pp. 243–45; skeptical of the Party in all other matters, accepts the Party allegations concerning white chauvinism.

38. Among district leaders, Stong and Dave Davis, the UE leader, seemed the most popular and respected. The least liked was clearly Robert Klonsky. Sam Darcy, the most controversial, seems to have been the most able.

39. Maxwell Whiteman, "Philadelphia's Jewish Neighborhoods," in *The Peoples of Philadelphia,* ed. Allen F. Davis and Mark Haller (Philadelphia: Temple University Press, 1973), pp. 231–54; Peter Muller, Kenneth C. Meyer, and Roman A. Cybriwsky, *Philadelphia: A Study of Conflicts and Social Change* (Cambridge: Harvard University Press, 1976), pp. 14–20, 40–41.

40. One must consider the likelihood that some moves to ethnically homogeneous sections had less to do with an abandonment of integrationist ideals than with an attempt to find security and a sense of identity.

41. Morris U. Schappes, "A Secular View of Jewish Life," in *Jewish Currents Reader* (New York: Jewish Currents, 1966), pp. 46–53; Isaac Deutscher, *The Non-Jewish Jew and Other Essays* (New York: Hill and Wang, 1968), esp. ch. 1 and 2.

42. William Kornblum, *Blue Collar Community* (Chicago: University of Chicago Press, 1974), pp. 7–87.

43. For criticisms of the Party's subordination of socialist goals, see James Weinstein, *Ambiguous Legacy: The Left in American Politics* (New York: New Viewpoints, 1975), pp. 57–113. See also Richard H. Pells, *Radical Visions and American Dreams* (New York: Harper & Row, Harper Torchbooks, 1974), pp. 292–98.

■ *chapter 5*

1. The most promising effort along such lines is the recent study of New Left women by Sara Evans, *Personal Politics: The Roots of Women's Liberation in the Civil Rights Movement and the New Left* (New York: Alfred A. Knopf, 1979). See also Ellen Kay Trimberger "Women in the Old and New Left: The Evolution of a Politics of Personal Life" and "Afterword," pp. 432–50, 460–61, Peggy Dennis's response, pp. 451–60, and Trimberger's afterword, pp. 460–61, in *Feminist Studies* (Fall 1979).

2. Harvey E. Klehr, *Communist Cadre* (Stanford: Hoover Institution Press, 1978), p. 75; Annie Kriegel, *The French Communists Profile of a People* (Chicago: University of Chicago Press, 1972), pp. 59–63. Kriegel indicates that the French Communist Party was only 11.1 percent female in 1946, 20.2 percent in 1954, and 25.5 percent in 1966. She adds, significantly, that 46 percent of the 1966 female members are listed as housewives and that women's role in the Party has always been "very modest."

3. Glen H. Elder, Jr., *Children of the Great Depression: Social Change in Life Experience* (Chicago: University of Chicago Press, 1974), pp. 157, 206, citing J. Joel Moss, "Teenage Marriage: Cross-National Trends and Sociological Factors in the Decision of When to Marry," *Acta Sociologica* 1964, pp. 98–117, indicates that the median age for American males to marry was 24.6 in 1920 and 24.3 in 1940; for females it was 21.3 in 1930 and 21.5 in 1940.

4. On the domestic life of the foremost Bolshevik, see Robert Payne, *The Life and Death of Lenin* (New York: Simon and Schuster, 1964), pp. 201–11, 233–36, 239–41, 528–29.

On Karl Marx's Victorian household, see Isaiah Berlin, *Karl Marx* (New York: Oxford University Press, Galaxy Books, 1967), pp. 70, 79–80, 159, 280; Erich Fromm, *Marx's Concept of Man* (New York: Frederick Ungar, 1969), pp. 80–83, 221–556; Joel Carmichael, *Karl Marx* (London: Rapp & Whiting, 1968), pp. 87, 105–6, 202.

5. Peggy Dennis, *The Autobiography of an American Communist* (Berkeley: Creative Arts Book Company, 1977), pp. 36–37. Albert Weisbord, the youthful leader of the 1926 Passaic textile strike, offered a Bolshevik relationship to Vera Buch in what she called a "businesslike way," saying, "I want to live with you on a permanent basis. I believe you have the qualities I want in a partner. You have courage, intelligence, and the desire to be a Bolshevik. You'll be my Krupskaya. You will go with me from one strike to another. This is just the beginning. When we have the textile industry organized, we'll move on to steel, and so on, building the Party. You can never have children, not even a home. But you'll be always by my side, fighting with me, helping me" (Vera Buch Weisbord, *A Radical Life* [Bloomington: Indiana University Press, 1977], p. 115). The Bolshevik model was in its own fashion decidedly patriarchal, as Vera soon found out when Albert opposed her taking an important post that would separate them (pp. 140–41). Vera Weisbord also experienced the trauma of an illegal abortion alone. Albert insisted, "My responsibility is to provide the money, that is all" (pp. 165–69).

6. James Weinstein, *Ambiguous Legacy: The Left in American Politics* (New York: New Viewpoints, 1975), p. 162.

7. Michael Young and Peter Willmot, *The Symmetrical Family* (London: Penguin, 1973), pp. 28–33; See also Elder, *Children of the Great Depression*, p. 287, for the continuing gradual shift toward a more companionate family model in the 1930s.

8. Elizabeth Bott, *Family and Social Network* (London: Tavistock, 1957), pp. 92–96. Bott and her associates find "no families" in which a joint conjugal role relationship was associated with "a close-knit network" and conclude that "the closer knit the network, the greater degree of segregation between the roles of husband and wife" (pp. 60, 62). This sample offers an alternative option of close-knit network with relatively equal conjugal role relationship.

9. See Vivian Gornick, *The Romance of American Communism* (New York: Basic Books, 1977), pp. 133–34, on hostessing. Sara Evans, *Personal Politics*, pp. 111–12, discusses the invisibility of the paired woman, the invisible teammate of the 1960s. She admires the Old Left households for their greater political consciousness (compared with New Left marriages and relationships) about the oppression of women. Recognizing the tensions between egalitarianism and patriarchy, Evans notes that few Old Left women "became primarily housewives" and that they seem to have taught feminism to their daughters.

10. Gabriel Almond, *The Appeals of Communism* (Princeton: Princeton University Press, 1954), p. 155, states, "Male party members were generally urged to bring their wives into the party; and wives their husbands. As a former American party member said, "Anyone whose spouse was not a CP member was not fully trusted, and it was made clear to the person involved."

11. Mark Tarail, "Child Psychology," *Daily Worker* (Sunday supplement), 14 April 1946.

12. *Daily Worker*, 17 November 1946.

13. *Daily Worker*, 14 April 1946, 17 April 1946.

14. Ibid., 27 October 1946.

15. Dennis, *Autobiography*, pp. 76–77.

16. Ibid., p. 131.

17. Christopher Lasch, *Haven in a Heartless World: The Family Besieged* (New York: Basic Books, 1977), pp. 3–8, describes the changes that occurred in family structure beginning in the late nineteenth century.

18. Almond, *Appeals*, p. 156. On the Popular Front's effects on Party personal and family life, see James Weinstein, *Ambiguous Legacy*, pp. 161–62, and Robert Shaffer, "Women and the Communist Party, 1930–1940," *Socialist Review* (May–June 1979), pp. 73–118.

19. Betty Yorburg, *The Changing Family* (New York: Columbia University Press, 1973), p. 1. Yorburg finds liberalized sexual practices developing in the 1920s among "those whose ties to traditional organized religion and to the conventional morality are weakest: the highly educated, men in general, blacks, political radicals, and non-church-goers" (p. 63).

20. Shaffer, "Women and the Communist Party," argues that during the 1930s, the Party was "an important institution of struggle for women's liberation," but concedes that under the conformist pressure of the Popular Front it "also contained . . . strong tendencies toward the uncritical adoption of many sexist cultural traditions and toward an increasingly conservative approach to sexuality and the family" (pp. 74, 110).

21. The median and mean year of marriage was 1940, with 63 percent of those interviewed marrying between 1936 and 1945. Of the forty-eight children fully accounted for, only three were born prior to 1939, and in all such cases the marriages significantly predate the Popular Front period. Fully 63 percent of the children were born in the 1940s, nineteen during

World War II and thirteen in the immediate postwar period. The average time span between marriage and the first child was approximately five years, a notable wait attributable both to the reluctance of activists, particularly men, to be tied down to family responsibilities and to the uncertainties of the times.

22. Yorburg, *Changing Family,* pp. 63, 125.

23. Klehr, *Cadre,* pp. 80, 82.

24. Dennis, *Autobiography,* p. 191.

25. Kriegel, *French Communists,* pp. 68–69. Peggy Dennis, "Response," p. 453, argues that American Communist Party women, in contrast, typically had no children and "no permanent personal relationship."

26. Weinstein, *Ambiguous Legacy,* p. 162.

27. Yorburg, *Changing Family,* p. 63.

28. Most notable is how the belief in their work and the supportive social network of the Party subculture enriched and strengthened activists' lives. Communist couples consequently avoided to some extent the modern malaise so incisively analyzed by Christopher Lasch in *The Culture of Narcissism* (New York: W. W. Norton, 1978), pp. 194–95: "The degradation of work and the impoverishment of communal life force people to turn to sexual excitement to satisfy all their emotional needs." Ellen Kay Trimberger, "Women in the Old and New Left," p. 436, suggests that there was more opportunity for women in the Old than in the New Left.

■ *chapter 6*

1. James Weinstein offers the Debsian Socialist Party of the first two decades of this century as a plausible alternative in *The Decline of American Socialism, 1912–1925* (New York: Vintage Books, 1969).

2. Irving Howe and Louis Coser, *The American Communist Party* (New York: Frederick A. Praeger, Praeger Paperbacks, 1962); Wilson Record, *The Negro and the Communist Party* (Chapel Hill: University of North Carolina Press, 1951); Wyndham Mortimer, *Organize! My Life as a Union Man* (Boston: Beacon Press, 1971); Mark Naison, "The Communist Party in Harlem in the Early Depression Years: A Case Study in the Reinterpretation of American Communism," *Radical History Review* (Fall 1976).

3. For oral histories of a variety of left-wing organizers, see Alice and

Staughton Lynd, eds., *Rank and File* (Boston: Beacon Press, 1973); on the Socialists, see Betty Yorburg, *Utopia and Reality: A Collective Portrait of American Socialists* (New York: Columbia University Press, 1969); Bruce M. Stave, ed., *Socialism and the Cities* (Port Washington, N.Y.: National University Publications, Kennikat Press, 1975); Frank A. Warren, *An Alternative Vision: The Socialist Party in the 1930s* (Bloomington: University of Indiana Press, 1974).

4. On political influence, see Howe and Coser, *American Communist Party*, pp. 319–436. On the role of blacks, see Wilson Record, *Negro and the Communist Party* and Naison, "The Communist Party in Harlem," *Radical History Review*, pp. 68–95. The American Labor Party was established in 1936 in New York State to provide a way for radicals to vote for Roosevelt and the New Deal without becoming Democrats. The Communists elected two city councilmen, Peter Cacchione and Benjamin Davis, Jr., during the war and were a significant force behind American Labor Party candidates and officeholders like Congressman Vito Marcantonio.

5. The distribution within the sample according to Party function and role is not reflective of the district. For one thing, those who stayed with the Party for some time were more likely to become cadres or functionaries. In addition, people encountered through old Party networks are likely to have had more than the average number of years of Party affiliation. The sample is thus tilted toward cadres. Over 70 percent (twenty-six subjects) were Party cadres; only 30 percent (ten) were rank-and-filers. Of the ten rank-and-file members, one-half were women, and four of them were wives of male cadres. Among the twenty-six cadres, were three union leaders, three professionals, and six functionaries. Fully twenty subjects (54 percent), did their main Party work within the labor movement, and seven had district- or section-level status. Another ten (29 percent) worked primarily through mass organizations, of which the Progressive Party was the most prominent.

6. Vivian Gornick, *The Romance of American Communism* (New York: Basic Books, 1977), p. 110.

7. Gabriel Almond, *The Appeals of Communism* (Princeton: Princeton University Press, 1954), p. 150, claims that nonfunctionaries attended four to five meetings per week. I found that most members had anywhere from six to twelve meetings a week; only least-involved rank-and-filers had fewer.

8. Gornick, *Romance*, p. 45.

9. *The French Communists: Profile of a People* (Chicago: University of Chicago Press, 1972) pp. 1–2, 25, 27.

10. Harvey E. Klehr, *Communist Cadre* (Stanford: Hoover Institution Press, 1978), pp. 86, 4–5, 6; See also Frank Meyer, *The Moulding of Communists* (New York: Harcourt, Brace, 1961), p. 92. One informant described cadres as the skeleton that survives and reorganizes if the army is decimated.

11. Almond, *Appeals*, pp. 65, 15. "A person who has simply assimilated the pattern of political action represented in the American *Daily Worker* has no conception whatever of what the Communist movement really is. He has identified himself with a rather pallid champion of generalized virtue and has accepted a somewhat watered-down version of the Communist demonology" (p. 93).

12. Klehr, *Cadre*, pp. 6, 8; Kriegel, *French Communists*, p. 198; Philip Selznick, *The Organizational Weapon: A Study of Communist Strategy and Tactics* (New York: McGraw-Hill, 1952), p. 18; Meyer, *Moulding*, pp. 132–58.

13. Selznick, *Organizational Weapon*, p. 20.

14. Kriegel, *French Communists*, p. 198. Several informants use the words interchangeably, but Selznick, *Organizational Weapon*, pp. 18–20, makes the useful distinction between cadre and functionary. See also Meyer, *Moulding*, p. 15.

15. Almond, *Appeals*, p. 93. Klehr, *Cadre*, p. 4. states that "even party veterans may not be part of the inner core."

16. I do not wish to ignore the important debate concerning the alternative strategies available to labor organizers in the thirties. For an introduction to the issues, see Max Gordon, "The Communist Party of the Nineteen-Thirties and the New Left," with a response by James Weinstein and a reply by Gordon, pp. 11–66, *Socialist Revolution* (January–March 1976). It is clear that the Party was essentially demagogic about its "hidden agenda" and that the NLRB structure shackled working-class initiative; however, Philadelphia Communist organizers almost unanimously argue that their approach was the most appropriate one, given the unionist but hardly socialist aspirations of workers. Like Max Gordon, they ask why all of the alternative, more aggressively ideological strategies failed. See also Roger Keeran, "'Everything for Victory': Communist Influence in the Auto Industry During World War II," *Science and Society* (Spring, 1979).

17. Quoted in Paul Buhle, "Questions for the Thirties," *Radical History Review* (Spring–Summer 1977), p. 123.

18. Let me make it clear that such intimidation stopped short of murder.

19. Peggy Dennis, *The Autobiography of an American Communist* (Berkeley: Creative Arts Book Company, 1977), p. 71.

20. Joseph R. Starobin, *American Communism in Crisis, 1943–1957* (Berkeley: University of California Press, 1972), p. 27.

21. For purposes of this study, "Stalinism" signifies the perversion of the ideal of democratic centralism—that is, the solidification of party dictatorship over the populace and the elimination of internal democracy within the Party.

22. For example, a humane and decent person like Dalton Trumbo had no qualms about reporting the names of correspondents to the F.B.I., believing that anyone who wrote to him about his antiwar novel *Johnny Got His Gun* after the United States and the Soviet Union entered World War II was likely to be fascist and therefore deserving of no consideration. See his *Additional Dialogue* (New York: Bantam Books, 1972), pp. 6–7. Communists have chronically been too quick to excoriate opponents with the most insulting and vituperative epithets. For charges of treason that, if made by a person in power, would make one tremble, see the *Daily Worker* during the period of World War II from June 1941 to August 1945.

23. Starobin, *American Communism in Crisis,* pp. 208–9; see also Eric Bentley, ed., *Thirty Years of Treason* (New York: Viking Press, 1971), pp. 940–53; Jessica Mitford, *A Fine Old Conflict* (New York: Alfred A. Knopf, 1977), p. 115.

24. Howe and Coser, *American Communist Party,* p. 422, argue that cadres often avoided having to promote and implement unpleasant Party policies, such as the Nazi-Soviet Pact, by pouring themselves into their local organizing work.

25. See Gornick, *Romance,* pp. 33–39, for a portrait of such a transformation.

26. Sara Evans, *Personal Politics: The Roots of Women's Liberation in the Civil Rights Movement and the New Left* (New York: Alfred A. Knopf, 1979), passim. Evans's study provides some insightful observations about the organizing skills of women during the 1960s. See also Ellen Kay Trimberger, "Women in the Old and New Left: The Evolution of a Politics of Personal Life," *Feminist Studies* (Fall 1979), p. 434.

27. See James Weinstein, *Ambiguous Legacy: The Left in American Politics* (New York: New Viewpoints, 1975), pp. 68–71, on Communist union officials and their status within the CIO.

28. Starobin, *American Communism in Crisis,* calls this ‚group "influentials" and "submarines" (pp. 39–41) and suggests that they "were living in two worlds" (pp. 187–88).

29. Harry Lore, "Apostasy at the Bar: Lawyers and McCarthyism,"and Joseph S. Lord III, "Communists'Trials," *The Shingle* (November 1978); D. Weinberg and M. Fassler, "A Historical Sketch of the National Lawyers Guild in American Politics, 1936–1968" (New York: National Lawyers Guild, 1968).

30. Michael R. Belknap, *Cold War Justice: The Smith Act, the Communist Party, and American Civil Liberties* (Westport, Conn.: Greenwood Press, 1977), pp. 13–15, 67.

31. George Charney, *A Long Journey* (Chicago: Quadrangle Books, 1968), pp. 187–88.

32. Mitford, *Fine Old Conflict*, p. 67.

33. Gornick, *Romance,* p. 252.

■ *chapter 7*

1. William Kornblum, *Blue Collar Community* (Chicago: University of Chicago Press, 1974), pp. 34–35. Although Christopher Lasch, *The New Radicalism in America* (New York: Vintage Books, 1965), pp. 290–307, criticizes the tendency of radical intellectuals to abnegate their responsibilities through compulsive political behavior, there has yet to be an analysis of the ways in which political activists enter the realm of group loyalty. On Party contempt for intellectuals, see Daniel Aaron, *Writers on the Left* (New York: Avon Books, 1965), passim.

2. During the period of the Pact, the American Peace Mobilization, a Party front, argued that "The Yanks Are Not Coming," that is, that the United States should stay clear of involvement in the war in Europe. See Irving Howe and Louis Coser, *The American Communist Party* (New York: Frederick A. Praeger, Praeger Paperbacks, 1962), pp. 387–405.

3. See Maurice Isserman, "The 1956 Generation: An Alternative Approach to the History of American Communism," *Radical America* (March–April 1980), p. 44, for an excellent overview of this Depression Communist generation and its traumatic break with the Party in the mid-fifties.

4. Robert A. Rosenstone, analyzing Lincoln Brigade volunteers in *Crusade of the Left* (New York: Pegasus, 1969), p. 266, suggests that "the chief object of hate in their world—even more so than Hitler himself—was . . . Trotsky." Frank Warren, *Liberals and Communists* Bloomington: University of Indiana Press, 1966), p. 142, argues that "the Popular Front mind could not tolerate ambiguity; it did not understand critical support." In fact, one finds that Popular Front Communists, while suffering from such dogmatism, experienced greater ambivalence about Party intransigency than did pre-Popular Front members. Andrei Vyshinsky was the chief prosecutor during the late thirties purge trials. V. M. Molotov was the Soviet foreign minister who negotiated the Non-Aggression Pact with German Minister Joachim von Ribbentrop in 1939.

5. Twenty-seven of those interviewed recall supporting the Pact; eight were not sufficiently involved by 1939; and one, a professional who was not formally in the Party, vigorously opposed it. Of the twenty-seven supporters, fully twenty-five maintain that support today.

6. Al Richmond, *A Long View from the Left* (Boston: Houghton Mifflin, 1973), p. 284.

7. Burton K. Wheeler was a Democrat from Montana and a leading isolationist in the thirties.

8. Joseph R. Starobin, *American Communism in Crisis, 1943–1957* (Berkeley: University of California Press, 1972), p. 34; Michael R. Belknap, *Cold War Justice: The Smith Act, the Communist Party, and American Civil Liberties* (Westport, Conn.: Greenwood Press, 1977), p. 202; David A. Shannon, *The Decline of American Communism* (New York: Harcourt, Brace, 1959), p. 109.

9. Of the twenty-six men in the sample, fully thirteen served in the United States armed forces during World War II; another two served in the merchant marine. Two others were too young to be draft-eligible, and nine were exempted for a variety of reasons, most often because of war-related jobs. Many of the ten women served in defense plants for at least a part of the war years.

10. George Charney, *A Long Journey* (Chicago: Quadrangle Books, 1968), p. 129; John Gates, *The Story of an American Communist* (New York: Thomas Nelson & Sons, 1958), pp. 82–83. Charney exulted, "We were not only Communists, we were Americans again" (p. 60).

11. See *The Communist* (February, April, May, and June 1943) for typical pieces calling for action against "fifth columnists," including

Socialist Norman Thomas. For a defense of the Party's record in organized labor during the war, see Keeran, "'Everything for Victory': Communist Influence in the Auto Industry During World War II."

12. See the Philadelphia *Inquirer* and Philadelphia *Record* for daily accounts, and the Philadelphia *Tribune*, a black biweekly, 1–31 August 1944; see also Philip S. Foner, *Organized Labor and the Black Worker, 1619–1973* (New York: Praeger, 1974), pp. 266–67, and Aden M. Winkler, "The Philadelphia Transit Strike of 1944," *Journal of American History* (July 1972).

13. The political advertisement supporting federal action in the Philadelphia *Tribune*, 12 August 1944, p. 2, mentions a rich array of church and religious organizations, community groups, labor unions, and Party fronts.

14. Samuel Adams Darcy, "The Last Crusade" (manuscript in Mr. Darcy's possession), pp. 542–64: *Daily Worker*, 8 August 1943. Samuel defeated Bullitt overwhelmingly, whereas Abercauph received only several thousand votes. See the account of the election in Chapter Three.

15. *The Communist* (February 1944), p. 101; *Daily Worker*, 5 June 1944.

16. For a sense of Earl Browder's political positions, see *The Second Imperialist War* (New York: International Publishers, 1940) and *Victory—and After* (New York: International Publishers, 1942).

17. See *The Communist* (June 1944), an issue devoted to eulogizing Browder. Jacques Duclos was a leading member of the French Communist Party; his letter criticizing Browder for "revisionism" in the French journal *Cahiers du Communisme* in April 1945 signaled a new turn in Communist strategy. See Howe and Coser, *American Communist Party*, pp. 437–57.

18. As James Weinstein argues in *Ambiguous Legacy: The Left in American Politics* (New York: New Viewpoints, 1975), p. 98, William Z. Foster, in repudiating Browder, remained committed to a Left-Center alliance and to reformist goals. The rub was that foreign policy considerations—the need to spearhead a militant assault on U.S. Cold War policies directed at the Soviet Union—made such an alliance impossible. See also Norman D. Markowitz, *The Rise and Fall of the People's Century* (New York: Free Press, 1973), pp. 201, 206.

19. Peggy Dennis, *The Autobiography of an American Communist*

(Berkeley: Creative Arts Book Company, 1977), p. 159; Shannon, *Decline of American Communism*, pp. 3, 364. Starobin, *American Communism in Crisis*, p. 114, describes the Party in 1948 as having 1,700 community clubs, 3,425 industrial clubs, 300 shop branches, and 200 student clubs in 600 cities, towns, and rural areas. Belknap, *Cold War Justice*, p. 190, insists that from early 1946 until January 1950 membership actually increased from 52,000 to 54,174. In Philadelphia one finds that until 1948 prospects were still hopeful and membership was at least firm after wartime and immediate postwar gains.

20. Irwin Ross, *The Loneliest Campaign* (New York: New American Library, Signet Books, 1969), pp. 18–34; Allen Yarnell, *Democrats and Progressives: The 1948 Presidential Election as a Test of Post War Liberalism* (Berkeley: University of California Press, 1974), passim; Markowitz, *People's Century*, passim.

21. Markowitz, *People's Century*, pp. 201, 211.

22. Ibid., pp. 212, 246–49. On the ADA, see Clifton Brock, *Americans for Democratic Action* (Washington: Public Affairs Press, 1962), and Arthur Schlesinger, Jr., *The Vital Center* (Boston: Little, Brown, 1948).

23. Markowitz, *People's Century*, passim. On Truman's co-optation of Wallace's domestic program, see pp. 257, 292.

24. Luce, the publisher of *Time* magazine and founder of the Time-Life publishing company, prophesied an "American Century" in 1941 and publicized its capitalist and democratic aspirations over the next years; see Henry R. Luce, "The American Century," in *Culture and Commitment 1929–1945*, ed. Warren Susman (New York: George Braziller, 1973), pp. 319–26.

25. Starobin, *American Communism in Crisis*, pp. 173–77. Mike Quill was the head of the Transport Workers Union and a long-time ally of the Party until the 1948 campaign. Walter Reuther became the leader of the United Automobile Workers after defeating Communist-backed rivals.

26. In Pennsylvania, Wallace drew 55,161 votes; in Philadelphia, he received 20,745. See Philadelphia *Bulletin Almanac* (Philadelphia: Philadelphia Bulletin, 1949), pp. 35–38.

27. William L. Patterson, *The Man Who Cried Genocide* (New York: International Publishers, 1971), pp. 156–68. The Martinsville Seven were blacks convicted of raping a white woman in West Virginia. Also executed, these men were considered by many to have been wholly innocent.

28. Michael Harrington, *Fragments of the Century* (New York: Saturday Review Press, 1973), p. 64.

29. Robert K. Murray, *Red Scare* (Minneapolis: University of Minnesota Press, 1955). On Truman's role in establishing new loyalty procedures, see Athan Theoharis, "The Rhetoric of Politics: Foreign Policy, Internal Security, and Domestic Politics in the Truman Era, 1945–1950," and "The Escalation of the Loyalty Program," in *Politics and Policies of the Truman Administration,* ed. Barton J. Bernstein (Chicago: Quadrangle Books, 1970), pp. 196–268.

30. On the political repression of the McCarthy period, see Belknap, *Cold War Justice,* passim; Mary Sperling McAuliffe, *Crisis on the Left: Cold War Politics and American Liberals, 1947–1954* (Amherst: University of Massachusetts Press, 1978); David Caute, *The Great Fear: The Anti-Communist Purge under Truman and Eisenhower* (New York: Simon and Shuster, 1978); Michael Paul Rogin, *The Intellectuals and McCarthy* (Cambridge: Harvard University Press, 1967).

31. *Daily Worker,* 3 April 1950, 20 April 1950, feature editorals. Two and one half million signatures to the pledge were collected in the United States. The Stockholm Peace Pledge called for U.S. efforts at friendship with the Soviet Union in the interest of world peace. See Howe and Coser, *American Communist Party,* p. 478.

32. Belknap, *Cold War Justice,* p. 190. The Taft-Hartley Act included a provision requiring union officials to sign affidavits that they were not members of the Communist Party.

33. On suburbanization, see Peter Muller, Kenneth C. Meyer, and Roman A. Cybriwsky, *Philadelphia: A Study of Conflicts and Social Change* (Cambridge: Harvard University Press, 1976), pp. 39–40, who discuss the pairing of the new U.S. Steel plant in Fairless Hills with the new Levittown community. See also pp. 49–55 of the same work. Starobin, *American Communism in Crisis,* p. 236, argues that the Party was not at all prepared for the postwar affluence. Shannon, *Decline,* p. 110, suggests that "the Levittowns broke up most of the Communist neighborhoods of New York."

34. Jessica Mitford, *A Fine Old Conflict* (New York: Alfred A. Knopf, 1977), p. 117.

35. See the *Daily Worker,* 3 July 1949, 5 March 1950, 23 June 1950, 9 May 1951, for Party coverage of important civil rights cases.

36. The McCarran Act, or the Subversive Activities Control Act,

among other repressive features, required the officers of Communist and "front" organizations to register with the Attorney General as foreign agents.

37. Starobin, *American Communism in Crisis*, pp. 219–23.

38. Ibid., p. 223; Belknap, *Cold War Justice*, p. 195. Starobin says that virtually everyone who had anything to do with the underground left the American Communist movement between mid-1956 and mid-1957."

39. Belknap, *Cold War Justice*, pp. 191–95; Starobin, *American Communism in Crisis*, p. 198.

40. Arthur Liebman, *Jews and the Left* (New York: John Wiley & Sons, 1979), pp. 310–22; Sara Evans, *Personal Politics: The Roots of Women's Liberation in the Civil Rights Movement and the New Left* (New York: Alfred A. Knopf, 1979), pp. 120–24, provides a favorable impression of the experiences of the children of Communists during the fifties.

41. Teachers Union of Philadelphia, *The Case against the School Board* (Philadelphia: Teachers Union of Philadelphia, 1955); Teachers Union of Philadelphia, 1937–1958, URB 36, Urban Archives, Temple University, Philadelphia; Robert W. Iverson, *The Communists and the Schools* (New York: Harcourt, Brace, 1959), pp. 117, 335–3; Caute, *The Great Fear*, pp. 94, 419.

42. On the Philadelphia Smith Act prosecution and case, see Belknap, *Cold War Justice*, pp. 154, 167–68, 179; Joseph S. Lord III, "Communists' Trials," and Harry Lore, "Apostasy at the Bar: Lawyers and McCarthyism," both in *The Shingle* (November 1978), give credit to the Philadelphia lawyers, both radical and mainstream, who defended those facing prosecution for their political affiliations and beliefs.

The goal of the Fletcher-Mills campaign, spearheaded by the Civil Rights Congress was to prevent the extradition of two blacks to the South for imprisonment.

43. Belknap, *Cold War Justice*, p. 244. Like most accounts, Belknap's stresses the primary importance of the California trial and defense strategy. See also Richmond, *Long View*, pp. 331–66.

44. Many Philadelphia Old Leftists emphasized the skill and loyalty of the local Smith Act defendants' wives.

45. Lord, "Communists' Trials," p. 146.

46. Gabriel Almond, *The Appeals of Communism* (Princeton: Princeton University Press, 1954), p. 300, suggests that Party members experienced conflict in five areas: career, personal relations and personality, non-Party group loyalties, values and moral standards.

47. Elizabeth Gurley Flynn, "He Loved the People," p. 43, *Political Affairs* (April 1953). The entire issue was devoted to this theme, including an editorial from the Central Committee, "The Death of Joseph V. Stalin." See also *Masses and Mainstream* (April 1953) for more eulogies of Stalin.

48. See the *Daily Worker*, 5, 6, and 10 June 1956, for publication of Khrushchev's speech and editoral comments.

49. Starobin, *American Communism in Crisis,* pp. 274–77. See also *Political Affairs* (October 1956), including an article by William Z. Foster, "On the Structure of the Communist Party," in which he admits to three major errors: first, giving the CIO an excuse to expel left-wing unions during the Progressive Party campaign; second, failing to pay more attention to electoral possibilities in the period of the Smith Act trials; third, taking excessive and demoralizing security measures as a counter to McCarthyism. By late 1957, however, Foster was back on the attack; see "The Party Crisis and the Way Out," parts 1 and 2, *Political Affairs* (December 1957 and January 1958).

50. John Gates, "Time for a Change," and Steve Nelson, "On a New United Party of Socialism," *Political Affairs* (November 1956); see also the entire March 1957 issue for both sides' arguments as they prepared for the sixteenth national Party convention. A detailed but partisan view can be found in Gates, pp. 157–91.

51. Eugene Dennis, "Questions and Answers on the XXth Congress, CPSU," *Political Affairs* (April 1956). For participants' reflections on these battles, see Richmond, *Long View*, pp. 367–82; Charney, *Long Journey*, pp. 269–85; Dennis, *Autobiography,* pp. 219–33. See also the *Daily Worker's* extensive coverage, including the remarkable letters to the editor that filled the paper between March 1956 and mid-1957. Finally, for a sense of the personal dimension, see the correspondence in *Masses & Mainstream* (March, April, and June 1957) concerning the resignation from the Party of the writer Howard Fast.

52. Starobin, *American Communism in Crisis*, pp. 313, 243; *Daily Worker,* 10 October 1956 through early January 1957.

53. Laszlo Rajk was a Hungarian Communist leader purged and executed in the early fifties after an induced confession.

54. Shannon, *Decline*, p. 248, indicates that by 1953, 60 percent of the national membership was between thirty-five and forty-five, born between 1907 and 1918, and that more than half of the membership was female. In 1955 the underground period officially ended. Nathan Glazer,

The Social Basis of American Communism (New York: Harcourt, Brace and World, 1975), p. 93, relying on FBI figures, cites Party membership in 1955 as 22,663.

55. Caute, *The Great Fear*, p. 537.

56. Isserman, "The 1956 Generation," p. 44. Of those respondents who express opinions on the mid-fifties crisis, nearly 60 percent say that they felt then, and still do now, that it was "salutary"—"traumatic" and yet "a relief." Four claim that they were oblivious to it, being absorbed by personal matters. Close to one-third (six) feel that in one way or another the Khrushchev revelations were detrimental to the movement and contributed to a heightened "revisionism."

A majority accepted and still accept the Soviet intervention in Hungary, although with differing analyses and qualifications. Sixty-two percent (13) supported it at the time, whereas only 55 percent (9) now see it as justifiable. Many of those who accept the intervention—at least half—say that it remains a painful memory. They deplore Soviet behavior and are uncomfortable with the kinds of justifications made by Moscow and the national leadership in New York; yet they believe that there was a genuine fascist and anti-Semitic counterrevolution threatening, and so they accept the legitimacy of intervention. The "hard-liners," critics of both Khrushchev's speech and local reform efforts, argue that criticism of Stalin and Stalinism "made us the laughingstock of the world" and "played footsie-wootsie with the capitalist world." One unrepentant Stalinist agrees that Stalin "did a lot of bad things and good things, too," but "if it wasn't for the Soviet Union we wouldn't be sitting here today, talking as freely," a reference to the victory of the Red Army over the Nazis. Another orthodox subject put it this way: "I disagree with Khrushchev in one respect; I don't share his opinion on Stalin."

57. Glazer, *Social Basis*, p. 164; Charney, *Long Journey*, pp. 148, 276, 282–83; Richmond, *Long View*, p. 381; Starobin, *American Communism in Crisis*, pp. 20–21; Almond, *Appeals*, pp. 149, 396; Harvey E. Klehr, *Communist Cadre* (Stanford: Hoover Institution Press, 1978), pp. 23, 32 112; Jon Weiner, "The Communist Party: An Interview with Dorothy Healey," *Radical America* (May–June 1977), p. 33.

58. Liebman, *Jews and the Left*, pp. 517–26. See also Isserman, "The 1956 Generation," p. 49.

59. Starobin, *American Communism in Crisis*, pp. 20–21; Klehr, *Cadre*, p. 32; Almond, *Appeals*, p. 149.

60. Charney, *Long Journey,* p. 283.

61. Ibid., p. 276. Dorothy Healey, who stayed in the Party, nevertheless speaks of the mid-fifties loss of "our most able, experienced mass leaders and Party leaders, particularly from my generation of the thirties" (Weiner, "Interview with Dorothy Healey," p. 33). See also Richmond, *Long View,* p. 381, and Almond, *Appeals,* pp. 149, 396. In Communist imagery, "Bolshevik" suggested militant behavior associated with the barricades; it was extended to cover a willingness to assume unpleasant tasks.

62. Of the small sample of five Gentiles from the thirties generation, two remained orthodox and pro-Soviet while three fought for reform before finally resigning from the Party. Those who entered after 1939 do not constitute a large enough sample for analysis. Of the seven pre–Popular Front recruits in my slim sample, four remained orthodox and pro-Soviet, and a fifth was closer to the Fosterites than to the Party reformers. The results are, at best, suggestive.

Among those of industrial working-class origins, three of four remained orthodox, while the other abandoned the Left altogether. Within the Gentile sample, four opted for orthodoxy, three for reform. Women split into a majority of five reformers, one hard to categorize, and two orthodox. Finally, among those who had a sustained working-class orientation in their organizing efforts, although not necessarily in their backgrounds, five leaned toward orthodoxy, four toward reform. Given the smallness and lack of randomness within the sample, such figures have no statistical significance.

63. Weinstein, *Ambiguous Legacy,* p. 112. In Marxian terminology, "economistic" pertains to policies and behavior that depend on the assumed inevitability of socialism; economism denigrates the role of class consciousness and politics.

■ *chapter 8*

1. Daniel Boorstin, *The Image: A Guide to Pseudo-Events in America* (New York: Harper & Row, Harper Colophon Books, 1964), p. 57.

2. The highest proportion of subjects, nearly 40 percent, continued in or entered the human service area, including social work, education, and clinical practice; eight ultimately became administrators or directors, and six remained in direct practice. There is no significant distribution by sex of promotions to administrative positions. The second-largest category is

business, small and medium-size, which accounts for seven, or nearly 20 percent, of the subjects. Four are professionals, another four are in the arts and the academic world, three are skilled workers, three are housewives, and one is a trade-union official.

A rough estimate of the social-economic status of respondents yields the following breakdown: two upper class; nine upper-middle class, eighteen middle-class; and seven lower-middle class. The estimates are based on interview comments, general observations of appearance, home, and style of living, and commentary from other respondents. Certainly, the sample can be accurately described as "affluent," although "wealthy" would be appropriate to only the two upper-class respondents. Under the circumstances of long-delayed careers, blacklisting, and job harassment, the economic and career success of the sample's subjects is indeed impressive. Harvey E. Klehr, *Communist Cadre* (Stanford: Hoover Institution Press, 1978), p. 115, observes, "A large number of those who left the CPUSA became quite successful." Joseph R. Starobin, *American Communism in Crisis, 1943–1957* (Berkeley: University of California Press, 1972), p. 307, tantalizes his readers with the following remark: "One of the untold stories of the U.S. economic boom of the Sixties is the part played in it by former Communists."

3. See Armand L. Mauss, "The Lost Promise of Reconciliation; New versus Old Left," *Journal of Social Issues* 1971, pp. 1–20, for the "optimistic futurism" of the Old Left, as well as its sense of history, faith in central government, commitment to racial integration, and belief in democracy.

4. Vivian Gornick, *The Romance of American Communism* (New York: Basic Books, 1977), p. 190, describes post-Party activity as more conventional and private than this study suggests: They pay more attention to the work they do and to their family lives than they do to the stir of world events. They are on the whole excellent workers, superior in their capacity for achievement, and they occupy large and admirable spaces in nearly every sphere of American life."

5. Jessica Mitford, *A Fine Old Conflict* (New York: Alfred A. Knopf, 1977), p. 281.

6. In an earlier study, *The Appeals of Communism* (Princeton: Princeton University Press, 1954), Gabriel Almond describes his sample of former Party members as 41 percent moderate left, 6 percent extreme left, 12 percent trade-union activity, 18 percent indifferent, and 10 percent

right-wing and/or religious. In addition, he notes that whereas 46 percent of his sample had rejected Marxism and revolutionary socialism at the point of their resignation, by the time of the interviewing that percentage had risen to 66 percent (p. 353). One must keep in mind that Almond's sample includes many who left the Party in the 1920s and 1930s and therefore had spent many years outside the movement prior to being interviewed.

7. For a three-generational model, see Reuben Hill, *Family Development in Three Generations* (Cambridge: Schenkman, 1970).

8. Sara Evans, *Personal Politics: The Roots of Women's Liberation in the Civil Rights Movement and the New Left* (New York: Alfred A Knopf, 1979), pp. 116, 120, 122-24.

9. One of the limitations of Marxism, particularly of its Leninist version, is the flatness of its psychology. Its radical environmentalism, resting on a Pavlovian base, reduces the tragic to societal and class determinants. The rejection of psychoanalysis by most radicals, particularly Communists rests on a refusal to accept Freud's assumptions about human frailty. Although one can find the gloomiest views of human nature in Freud, he was ultimately, like many Communist activists, a Promethean, always seeking to expand the frontiers of civilization, hoping to increase the margin of sublimated activity and reduce the inroads of the destructive. At the same time, Freud's belief in the ability of psychotherapy to increase human freedom—that is, conscious choice—assumed certain limits—a bedrock of the irrational, the complicated dialectics of sexuality and aggression, sublimation and repression. As Freud proclaimed, "It is impossible to overlook the extent to which civilization is built up upon a renunciation of instinct" (*Civilization and Its Discontents*, in *The Standard Edition of the Complete Psychological Works of Sigmund Freud*, vol. 31, ed. James Strachey [London: The Hogarth Press, 1973]. p. 96).

Yet Freud, who believed that the usefulness of work as a form of sublimation was limited to those driven not by necessity but rather by professional and artistic ambitions, allows for a less utopian and altruistic vision of socialism in asserting that "it is quite certain that a real change in the relations of human beings to possessions would be of more help in this direction than any ethical commands" (ibid., p. 143). Freud made no affirmation of socialism and chastised its adherents for persisting in unrealistic theories of human behavior. He suggested that the recognition of the importance of property relations among socialists "has been obscured and made useless for practical purposes by a fresh idealistic misconception of human nature" (ibid.).

Both Lenin and Freud shared a belief and commitment to Promethean struggle balanced by an attention to human limitation. Lenin asserted that the necessary virtues of a revolutionary are patience and a sense of irony; Freud, though a bourgeois liberal, would have surely concurred. So would Old Leftists like Abe Shapiro.

Perhaps what these seminal and courageous thinkers most shared was an absence of fear that their awareness of human limitation would subvert their commitment to a humane social order. In this sense, they recall the stern but enthusiastic revivalists of the American Revolutionary period, who, in affirming that all were sinners, emphasized that all were *equally* sinners and thus equal. A belief in human equality does not require a faith in human perfectability, only a respect for human dignity. See Alan Heimert, *Religion and The American Mind* (Cambridge: Harvard University Press, 1961).

10. Kenneth Keniston, *Young Radicals* (New York: Harcourt, Brace and World, 1968), pp. 111–20.

11. Arthur Liebman, *Jews and the Left,* (New York: John Wiley & Sons, 1979), pp. 316–21.

12. Such a group tends to identify with the perspective of I. F. Stone, the iconoclastic radical journalist, and Noam Chomsky, the linguist and Cold War critic.

13. See Harry C. Boyte, *The Backyard Revolution: Understanding the New Citizen Movement* (Philadelphia: Temple University Press, 1980), passim.

14. Starobin, *American Communisn in Crisis,* p. 235.

15. A recent article by Robert Shaffer, "Women and the Communist Party, 1930–1940," *Socialist Review* (May–June 1979), scratches the surface.

16. See Daniel Bell, *The Cultural Contradictions of Capitalism* (New York: Basic Books, 1976).

17. A good example is J. L. Talmon, *The Origins of Totalitarian Democracy* (New York: W. W. Norton, The Norton Library, 1970); the best effort to incorporate conservative insights into a socialist perspective is Peter Clecak, *Crooked Paths: Reflections on Socialism, Conservatism,*

and the Welfare State (New York: Harper & Row, Harper Colophon Books, 1977).

18. See my article, "The New Left and the Cuban Revolution" and those by Martin Duberman, Ronald Radosh, and Frances Fitzgerald in *The New Cuba: Paradoxes and Potentials,* ed. Ronald Radosh (New York: William Morrow, 1976).

19. James Weinstein, *Ambiguous Legacy: The Left in American Politics* (New York: New Viewpoints, 1975), pp. 161–62.

20. Christopher Lasch, "Politics and Social Theory: A Reply to the Critics; Symposium: Christopher Lasch and the Culture of Narcissim," *Salmagundi* (Fall 1979), p. 179.

21. Eric Bentley, *Thirty Years of Treason* (New York: Viking Press, 1971), p. 944.

22. Ibid., p. 950.

23. Sidney Hook, *Towards the Understanding of Karl Marx* (New York: John Day, 1933), p. 99.

bibliographic essay

Much of the literature concerning the Communist Party, U.S.A., is quite useless, even counterproductive, to an effort to make sense of the Communist experience. Too many studies are marred by the ideological distortions of partisan writers.

First and foremost are the autobiographies and memoirs of veterans of the American Communist movement. Most of those written by Party loyalists and published by Party outlets are of limited value insofar as they serve as apologetics rather than as critical evaluations of political careers. Examples include: Hosea Hudson, *Black Worker in the Deep South* (New York: International Publishers, 1972); William L. Patterson, *The Man Who Cried Genocide* (New York: International Publishers, 1971); Al Richmond, *Native Daughter: The Story of Anita Whitney* (San Francisco: Anita Whitney 75th Anniversary Committee, 1942); John Williamson, *Dangerous Scot* (New York: International Publishers, 1969); William Z. Foster, *Pages from a Worker's Life* (New York: International Publishers, 1939); Joseph North, *Robert Minor: Artist and Crusader* (New York: International Publishers, 1956).

231

The best of such relatively orthodox memoirs include Wyndham Mortimer's *Organize!* *My Life as a Union Man* (Boston: Beacon Press, 1971), a lively account of organizing in the auto industry, and Len DeCaux's *Labor Radical* (Boston: Beacon Press, 1970), a colorful account of an old Wobbly's role in the rise of the CIO. Both Mortimer's and Decaux's memoirs suffer from the same limitation as James J. Matles and James Higgins's account of the history of UE, *Them and Us* (Englewood Cliffs, N.J.: Prentice-Hall, 1974): a tendency to avoid the issue of the role of the Communist Party.

Accounts by ex-Communists who have "seen the light" and wish to demonstrate their newly found orthodoxy have virtually no value for the historian. Most, like Louis Budenz, *This Is My Story* (New York: McGraw-Hill, 1947); Bella Dodd, *School of Darkness* (New York: P. J. Kennedy & Sons, 1954); and Benjamin Gitlow, *I Confess* (New York: E. P. Dutton & Co., 1940), melodramatically exaggerate Communist espionage and subversion and ignore the more substantial organizing efforts that took place in various districts and involved many more people.

The most useful autobiographical material comes from those former Party members who have deserted the Party but not the cause, that is, who have remained essentially consistent in their political values and goals over decades. Such participants, most of whom spent several decades in the Party, have been better able to reflect on the contradictory qualities and consequences of American Communism. While humbled by their experiences, they have not repudiated their vision; consequently, their recollections are less melodramatic and more considered. Nevertheless, they are creatures of their pasts and inevitably engage in some self-justification. Most such memoirs are by anti-Stalinist Party reformers who split during the mid-fifties crises associated with Khrushchev's Twentieth Party Congress revelations about Stalin and the Soviet intervention in Hungary; a few are by members who resigned in the aftermath of the Soviet military action in Czechoslovakia in 1968.

The earliest accounts are the least reflective, although they provide an excellent sense of how the failed Party reformers felt in the mid-Fifties. John Gates, *The Story of an American Communist* (New York: Thomas Nelson & Sons, 1958), is useful, but the most insightful account remains George Charney's *A Long Journey* (Chicago: Quadrangle Books, 1968), especially for its sensitivity to racial tensions and to the process of disengagement from Party orthodoxy.

More recent memoirs are more reflective. Al Richmond, *A Long View From the Left* (Boston: Houghton Mifflin, 1973), particularly valuable for its picture of the important West Coast Party districts; Jessica Mitford, *A Fine Old Conflict* (New York: Alfred A. Knopf, 1977), which displays a rarely seen left-wing humor and provides a unique perspective on Party life during the McCarthy period; Kenneth Kann, *Joe Rapoport: The Life of a Jewish Radical* (Philadelphia: Temple University Press, 1981), an entertaining reflection of a twenties-generation Communist with roots in the Yiddish-socialist subculture of the garment industry.

Two other autobiographical works provide particular insight into the role of women within the Communist Party: Peggy Dennis, *The Autobiography of an American Communist* (Berkeley: Lawrence Hill, Creative Arts Books, 1977), and Vera Buch Weisbord, *A Radical Life* (Bloomington: Indiana University Press, 1977). Weisbord's account focuses on the twenties and early thirties; Dennis's covers almost five decades of Party history. In both cases, the portrait of the author's Party leader spouse devastatingly reveals his sexism and yet is loving and empathetic.

Much of the scholarly work on the American Communist Party is dominated by Cold War ideology and passion. Anti-Communist scholars, sometimes veterans of the intraradical battles of the twenties and thirties, sought to analyze American Communism for particular political purposes. For example, Philip Selznick, the pioneer organizational theorist, concludes in his *Organizational Weapon: A Study of Bolshevik Strategy and Tactics* (New York: McGraw-Hill, 1952) that there must be a "denial to communists of legitimate participation in labor and reformist organizations," and the development of anti-Communist elites as a counter-force as well (pp. 328–29). Though such scholars as Selznick, Gabriel Almond, Nathan Glazer, Irving Howe, Louis Coser, David Shannon, and Daniel Bell have made real contributions, most Cold War–inspired studies suffer from excessive partisanship. Either they place the darkest and most sinister interpretation on every act the Party took, or they construct social-psychological typologies that correlate adherence to the Communist Party with neurotic behavior and psychopathology. The worst examples of this type include: Frank Meyer, *The Moulding of Communists* (New York: Harcourt, Brace, 1961); Max Kampelman, *The Communist Party vs. the CIO* (New York: F. A. Praeger, 1957); Robert Iverson, *The Communist and the Schools* (New York: Harcourt, Brace, 1959); Morris Ernst and David Loth, *Report on the American Communist* (New York: Praeger, 1952). Gabriel Almond, *The Appeals of Communism* (Princeton: Princeton University Press, 1954), presents useful comparative crossnational data but is marred by psychological reductionism and an obsession with "the vulnerability of the free world to Communist penetration" (p. ix). Nathan Glazer, *The Social Basis of American Communism* (New York: Harcourt, Brace & World, 1961), is rich in data and especially insightful in matters of ethnicity.

The various histories of the CPUSA are essential reading despite their obvious anti-Party biases. There have been sufficient examples of cynical and manipulative Communist Party behavior for the following studies to include a sufficient quantity of accurate data and reasonable if harsh interpretations: Irving Howe and Louis Coser, *The American Communist Party* (New York: Frederick A. Praeger, Praeger Paperbacks, 1962); Daniel Bell, *Marxian Socialism in the United States* (Princeton: Princeton University Press, 1967); David A. Shannon, *The Decline of American Communism* (New York: Harcourt, Brace, 1959). All such accounts tend to emphasize the Party's responsiveness to Soviet directives and its adherence to a Stalinized model of political action that dehumanized both members and those touched by the Party. Such analyses, however, have been incapable of explaining the idealism of Party members except by the most reductionist psychological means. Theories of inner and outer membership (Howe and Coser, pp. 536–42, and Almond, pp. 65, 93) account for the behavior of Party leaders but remain too crude and abstract to shed any light on the lives of most participants.

More recently, younger scholars have begun to provide us with less ideologically oriented studies. Such studies, in addition, have taken a more modest, empirical approach rather than the more abstract and theoretical accounts of the past. The broadest of such studies is Harvey E. Klehr, *Communist Cadre* (Stanford: Hoover Institution Press, 1978), which provides useful data and perceptive observations concerning the national leadership of the Party but, despite its title, does not focus on the actual cadres, that is, the full-time activists who typically did not become national functionaries.

A number of younger scholars have focused on local or sectoral Communist Party experience. The most prolific and insightful work is that of Mark Naison, "The Communist Party in Harlem, 1928–36" (Ph.D. dissertation, Columbia University, 1976); "Marxism and Black

Radicalism in America," *Radical America* (May-June 1971); "The Communist Party in Harlem," *Radical History Review* (Fall 1976); "Harlem Communists and the Politics of Black Protest," *Marxist Perspectives* (Fall 1978). Naison's major contribution has been to provide scholars with a reinterpretation of the Party's anti-racist and civil rights efforts, a much needed revision. Other valuable efforts include Maurice Isserman's perceptive overview, "The 1956 Generation: An Alternative Approach to the History of American Communism," *Radical America* (March-April 1980); James Prickett, "Communists and the Communist Issue in the American Labor Movement, 1920-1950" (Ph.D. dissertation, U.C.L.A., 1975); and Roger Keeran, 'Everything for Victory': Communist Influence in the Auto Industry during World War II," *Science & Society* (Spring 1979).

A few studies of European Communist parties are particularly suggestive. Annie Kriegel, *The French Communists: Profile of a People* (Chicago: University of Chicago Press, 1972), is informative and incisive despite its ideological biases. Donald L. M. Blackmer and Sidney Tarrow, editors of *Communism in Italy and France* (Princeton: Princeton University Press, 1975), criticize studies that "have tended to treat 'the party' as a monolithic structure, ignoring the significance of local and regional differences in composition and in implementation of party policies" (p. 16).

Stimulated by the memoirs of Peggy Dennis, Jessica Mitford, and Vera Buch Weisbord, young scholars are beginning to examine the role of women within the Communist Party. Such efforts have tended so far to focus too much on Party women in leadership positions and not enough on rank-and-file and district cadres: Robert Shaffer, "Women and the Communist Party, 1930-1940," *Socialist Review* (May-June 1979); Ellen Kay Trimberger, "Women in the Old and New Left: The Evolution of a Politics of Personal Life," *Feminist Studies* 31 (Fall 1979), including a response by Peggy Dennis and an afterword by Trimberger.

Young scholars have responded to Nathan Glazer's pioneer call for sensitivity to the issue of ethnicity within the Party. Arthur Liebman, *Jews and the Left* (New York: John Wiley & Sons, 1979), includes a section on Communism but is particularly useful in analyzing the Jewish-socialist subculture. The work of Klehr, Naison, Cruse, Record, and Schappes is essential; see Harold Cruse, *The Crisis of the Negro Intellectual* (New York: William Morrow & Company, 1969), Wilson

Record, *The Negro and the Communist Party* (Chapel Hill: University of North Carolina Press, 1951), and Morris U. Schappes, "The Jewish Question and the Left: Old and New," *Jewish Current Reprint* (New York: Jewish Currents, 1970). Paul Buhle has recently contributed a thoughtful essay, "Jews and American Communism: The Cultural Question," *Radical History Review* (Spring 1980).

Explanations of the ultimate decline of the American Communist Party are abundant and, though involving considerable controversy, fairly well defined. David Shannon argues that Soviet domination and dictation destroyed the Party, shattering its integrity and aborting any possibility of indigenous policies. Many others agree that the inability to respond to the American environment crippled Party activities (see Howe and Coser, Richmond). An adherence to Marxist-Leninist formulas further warped by Stalinist dogma made it virtually impossible for the American Communist Party to develop a native strategy appropriate to a highly industrialized democracy.

Analysts emphasize the inadequacies and contradictions of the policy imposed from Moscow but fashioned and carried out at home. Joseph R. Starobin, perhaps the most perceptive historian of the Party, suggests in *American Communism in Crisis, 1943–1957* (Berkeley: University of California Press, 1972) that the Party found itself caught between two strategies: reform and revolution, a pragmatic response to American circumstances and a dogmatic application of abstract theory. As Starobin persuasively demonstrates, "The American Communists did not choose either alternative: *their story resides in having tried both,* within a single decade (and at times simultaneously) and having succeeded at neither" (p. 237). James Weinstein, *Ambiguous Legacy: The Left in American Politics* (New York: New Viewpoints, 1975), supports Starobin's thesis but strongly criticizes the reformist Popular Front strategy the Party followed in the late thirties. In Weinstein's view, neither the Fosterite syndicalist approach nor the Browderite reformist strategy offered any solutions to the problem of maximizing socialist consciousness within particular segments of the population. As the Sixties reaffirmed, rhetorical militancy and obsequiousness to foreign models do not provide socialist strategies. In fact, they often disguise their absence.

Analysts also differ over the causes of the decline of the Party in the mid-fifties. While most scholars emphasize the above-stated limitations and contradictions, others, such as Michael R. Belknap, *Cold War Justice: The Smith Act, The Communist Party and American Civil Liberties* (Westport, Conn.: Greenwood Press, 1977), stress governmental prosecutions under the Smith Act and the generally repressive atmosphere of the McCarthy red scare. These factors certainly guaranteed that the Party, unable to revive the Popular Front to ensure its political survival, was in a weakened state when it faced the mid-fifties crises of Khrushchev's revelations, the exposure of Soviet anti-Semitism, and the invasion of Hungary. Norman D. Markowitz, *The Rise and Fall of the People's Century* (New York: The Free Press, 1973), provides the best account of the second Popular Front of the Progressive Party period; and Richard H. Pells's excellent *Radical Visions and American Dreams* (New York: Harper & Row, Harper Torchbooks, 1974) presents a framework for understanding the culture of Popular Frontism.

Whether the Party could have weathered its own international and national storms and salvaged at least the core of loyal supporters in a less repressive setting remains unresolved. New Left critics of the Party have argued that the Party's reformism, its refusal to establish a socialist strategy in the thirties, and its propensity to maintain a "private vision" contributed to its demise. Old Left veterans and scholars have countered that the Party's socialist vision was quite explicit during Popular Front periods and that its limited success in generating socialist consciousness was a result of deeply rooted ideological and cultural factors within the United States. (For a sample of such disputes see Max Gordon, "The Communist Party of the Nineteen-thirties and the New Left," *Socialist Revolution* [January–March 1976], including a response by James Weinstein and Gordon's reply.) New Left criticisms, somewhat tempered by a growing recognition of the difficulties of building a socialist movement, remain persuasive but at the margins of historical contingency. The CPUSA limited its ability to build a socialist presence within organized labor and in the political arena by its idolatrous relationship to the Soviet Union, its chronic dogmatism and intolerance, and its often cynical manipulation of indigenous values and liberal-reformist goals. However, it seems clear that the Communist Party's failures stem more from repression and unique American circumstances than from its own deficiencies. Indeed, the French and Italian Communist parties suffered from the same limitations but had the differential of wartime resistance to catapult them into the status of mass, working-class parties, while the old orders were repudiated for either outright fascism or at least collaboration with the occupying enemy. The American party, despite its wartime support for the antifascist cause, was limited by the strength of its bourgeois adversary in both the liberal New Deal and the conservative Republican versions.

Finally, to revise one of Marx's most notable comments, scholars have only interpreted radical history in various ways; the point is to change its direction toward a socialist cultural hegemony. I hope that I have made a minor contribution toward that end.

interviews

*Henry Blum. Philadelphia, Pa. 29 January, 1979.
*Laura Blum. Philadelphia, Pa. 29 January 1979.
*Mike Caldwell. Philadelphia, Pa. 6 July 1979.
*Sammy Cohen. Philadelphia, Pa. 18 December 1978.
Samuel Adams Darcy. Long Beach Island, New Jersey. 7 October 1978
and 4 January 1979.
*Sol Davis. Philadelphia, Pa. 29 April 1979.
*Harry Freedman. Philadelphia, Pa. 24 March 1979.
*Fred Garst. Philadelphia, Pa. 14 January 1979.
*Milt Goldberg. Philadelphia, Pa. 14 December 1978.
*Ben Green. Philadelphia, Pa. 24 January 1979.
*Mark Greenly. Philadelphia, Pa. 16 May 1977.
*Paul Jackson. Philadelphia, Pa. 16 May 1977.
*Marion Jackson. Philadelphia, Pa. 16 May 1977.
*Sam Katz. Philadelphia, Pa. 15 October 1978 and 6 January 1979.
*Otto Kramer. Philadelphia, Pa. 24 February 1979.
*Tessie Kramer. Philadelphia, Pa. 17 March 1979.

*Moe Levy. Philadelphia, Pa. 10 January 1979.
*Sarah Levy. Philadelphia, Pa. 10 January 1979.
*Mort Levitt. Philadelphia, Pa. 10 February 1979.
*George Paine. Philadelphia, Pa. 29 March 1979.
*Ethel Paine. Philadelphia, Pa. 21 March 1979.
*Tim Palen. Philadelphia, Pa. 8 January 1979.
*Al Rein. Philadelphia, Pa. 9 February 1979.
*Angelina Repice. Philadelphia, Pa. 17 February 1979.
*Mario Russo. Philadelphia, Pa. 3 March 1977.
*Jack Ryan. Philadelphia, Pa. 6 March 1979.
*Edith Samuels. Philadelphia, Pa. 23 October 1978.
*Ike Samuels. Philadelphia, Pa. 29 October 1978.
*Al Schwartz. Philadelphia, Pa. 23 May 1977.
*Vera Schwartz. Philadelphia, Pa. 21 January 1979.
*Abe Shapiro. Philadelphia, Pa. 14 November 1978.
*Ruth Shapiro. Philadelphia, Pa. 9 December 1978.
Johnny Tisa. Camden, New Jersey. 29 June 1979.
*Sally Turpin. Philadelphia, Pa. 7 February 1979.
*Stan Wax. Philadelphia, Pa. 30 April 1979.
*Meyer Weiner. Philadelphia, Pa. 7 March 1979.
*Pseudonym.

index

Almond, Gabriel, 13, 43–44, 114–15, 166
American Communism. *See* Communist Party, U.S.A. (CPUSA); Communist Party, U.S.A. (CPUSA), District 3
Americans for Democratic Action (ADA), 149–50

Bentley, Eric, 188
Black Communists. *See* Communist Party, U.S.A. (CPUSA); Communist Party, U.S.A. (CPUSA), District 3
Blum, Henry (pseud.): on present attitudes, 181–82; and "significant other," 46; and World War II, 145–46
Blum, Laura (pseud.): and children, 179–80; on Depression generation, 177; and "significant other," 46; trade-union experiences of, 100
Boorstein, Daniel, 169

Bott, Elizabeth, 92, 211
Boyte, Harry, 74
Browder, Earl, 76, 147
Brown, Norman O., 5
Buhle, Paul, 206
Bullitt, William C., 147

Cadres, 114–16
Caldwell, Mike (pseud.): on Jews and blacks, 83; and the McCarthy period, 123–24, 155, 160; and World War II, 146
Catholic Communists, 71
Charney, George, 67; on Depression generation, 166; on Jews and blacks, 75; on union leadership, 135–36; and World War II, 144
Clecak, Peter, 7
Cohen, Sammy (pseud.), 67; and Jewishness, 73; and the McCarthy period, 156; marriage of, 95, 179; radicalization of, 29–30; and World War II, 145, 146

241

Communist Party, U.S.A. (CPUSA),
9; and anti-white chauvinist
campaigns, 78; Depression
generation within, 166–67; and
ethnicity, 21–23, 27, 131; during the
McCarthy period, 153; marriage and
the family within, 87–90, 92, 96;
during the Nazi-Soviet Pact, 141–43;
during the 1956 crisis, 160–66;
organizational structure of, 51, 56;
personal behavior of members of,
65–66, 129, 139–40; during the
Popular Front, 23–24, 138–41;
during the Progressive Party period,
148–53; subculture within, 61–69;
during the Third Period, 22–23;
during World War II, 143–48
Communist Party, U.S.A. (CPUSA),
District 3: activities within, 63–64;
and blacks, 71, 76–84; and Browder
expulsion, 148; child-rearing within,
91, 101–3, 179–80; coping skills
within, 170–71; ethnic dynamics
within, 68, 71, 76–84, 145; Jewishness of, 58, 71, 145, 180–81; during
the McCarthy period, 153–60;
marriage and the family within, 88,
89, 91, 101–5, 107, 176–80; members'
views of the 1960s, 177–78; members'
views of socialism, 175–76; and the
1943 mayoral election, 147–48;
organizational structure of, 52–60,
111–12, 114–16, 131–36; and the
Philadelphia Transit Company
(PTC) strike of 1943, 146–47; post-
1956 lives of veterans of, 170–71,
174–75; sexual attitudes within,
97–98, 177–78; and Smith Act
prosecutions, 159–60; social network
within, 63, 181–82; underground
experiences within, 156–57; and
women, 88, 104–5, 107, 132–33, 178;
during World War II, 144–46. *See
also* Philadelphia
Cruse, Harold, 76–77

Darcy, Sam: expulsion of, 147–48; as
functionary (D.O.), 57, 133;
marriage of, 89; role of, in 1943
mayoral election, 147

Davis, Dave, 133–34
Davis, Sol (pseud.): as a colonizer,
121–23, 136; on Jewishness, 73
Dennis, Eugene, 162
Dennis, Peggy, 149; on Bolshevik ideal,
129; marriage of, 90, 97; on women in
CPUSA, 104
Depression generation, 14, 20, 25–26,
41–43
Dimitrov, Georgi, 23

Ethnicity. *See* Catholic Communists;
Communist Party, U.S.A.
(CPUSA); Communist Party,
U.S.A. (CPUSA), District 3; Jews

Feminism, 87. *See also* Communist
Party, U.S.A. (CPUSA); Communist Party, U.S.A. (CPUSA),
District 3
Freedman, Harry (pseud.): on Browder
expulsion, 77; marriage and family
of, 88, 103; on Progressive Party,
151; on racial harmony in Party, 77;
radicalization of, 25, 42, 47; and
World War II, 144

Gannett, Betty, 47
Garst, Fred (pseud.), 28, 66, 162; as a
cadre, 115; on ethnicity, 73; marriage
of, 95; and "significant other," 47;
and World War II, 145
Gates, John, 47, 161
Glazer, Nathan, 13, 32, 43, 72, 81
Goldberg, Milt (pseud.), 177; as cadre,
124–26; on Jewishness, 73; radicalization of, 33, 45–46; and World War
II, 144–45
Gornick, Vivian, 70–71, 132; on
behavior of Communists, 65, 69; on
everyday life, 50, 65, 182; interview
sample of, 13; on legacy of CPUSA,
136–37
Green, Ben (pseud.), 183; on child
neglect, 103; and 1956 crisis, 164;
as rank-and-file member, 113; on
Sholom Aleichem Club, 180